A LIFE OF SPICE

SIR JOHN LEAHY

Sally

With my love and very best wishes

John

June 2008

Published by BookPublishingWorld
www.bookpublishingworld.com

Copyright © John Leahy 2006
The right of John Leahy to be identified as author of this work has been asserted by him in accordance with the Copyright, Design and Patents Act 1988

First published 2006. First edition.
All rights reserved.
No part of this publication may be reproduced or transmitted in any form or by any means, electronic or mechanical, including photocopy, recording, or any information storage and retrieval system, without permission in writing from the publisher.

ISBN10: 1-905553-12-9
ISBN13: 978-1-905553-12-9

Printed in the United Kingdom
Typeset in Stone Sans by Bookcraft Limited, Stroud, Gloucestershire

A LIFE OF SPICE

Contents

Preface	vi
Foreword by Nicholas Shakespeare	vii
Photographs	viii
Career Details	ix
My Family	1
School Days	8
Cambridge	14
Yale	17
RAF National Service	25
Foreign Office	32
Singapore	47
Western Department	57
Paris	58
Permanent Under-Secretary's Department	66
Tehran	68
Administration	76
News Department	78
Paris Again	91
Northern Ireland Office	97
Assistant Under-Secretary	106
South Africa	112
Deputy Under-Secretary	135
Australia	147
Retirement	164
Lonrho	168
Senior Citizen	176
Latter-Day Free-thinker	180
Over and Out	188
Appendix I	189
Appendix II	193
Index	197

Preface

I have never kept a diary and these memoirs have been based on my own recollections, supported by newspaper cuttings, letters, references in various books and, not least, by frequent requests to my wife, Anne, to remind me of names and put me right on dates. All this means that the accuracy of some of the details in my account must be regarded as inherently fallible. Both Anne and our children have been through the text and done their best to eliminate mistakes, for which I am extremely grateful. Any that may have escaped their attention are solely my responsibility.

In the customary way, I offer my apologies to anyone whom I may have offended by something I have either written or omitted to mention.

Perhaps I should also explain the title of this book. I hope the reader will not be too disappointed to find that it is about me, rather than Mrs Beckham. It is meant to reflect the unpredictable nature of my career. Unlike some of my Foreign Office colleagues, I did not become a specialist in a particular area of the world or branch of diplomacy. I was a generalist and as such I rarely knew in advance where I was going to be sent next. I went where I was told. As things turned out, I had a stimulating variety of postings.

John Leahy
Eastbourne
September 2006

Foreword

Diplomacy is well described as the practice of saying "Nice doggy" while looking for a stone. It requires – apart from the stone – the gifts of patience, discretion, even-handedness, humour, curiosity, and every bit as much intelligence as humility. These are skills that no technological advance will make redundant, and it is a rare creature who can combine them all. John Leahy is such a beast. The natural modesty that vibrates through the following pages – rather as visitors to 50 Stanford Road will recall the vibrations made by the London Underground – will surprise very few who have known him. The author's modesty is part and parcel of what makes him in the flesh such a singular human being: urbane, compassionate, committed and with an ability unlike anyone I have come across to make you feel his intellectual equal (First Class Honours, Cambridge). But it is also the quality which has enabled him to be a formidable diplomat over four decades. This is someone who has sat in the front row in several of the late twentieth century's most important arenas and been involved at close hand with many of its leading players, including Margaret Thatcher and Alec Douglas-Home. At various times he incurred the wrath of Anthony Eden, Chou En-lai and Tiny Rowland. He was sent on delicate missions to those mercurial characters, Messrs Gadaffi and Savimbi, the Angolan rebel-leader. He even tried to harness Graham Greene's services to the cause of peace in Northern Ireland.

A Life of Spice encompasses much more than diplomacy. I read it in a single sitting, in awe of the life he has lived, but with delighted shocks of recognition too. Collobrières, Wimbledon, that Triumph Stag. Even that "nice dog" Milly. Above all the Leahy family, whom I came to regard as an extension of my own. It is impossible for me to think of early childhood without remembering Emma's lanky beauty, Peter's great good humour, James' warm kind-heartedness and Alice's mischievous intelligence. And permeating everything, holding the whole show together with a serenity and spiritual strength that for me, at that age, resisted analysis or logic: Anne. I defy anyone not to be moved by John's account of her polio or the miraculous circumstances surrounding James' birth. It is clearer than any Mediterranean afternoon that Anne has been John's strength, too; his halfness.

Nicholas Shakespeare

Photographs

My Leahy grandparents	2
Pa, Ma and Roly	5
Bet and Pam	6
From the sublime to the ridiculous *c.* 1936	9
Wedding day, August 1954	40
What a lovely girl!	45
Le Clos, Collobrières	62
Arrival in Salisbury, 1971	82
Never out of earshot	84
Visit to Pakistan, 1972	86
Take no notice of Leahy, Peking 1972	88
My head was still too big, Pretoria 1979	113
Our Cape Town digs	115
In borrowed finery	129
KCMG, October, 1981	130
Umfalosi Trail	131
Farewell party	133
Rescue mission, May 1984	140
My first meeting with Bob Hawke, 1984	148
Westminster House	149
Foreign Secretary's visit, 1987	157
Papal visit	159
Young Endeavour	160
Young Endeavour's Handover, Sydney, 1988	161
Manor Stables, front	165
Manor Stables, back	165
Rosella II	177
Anne's 70th Party	178

Career details

DATE OF BIRTH 7 February 1928

MARITAL STATUS Married (Anne), two sons and two daughters

EDUCATION
1941–1946	Tonbridge School
1946–1949	Clare College, Cambridge, BA Hons (Classics)
1949–1950	Yale University, USA, MA (International Relations)

NATIONAL SERVICE
1950–1952	RAF, Flying Officer

DIPLOMATIC CAREER
1951	Entered Foreign Service
1952–1953	Central Department, Foreign Office
1953–1954	Assistant Private Secretary to Minister of State
1955–1957	Third Secretary, Commissioner-General's Office, Singapore
1957–1958	Western Department, Foreign Office
1958–1962	Second, and later, First Secretary, Paris
1962–1965	Permanent Under-Secretary's Department, Foreign Office
1965–1968	First Secretary and Head of Chancery, Tehran
1969–1970	Head of Personnel Services Department, FCO
1971–1973	Head of News Department, FCO
1973–1975	Counsellor and Head of Chancery, Paris
1975–1976	Under-Secretary Northern Ireland Office, Belfast (Political and Public Relations)
1977–1979	Assistant Under-Secretary (UN, North America, Information), FCO
1979–1982	Ambassador to South Africa
1982–1984	Deputy Under-Secretary (Africa and Middle East), FCO

1984–1988	British High Commissioner to Australia
	Director of the *Observer* (1989–1993)
	Chairman Lonrho plc (1994–1997) (Non-Executive Director 1993–98)
	Chairman of the Council and Pro-Chancellor City University (1991–1997)
	Chairman, Urban Foundation (London) (1991–1994) Member Franco-British Council (Chairman 1989–1993)
	Master of Skinners' Company (1993–1994)
	Governor English-Speaking Union (1989–1995)
	Chairman Britain–Australia Society (1994–1997)
HONOURS	CMG (1973) KCMG (1981) Officier Légion D'Honneur (1996) Honorary Doctor of Civil Law, City University (1997)

My Family

My father's family is of Irish origins and, like many Irish families, is scattered all over the place. Recent generations have made their lives in various different countries, including the UK, the USA, India, Australia and New Zealand. In the course of some genealogical research I have not come across any family members living in Ireland today, though the name Leahy is common enough there.

My father, known to his children as "Pa", spent all his working life in India as a tea planter and by the time I was born in 1928 he was already 59 and retired in this country. He was the eighth of twelve children whom my grandmother, Alice, produced over a period of 18 years, before expiring, poor woman, at the tender age of 36. She was 16 when she married my grandfather, John, in 1854 at the Catholic Chapel of Jesus in Aden, where he was serving as an army "apothecary" or junior medical officer. John was still young when both his parents died in quick succession and he and his younger sister, Mary, acquired Protestant step-parents who brought them up as Anglicans. His procreative instincts were obviously not affected by the change. Succeeding generations have been less prolific. For his part, my father did pretty well, considering he was not married until he was forty-three, to sire six children. I was the youngest and it still astonishes me that no less than 98 years elapsed between my grandfather's birth on 26 January 1830 and mine on 7 February 1928.

To go back a further generation, my paternal great-grandfather, Daniel, seems to have been regarded as the black sheep of the family. Certainly he was taboo as a subject of conversation and the information we have about him is sketchy. On the only occasion when my elder sister, Betty, recalls my father having spoken about him, he said, in a half-joking rather dismissive way, that he had been had up for stealing sheep. Daniel's daughter, Mary, my great-aunt mentioned above, confessed in a letter "I never heard what my father was".

Further light of a sort was thrown on the subject in April 1983 when out of the blue a cousin I was not even aware of arrived in London from America with her husband. Joyce Leahy-Johnson turned out to be a first

My Leahy grandparents (I think)

cousin once removed, i.e. one generation down from me although ten or so years older: her grandfather was my father's elder brother, Jack (John), who had migrated to America and married much earlier in life. On arrival she looked up the name Leahy in the London telephone book and knowing my father's initials were W.H.G. plumped for the entry J.H.G. and telephoned straightaway. My brother, Peter, was staying with us at the time and we had an impromptu family get-together. Joyce told us that over a period she had picked up some apocryphal family stories and had put them down on paper. She showed us what she had written. It included the fascinating assertion that Daniel got into trouble during the days of the rebellion in Ireland, had his farm taken away from him and was shipped to Australia along with his wife, Mary, son, Alfonso (sic) and daughter, Mary.

When I was appointed High Commissioner to Australia the following year I dined out on the story for quite some time. As the bicentenary of the landing of the first fleet of convict ships in 1788 approached, many Australians began to feel a certain pride at discovering one of their ancestors among the "passengers", and I made the most of this. Eventually, however, the laugh was on me: an Australian genealogical expert I had commissioned to do some more research confirmed that Daniel had indeed been sent to Australia, but as a corporal in the army guarding a shipload of convicts. It was even suggested that his regiment had been responsible, amongst other things, for looking after women prisoners. It goes without saying that during the latter part of my stay in Australia I talked about other things at the dinner table.

Since that time, another cousin, Mirabelle Hollingsworth, and I have delved into a number of relevant genealogical sources, with the following results. Daniel was born in Bruff, Co. Limerick; but there is no record of his date of birth. Army records indicate that he enlisted in the army on 24 June 1823 and at the time his trade was described as "clerk". Over the next seven years he saw service in England, Scotland and Ireland and during that time he met a young Irish girl, called Mary Hieland, to whom a son, John, was born on 26 January 1830. We have no record of when and where they were married. We do know that he left for Australia on 6 June that year in the convict ship *Lord Melville*, arriving in Port Jackson, now Sydney, on 21 October. Whether or not Mary and son, John, accompanied him on the voyage we cannot be sure, but what is certain is that they were with him in Australia, where a second child, Mary, was born on 2 July 1833. After serving there for five years and being promoted to Sergeant, he sailed for Bombay with his regiment on 3 March 1836. He died at sea from cholera just before the ship reached Bombay. His young widow, Mary, along with her two small children, had been accompanying him on board and she lost no time in finding herself a new husband, just six weeks in fact, after she landed. He rejoiced in the name of Ebenezer Alexander and was a Sergeant in the "Honourable Company's Bombay European Regiment". He was a Protestant, but she did not allow this to deter her. Interestingly it appears from their marriage certificate that she "made her mark", that is to say she could not write her name. After only eighteen months of marriage she herself succumbed to cholera. She was then only 25, which means that when her son John, my grandfather, was born in January 1830 she was barely 17 years old. A little later Ebenezer took Jane McBean, also a Protestant, as his second wife and brought up his two stepchildren in that faith. Nice things are said about him in one or two contemporary family letters.

Beyond this the genealogical trail has gone cold, particularly about Daniel's Irish background and forebears. Unfortunately various parish records in Ireland which might have provided clues have been lost. What he had done to blot his copy book we can but speculate. Could it be that he was thought to have brought shame on the family by marrying an illiterate girl of 16 or that they were not indeed married when John was born? We do not know and for the time being at least he can rest in peace. I should add that no trace of an "Alfonso" has ever been found; as already noted, the name of Daniel's son, my grandfather, was John.

Most of the information I have about my mother's family is derived from researches recently begun by my nephew, Ro Lawrence. Her maiden name was Ethel Sudlow and she and her twin sister, Dorothy or "Doolie", were born in Weston-Super-Mare on 2 May 1892. Her father was Arthur Sudlow, a solicitor, but so far the only other thing we know about him is that he predeceased his wife, Anne (Annie). There is indeed a certain air of mystery about him, compounded by the fact that Annie, born on 17 May 1862, was also a Sudlow. It is of course possible that they were cousins. Anne was the daughter of Edward Sudlow, a silk broker, and Sarah née Astor. My mother ("Ma") liked to say that she was related to the Astors and it was no idle boast.

The story of how she and Pa came to be married is intriguing. That they already knew one another in 1908, when she was 16 years old, we can tell from a postcard he wrote to her on 29th January 1909. At the time he was on board ship going down the Suez Canal on his way back to India from leave. The tone of what he has to say clearly suggests that he had fallen for her and he ends it with the words "Fondest love – always thinking of you". He signs himself "Yours only W.H.G. O'Leahy", which may seem to our eyes a curious mixture of the personal and impersonal, but perhaps not in those days. The O' is also interesting: he apparently said on a number of occasions that that was the old form of the name, but I have not seen it in anything else he wrote. Perhaps he was trying to impress her? The next thing we can piece together in this story occurred nearly three years later, when he wrote a letter, dated 5 December 1911, to his elder brother, John, in America saying that he was going on home leave the following April and hoped to get married then. He went on to say "Mary and Kate [his sisters] have a selection of girls for me to choose from, which is quite embarrassing". These words raise all sorts of fascinating questions. Was it embarrassing because the rapport between him and Ethel was still close despite the long separation and they had become secretly engaged or at least had an "understanding" which he had kept from his sisters? Or did they not approve of her and felt he should cast his net wider? Had she perhaps cooled off a bit and was not sure about marrying him until they met again? Was she included in the selection? We do not know, but it is fun to speculate. What we do know is that a few months into his leave, on 30 October 1912, he and Ethel were married in St. Andrew's Church,

Pa, Ma and Roly

Worthing. To judge by the formal wedding photograph and a local newspaper account, it was quite a stylish wedding. Annie was not at all well off, so I wonder who paid for it?

Ma was a remarkable person. Like her twin sister, she had to cope with the onset of total deafness when she was in her early thirties. Severe handicap as it was, she managed it very well and had a lovely sense of humour. From an early age I learnt, like other members of the family, to speak in

Bet and Pam

such a way as to help her lip-reading and, if necessary, to use the hand alphabet to spell words out. Later, when Pa died in 1941, she was left a widow in fairly straitened circumstances. Most of the family were off her hands by then, but my elder brother Peter and I continued to live with her in the school holidays for a few more years. Then we too went our ways and she managed on her own for another 18 years until her death in 1967.

In all there were six of us children, of which I was the youngest. Before me were Betty, Patrick, Pamela, Roland (Roly) and Peter, in that order. The first three were born in India, the rest of us in England (Worthing). From little hints Ma dropped from time to time, I gathered that my arrival in the world was not something she and Pa had planned. Not that they ever showed themselves to be other than loving parents; and my elder siblings no doubt felt the youngest of the family was allowed to get away with things. But I also have a clear recollection of not seeing much of my father as a very small boy and of being paraded for his inspection for a short time each evening before going off to bed. My first memory, albeit a fairly vague one, is of No. 57 Grand Avenue, Worthing, the house where we lived until I was four, when we moved across the road to No. 68, which remained the family home until my mother died in 1967. It was a substantial family house of 1920s vintage with a mock-Tudor frontage and leaded-light windows and was appropriately called "Bruff". Apart from Winnie (the nanny), we had a cook and a "daily", though I am not sure that the first two coincided, since there would not have been room to house them both. What I do remember is that on a number of occasions my mother had to mollify the cook when she had been upset either by my father's comments at table on her cooking or by the names my elder brother, Peter, called her from time to time. I might add that when Winnie had her weekly afternoon off she used to give me a penny to go out with my mother instead. This is not to say that I disliked or feared my mother, far from it, but the fact was that my daily life revolved much more around Winnie than her. It is worthy of note, I think, that my father could keep up this sort of household since he had always been a man of fairly modest means and in retirement had had to watch the pennies carefully. So carefully indeed that when the Great Depression really made itself felt in 1932 he was obliged to take my eldest brother, Patrick, away from Tonbridge School because he could not afford the fees any more.

School Days

My elder sister, Betty, ran a small kindergarten class ("Sunshine School") in the nursery of No. 68, with me as one of its founder members. She tells me I embarrassed her by being cheeky in class, but relief was at hand because in May 1936 I was sent off to preparatory school at the Grange, Stevenage. I was the youngest of three brothers at the school and for one term was officially designated "Leahy Minimus". It was a classic prep school of the old kind. Classical would be more apt, perhaps, since Latin and Greek were drummed into us almost from the start. The be all and end all was to steer the boys through their Common Entrance exams into a Public School, and even better to force-feed a few of them into getting scholarships. I was one of the latter specimens, eventually getting a scholarship to Tonbridge. But I have happy memories of the Grange and the ordered life of the prep school boy in the sunlit, innocent days before the war, as they seem to me now. There were only two wars I knew about then: the "Great War" and, from the sublime to the ridiculous, Mussolini's more recent effort against Abyssinia, about which we young boys held very strong anti-Italian views.

Up to this point I had had a happy, uneventful boyhood as the youngest member of a large middle-class family which may have been hard up at times, but in which I was not aware of lacking for anything myself. Even the outbreak of the war when I was eleven years old did not make much difference to things, at least not at the start. In fact it was all rather exciting. As a young schoolboy, I had a fairly simplistic view of the world: British right would prevail over German might and the combination of the Royal Navy and the French army would be irresistible. We would indeed soon be "hanging out the washing on the Siegfried Line", as the song would have it. We were issued with gas masks in brown cardboard boxes and shown how to put them on. Pa donned a tin helmet as an Air Raid Warden and learned what to do if an air raid warning went off. I also remember going up with him to the Sussex Downs on one occasion to see the wreckage of a German Bomber which had been shot down and being shown the dead pilot's bloody harness.

It was not long before things began to change in earnest. The Grange was evacuated from Stevenage to Broughton Hall in Staffordshire, the family home of Delves Broughton of Nairobi "White Mischief" fame (although none of us knew anything about that at the time). One of my elder brothers, Patrick, joined the Indian Army; another, Roly, joined the RAF and went off to Rhodesia to train as a pilot in the Empire Flying Training Scheme. My brother-in-law, Phil Green, whom Betty had married the year before, was in the Royal Artillery. Pam's husband, Tudor, was a lawyer and was seconded as a senior member of the Ministry of Aircraft Production throughout the war. To complete the picture, when Peter reached the age of 18 in 1943, he joined the Army Intelligence Corps and undertook an Intensive Japanese language course so that he could join a team of translators of intercepted messages at Bletchley Park.

From the sublime to the ridiculous, c. 1936

My father had suffered from angina for some time and in January 1941, just before his 72nd birthday, he had a heart attack and died. He was in a nursing home at the time, so it was not unexpected. It must have come, nevertheless, as a terrible blow for Ma. I myself had never felt very close to him and cannot honestly say I was overcome with grief. Given wartime travel restrictions it would have been difficult to organise for me to attend his funeral from school, and I did not do so. Two years later came the dreadful news that Roly had been shot down in his Beaufighter aircraft and was presumed killed in action while on a Coastal Command operation near Brest. He was only twenty years old and had his life in front of him. (Years later, while I was at the British Embassy in Paris, I made some enquiries in Brest to check if his body might have been washed up on the shore, as happened to a number of RAF pilots, but while there were some unmarked graves no trace of Roly could be found.) It was a very sad time indeed for the whole family, particularly Ma, but a lot of families suffered similar, or worse, losses.

In any case there was no time for self-pity. The mores of the time were that of the stiff upper lip. Come what may, people just had to get on with their daily lives amid the ever-increasing problems of rationing of food, clothes and petrol, shortages of various kinds, the blackout, travel restrictions, and many other frustrations. For the most part such things affected my elders more than me and I myself was not conscious of much deprivation. We learnt to eat powdered eggs, spam and a South African tinned fish called snoek without too much fuss. Our meals may have been monotonous, but we never went hungry, and to supplement our rations in the holidays there was a fish and chip shop, or one of Lord Woolton's cheap and cheerful "British Restaurants", not far away. The seafront at Worthing was barricaded and we could not swim in the sea, but we made up for that by using our bicycles to visit, and swim in, various rivers all over Sussex. We continued to play cricket, tennis and hockey with our friends during the holidays and all in all we were a good deal fitter than today's young generation. We also went to the cinema or "flicks" once or twice a week. We saw pictures of the war in the Newsreels, heard something about it on the "wireless" and read about it in the newspapers, but we were on the periphery of great events happening elsewhere and in the pre-television era it did not loom that large in the everyday life of us boys and girls. Our main contribution to the war effort was to help local farmers with the "stooking" at harvest time.

I joined Peter, at Tonbridge, in 1941. Fortunately for Ma we both had scholarships. In fact I doubt if we could have gone there otherwise. The school was then down to just over 300 boys, less than half what it is today. I imagine its somewhat exposed position in the South of the country had something to do with this, though in fact the year before it had received Dulwich College as evacuees from their London suburb. This uncomfortable experiment was unpopular with both schools and was abandoned after only one term. The war also made itself felt in the amount of time devoted to Junior Training Corps activity and in the paucity of extra-curricular activities. In 1944 we saw, and heard, at close hand the V1 flying bombs. On 23 June one came down and exploded in the garden of Ferox

Hall, a boarding house just opposite the main school, which had been closed "for the duration" and let to the Kent County Home for the Aged. In terms of broken windows in our buildings the damage was spectacular, but the only casualty was the Headmaster, who received a cut on his face from some flying glass, as he was playing bridge (it was after supper on a Sunday evening). The boys loved that! Not maliciously, I should add, because he was not an unpopular figure, it was more a case of poetic justice. Moreover we all had the next morning off school to clear up the mess. For the last six weeks of the term daily morning chapel was dropped and the Sunday services were held on a voluntary basis. Skinners' Day, the annual speech day visitation by the Governors, was cancelled, for the first time in the recent history of the school (a quasi-Skinners' Day was held instead the following March). Other excitement was provided by the appointment of some senior boys as Fire Watchers and, for those over seventeen, by the possibility of joining a local unit of the Home Guard. For those taking their official exams there was an added bonus of 10% extra marks to make up for the fact that when, every now and then, a V1 flying bomb was heard to be approaching we were ordered to hide under our desks. This was a fatuous gesture in terms of the protection it afforded us, but the extra marks we received were a matter of life or death, of a less literal kind, for some borderline cases. Whether I was one I do not know. We were also told that if a V1 was heard to be approaching while we were on the cricket field we should lie down on the ground: this too was not likely to prove very effective advice, but happily it was not put to the test. I was myself put to the test in a different way and, unhappily, found wanting. Unlike my brother, Roly, I was not much of a cricketer, but I was good enough in a sparse year for talent to be included in the 1st X1 squad. Until, that was, a precocious little boy in his first term called Colin Cowdrey rapidly made his way up the junior teams and into the final 1st X1 trial game. He was a rotund little boy, but had all the cricketing skills with both bat and ball. He bowled me out twice in one afternoon with his fiendish leg-breaks and out of the team as well. In the ensuing annual match with Clifton College at Lord's he made a name for himself with both bat and ball. The surprising thing was that he was a delightfully modest little boy against whom one could not possibly bear any resentment. I got to know him well in later life, both in the Skinners' Company and when I was in Australia, and can vouch for the fact that despite all his achievements his head always remained the same size.

There is, of course, more I could, and perhaps should, say about my alma mater. I do not look back upon the academic education I received there with much sense of excitement or enthusiasm. In many respects I can be said to have done well. I had good academic results, moved up the hierarchy to become Head of the School and, Colin Cowdrey notwithstanding, was reasonably successful on the sports fields – the ideal Tonbridge all-rounder, you might say. But I was not in fact well-rounded, except physically. Like other boys who, as I mentioned earlier, had been force-fed with Latin and Greek at our prep schools, I developed the ability to learn things by heart and reproduce them like a parrot in exams. It mattered less to our teachers whether or not we gave much thought to the content of what we were learning. At Tonbridge I was made to specialise in the Classics at an early stage and was not given the chance to find out, even in the most rudimentary way, what the sciences were about. I never went into a laboratory of any kind. Instead, the teaching of my chosen subjects was geared to getting good results in the Higher Certificate examination and obtaining a scholarship to Cambridge, both of which I achieved. In my last term I successfully resisted the pressure to take the HC a third time, for the honour of the school, on the pretext that, amongst other things, I needed time to write the Latin Speech for Skinners' Day. I hasten to add that the school of today is much more ambitious in what it aims to do for the 750 or so boys in its care.

Very often these days school leavers have a "gap year" before they go up to university. It is too well known for me to have to explain this more, but it was virtually unknown in 1946. In any case, like other young men at that time I had two years' National Service ahead of me and, although I was allowed to defer the start of this until I had completed my university course, taking extra time off to go to Australia or wherever would have been frowned on, to say the least. But I did have one little treat: a two-week trip to Paris in September. No big deal these days, but an exciting adventure then for an 18 year old who had grown up during the war and had never been abroad before. Indeed I was so naïve that when I was first told that I could have an official foreign exchange travel allowance of £25 for the trip, I fondly imagined that it was a grant I would be getting from the government! I went in company with my school friend, David Gallop, on the Newhaven–Dieppe ferry and thence by train to Paris. He was to stay with a French relation, Madame Smol, and she in turn had kindly arranged for me to stay with friends, Monsieur and Madame Ferdinand Maillard, who lived nearby in a flat on the Rue Pierre Demours in the 17th arrondissement, with their family of one son and three daughters. The son, Philippe, became a good friend and we exchanged a number of visits later on. I was also quite smitten by the eldest daughter, Janine, but she took no interest in me.

As I got off the train in Paris my nostrils were assailed by an all-pervasive smell I had never encountered before. I soon discovered that it came from an intriguing and wholly distinctive mixture of Gaulloises, garlic and pissoirs and was known to many visitors as one of the charms of Paris. David and I carried with us supplies of things like coffee, tea and sugar, which were said to be in short supply. These were obviously welcome to our hosts, though we soon found out that at a price you could lay your hands on practically anything in the city. There were three different price levels: rationed goods could be had at one price with the appropriate ticket, and at a somewhat higher price without a ration ticket on the unofficial, but not illegal, "marché libre"; more exorbitant prices were charged on the extensive black market. As visitors we were allowed temporary ration cards and my host even arranged for us to receive petrol coupons for imaginary cars. M. Maillard worked either in a bank or an insurance company, I do not recall which, and was very proud of his time as an officer in the army. He spoke about the war in terms which suggested that he was a sympathiser, at least, with the Resistance, although I noticed he had on the wall a framed citation from Marshal Pétain dating from the First World War. During our stay we were taken up to Houlgate in Normandy to meet some Maillard cousins, and while there we learnt for the first time that by no means everybody was grateful to the British for helping to liberate them. It was pointed out that farmers who had things like butter and cheese to spare had done well out of supplying the black markets in the towns. Moreover the Germans had been correct in their dealings with them and, for the most part, had left them in peace, unlike the RAF who had flattened their buildings and damaged their farms. I could understand, but was a bit taken aback.

The rest of the time David and I spent seeing the sights of Paris, from the Eiffel Tower to the Sacré Coeur, the Bois de Boulogne to Notre Dame, the Flea Market to the Louvre, etc. I have never been a great rubber-necker, but I did my share of it then, and it would have been unthinkable to do otherwise, while we were young and had both the curiosity and the legs for it. I do not recall any sorties to restaurants and for the most part we ate round the family table with the Maillards. The meals were simple and meat was not in evidence, but the cook, or bonne-à-tout-faire, made the most of the ingredients she had and produced some excellent soups, pastas, salads and the like. There was also no shortage of bread and wine. All of which opened my eyes to the infinite possibilities of French cuisine and ensured that for ever after my saliva glands would go into overdrive at the prospect of eating even in the most modest of bistros.

Cambridge

My immediate reaction on going up to Cambridge was one of liberation. In 1946 it was a particularly exciting place to be, with the war just over and many ex-servicemen among the undergraduates. For those of us straight from school they provided a new dimension to what was in any case an invigorating change of environment. Many of the returning warriors took advantage of a special dispensation that allowed them to compress a three-year degree course into two years and to do that they had to work hard. They liked to play hard too and had a healthy disregard for some of the petty regulations governing undergraduate behaviour, such as having to be back in college by midnight or wearing a gown after dark. They brought a certain gaiety to what in some respects was an austere scene.

The winter of 1946 was severe and much of the country, including Cambridge, was snowed in and frozen solid. I still have photos I took at the time of what the "backs" looked like. The railways came to a standstill, coal was in short supply, electricity cuts were frequent, bread was rationed for the first time – it had not been during the war – and for many people life was at a low ebb. But not for me. Being well upholstered I do not feel the cold as badly as some people and I do not recall feeling desperately cold then. Moreover I could always warm up with a quick game of squash, and I found many other things as well to take my mind off the weather. I was not politically minded and did not join any of the party associations nor, at first, the Union. I also evaded the clutches of various Christian fellowship groups. But I did sign on for a bit of acting in the Amateur Dramatic Society and, for some reason which escapes me now, joined a rather cranky group of World Federalists. I was also fairly active on the sports scene: apart from squash, I played hockey and tennis for the college. In between times I did some work and found to my surprise that for the first time I was actually enjoying ancient history and Latin and Greek literature. Last but not least, I met a nice nurse from Addenbrooke's Hospital, Anne Betts. That is another story, though by modern standards it was all very innocent and there is nothing much to tell. The odd meal together, visits to the "flicks" and every now and then a game of tennis and a dance somewhere. Our staple drink was South African sherry; wine was a rarity. The height of the year's social life was the May Ball: Clare's was thought, by us at least, to be one of the best – a college having one of the "backs" on to the river had a romantic edge on other less fortunately situated rivals. I remember that year after year we had Tommy Kinsman and his band, as well as a Latin American group. The tickets were, and still are, expensive, but at least when Anne Betts came in my first year I did not have to pay for a hotel room for her as well. If this seems a distinctly unromantic attitude I can only say that it was more a case of being skint than skinflint, since I had to manage on narrow margins. After dancing the night through, we went by launch to Grantchester for breakfast. By then we all felt pretty jaded, to say the least, but some people had the energy, and the wherewithal, to go to another college ball that evening. I was definitely not one of them, on both counts.

At the end of my first summer term, I had a temporary job filling in for the Classics' Master at King's College, Taunton. He had unfortunately developed a serious illness a few weeks before the members of the sixth form were due to take their Higher Certificate exams and there was a desperate need for someone to help the boys with their revision. It was an interesting experience and earned me some pocket money, but it also helped me decide that schoolmastering was not for me. Nor did I stick around to find out how the boys had fared. I did, however, help run a summer camp of the school's Boy Scout Troop at Chard in Somerset. All good clean fun, but rather too hearty for my taste.

Looking back on my Cambridge days, I think it is fair to say that I worked quite hard. But the college authorities left me in no doubt that the 2.1 I achieved in Tripos Part I at the end of my first year was not good enough and a scholar was expected to get a First. For Part II I chose Ancient History as my special subject, in preference to Literature, Philosophy or Sanskrit and, with the help and guidance of an inspiring supervisor, Nick Hammond, Senior Tutor at Clare, I began to enjoy it as I had never done before. As a result of that and a bit of good luck I managed a First in Part II, the one that really counted. I was also awarded a college cup for being a good all-rounder in the JCR, the Junior Common Room.

Fairly early on in my last year I discussed with Nick Hammond what I might do for a living when I had done my National Service. I was not attracted by the idea of teaching, as I have already explained, or by an academic career. Not being at all numerate (for which I hold my previous schooling partly responsible) I doubted whether I was suited to the world of business or banking. I had often felt I would like to be a doctor, but had followed quite the wrong educational path for that (admittedly that did not stop our younger daughter, Alice, when she was faced with a similar choice at the end of her time at Cambridge, 35 years later). A lawyer? Possibly, but here again it would mean starting from scratch to acquire new qualifications and, unlike doctoring, it was not something I had ever even thought about. What else? As we ticked off the various possibilities Nick and I eventually got to talking about the Foreign Service. He said something to the effect that diplomatic life could be interesting and the FO took all sorts of funny people, so why not have a go? For want of a better idea I decided to do just that and applied to the Civil Service Commissioners to sit the requisite exam.

The competition was reputed to be tough and I was therefore agreeably surprised to get over the first hurdle in the form of a written qualifying test in which the numbers were whittled down to manageable proportions for the next stage, the two-day selection ordeal at a country house in Surrey, which A.P. Herbert sent up in his amusing spoof, "Number 9". But any thought of proceeding smoothly to this stage was upset by my nomination by the college, without my knowledge I should add, for the Mellon Fellowship at Yale University in the coming year. It seemed like an opportunity too good to miss and there was no problem about being allowed further deferment of my National Service to take it up. The Civil Service Commissioners were less accommodating and told me that if I went to the USA I would have to withdraw from the current competition and start again from scratch when I came back, always providing I was still within the eligible age limits. I accepted their kind "offer" with alacrity.

Yale

The Mellon Fellowship was a closed two-way scholarship between graduates of Clare College and Berkeley College, Yale, and was the gift of a great American philanthropist and benefactor, Paul Mellon, who had been at both institutions himself. There were few conditions attached, but I recall that the lucky recipient was expected to make an effort to see something of the country outside New England in the summer vacation, a stipulation with which I readily complied. That apart, one could have the Fellowship for one or two years, study whatever one liked in the Graduate School and take or not take a degree of some kind. It was worth between $3,000 and $4,000 a year: I forget the exact figure, but I do know that in 1949 it was considered to be a generous amount. Before leaving I had to go through the rigmarole of getting an American visa. In fact it was not really difficult, because it was still the era of quota visas for bonafide immigrants and the large British quota was never filled. I was not in fact a bonafide immigrant, but at the US Embassy I was encouraged to apply for this category of visa as it would make life much simpler for me than a Tourist Visa in terms of taking a job and travelling in and out of the country. It did involve my taking a Wasserman Test to make sure I did not have syphillis and swearing on oath that I was not a communist, fascist or anarchist and did not intend to assassinate the President or try to overthrow the US Government. To my mother's relief, the result of the test was as negative as my affirmations and I got the visa in time to board the SS *Nova Scotia* at Liverpool on the last day of August, bound for Boston via St. John's, Newfoundland, and Halifax. I was as excited as could be to be going to the bright new world after the drabness of the old.

The *Nova Scotia* was a small ship, compared with the big Atlantic liners, and I did not take long to find my way around and meet people. Amongst them was an attractive American girl, Charlotte Sears, who was returning to Boston after "doing Europe" with a couple of other girls who had just left college. We quickly struck up a friendship, in fact almost, but not quite, a classic shipboard romance, the inhibiting factor being that she was travelling first class and I was in cabin class, which meant that we had to adopt various ruses to overcome the physical barriers that were intended to keep the hoi polloi in their place. We had the will and found the way, but had to be a bit furtive about it at times.

My first sight of the new world at St. John's was a bit of a let down. It was then, and for all I know still is, a one-street town whose inhabitants were said to occupy themselves with fishing and fornication, except in the winter, when there was no fishing. As we went ashore to stretch our legs we were advised under no circumstances to drink the locally distilled spirit called "Screech", since it was known to afflict people with blindness (hence the expression blind drunk?). Instead I had my first taste of root beer, which was not too good either.

I do not recall much about Halifax, our next port of call. But our arrival in Boston on 12 September is clearly etched on my memory. After a fond farewell with Charlotte and promises to keep in touch, I went to the Railroad Express Office to forward my heavy luggage direct to Yale in New Haven, Connecticut, while I took a train to New York, where I was to spend my first day or two. There was a long line of people engaged in filling up forms, attaching labels and paying their dues, and before long a porter came over to me and, seeing the evidently bewildered look on my face, asked me if he could help me. In fact he did a good deal more than that. He got hold of a form and started filling it up for me. In the process he asked my name and when I said Leahy, pronouncing it in the way of our family Leehy, he corrected me and said that I must mean Layhy, and which part of the old country did I come from and how was the old place looking? "County Limerick" I said, omitting to add that I was born in England and am really Irish in name only. At once he took me to the head of the line, which caused one or two sour looks from the others, and saw me through the formalities in no time. I knew I ought to give him a tip for what he had done for me, but I was not sure how much. Eventually I handed him one dollar (this was just before the devaluation of sterling and there were still four dollars to the pound), but he insisted on handing it back to me. For a moment I thought I had offended him by not offering enough, but instead he leaned over towards me and whispered "No, Sir, no money need pass between the Irish". This was, of course, Boston and my education was just beginning: when anyone called me Layhy thereafter I did not argue. Leaving that aside, I will never believe that money does not pass between the Irish.

Unlike other American universities, Harvard and Yale have residential colleges along Oxford and Cambridge lines. Arriving at Berkeley College I entered by a familiar-style porters' lodge and was shown to a bedsitter room on a familiar-style staircase. As I unpacked and got my bearings one or two people in nearby rooms put their heads round the door to say hello and introduce themselves in the warm way that Americans have. Some could not help remarking, as I was to hear many times in the coming days, that they just loved my cute little accent, but it was meant nicely, I told myself. Out of self-defence it was not long before I began to acquire American intonations and to pronounce bananas etc the way the natives did. I also quickly came to terms with having the tray of food that I had just selected for lunch in the college cafeteria inspected by a dietician supervising the eating habits of the students. What she could not control, of course, was the frequent intake of high-cholesterol (but who had heard of cholesterol then?) milk shakes, chocolate sundaes and doughnuts at Liggett & Myers drugstore across the road. These were a revelation and a source of unending delight to me and my sweet tooth.

The devaluation of the pound I mentioned earlier had one beneficial effect for me. Shortly after my arrival in New Haven I bought a pair of "Daks" pants (trousers) and, as was then the custom, the bottoms had to be finished off to the customer's leg measurement. By the time I collected the finished article the next day the dollar cost of the import had gone down and I was given the benefit of the reduction. I remember also buying a portable typewriter about the same time, having learnt to my surprise that any papers I submitted for inspection in the Graduate School had to be in typed form.

By living in one of the residential colleges and working in the Graduate School, I had the best of both worlds at Yale. I was more or less the same age as the more senior of the undergraduates and enjoyed their fresh-faced company and the social life of the college. On the other hand, I would have found their academic disciplines rather undemanding, by comparison with what I had been used to at Cambridge. This was certainly not the case in the Graduate School, where the atmosphere was totally different. Many of its members seemed to think of themselves as perpetual students and lined themselves up for careers of never-ending graduate research in successive universities. In the International Relations faculty, where I signed up to sit for a Master's Degree, there were some first-class professors and lecturers, some of whom worked on a part-time basis in other institutions such as the National War College. One or two suffered at the hands of the notorious Senator Joe McCarthy and his fellow inquisitors on the Congressional Committee of Un-American Activities, which was then going full bore. Guilt by association seemed to be its guiding principle and for an academic to teach the theories of Marxism or even to examine the pros and cons of preventive war was to invite harsh grilling and castigation. Unlike the procedure at Oxford and Cambridge, taking a Master's Degree at Yale involves doing some work. I enrolled in a number of seminars, including European Diplomatic History between the Two World Wars, Introduction to International Law, the Analysis and Use of Power, and the Application of Anthropology to the Study of International Behaviour. I was required to write (type) papers on a variety of topics and these were given an alpha, beta etc rating. They did not have to involve original research material and I must have gone in for a good deal of plagiarism. How else could I have produced, and been highly commended for, a paper entitled "The Psychological Preconditions of Rational Consensualism", which I still have but cannot understand? If I wrote that all by my self, how clever I was. I should add that the mini-thesis I submitted at the end of my MA programme was a different kettle of fish. Not only was it a more substantial document in terms of its length, but it also contained quite a lot of material I had gleaned from primary sources. Its subject was the impact of German Propaganda in the United States prior to the latter's entry into the First World War.

I enjoyed a very full social life at Yale. In the first part of the year a lot of it revolved around football weekends and a lot of those revolved around Charlotte Sears, who had quickly become my "steady date". The pattern of such weekends was roughly as follows. Some time on the Friday before the big game Charlotte would arrive by train from Boston. She would be put up by the very nice and hospitable Master of Berkeley College, Sam Hemingway, and his wife, who made a number of beds available for visiting girlfriends on these occasions. There was normally a party in somebody's room to go to and we might even look in on the torchlight rally of football supporters held each eve of game on the campus, when the spherically-shaped coach, named Herman Hickman, would address some rousing words to the assembled throng. I particularly remember this rotund hulk shouting out "You may not have got the best coach in the East, but you certainly got the biggest". Also present would have been the first ever black captain of the squad, Levi Jackson (such names stick in my mind). Next day started fairly slowly and we made our way to the Yale Bowl in the late morning warmly clad against the cold and armed with the odd flask of internal life support. The best people had long racoon fur coats and white buckskin shoes, but I was not in that league. I never became an expert spectator, but I soon came to enjoy the game and, more than that, the spectacle and general razzmatazz, which helped to extend an encounter lasting from one hour to something like three hours.

The opposing teams came from other "Ivy League" universities like Princeton and Cornell, and the climax of the season was the Harvard game. I learnt and, much to my wife's embarrassment, can still belt out the old football songs such as "March, March on Down the Field" and "Bulldog, Bulldog". I can still sing the Whiffenpoofs Song too, for that matter, but that has nothing to do with football. After the game there was generally a dinner dance. With the exception of the one after the Harvard game, these were quite informal affairs, run by the students but quietly supervised by the Hemingways or other senior members of staff. The Harvard occasion was a bit grander and brought out dinner jackets for the men and corsages for their dates.

One social occasion worth a special mention was the wedding in the Yale Divinity School Chapel of two Drama School students, Ross Lewis and Betsey Bacon. Ross had come from Britain on a Commonwealth Fellowship and he asked me to be his Best Man. The wedding itself was a hilarious affair and was stage-managed, as far as such things as lighting and the positioning of the principals at the altar were concerned, with all the flair and attention one might have expected of would-be professional actors. Apart from the Best Man's usual duties, I was deputed to take care of a wild old uncle of Betsey's who had a reputation for rotting up weddings. I have forgotten what I did, but it worked. What I was not asked to do, but did, was to leave a live white rabbit in their going-away car. Betsey reminded me of this in a letter she wrote out of the blue in 1988 telling me that Ross had died two years earlier.

Another big event in my social calendar that year was a trip down to Florida at Christmas to stay in a beach house at Fort Lauderdale with the family of a fellow member of Berkeley, Ted White. There were three of us, Ted, another Berkeleyite called Draper (his first name escapes me), and me: none of us had money to burn. So we signed on to do what students used to do In such circumstances, deliver a new car to its purchaser in Florida. The car in question was a convertible and being intended for use in Florida it did not have a heater. We started out from New York with snow on the ground and we soon felt the cold – to the point where the two who were not driving at the time huddled up together on the back seat to get some added warmth. We drove through the night taking it in turns and some time in the early evening of the following day we reached Jacksonville in warm sunshine. We decided to lower the canvas top and soak up some sun. As the hours passed, however, it got colder and we put the top back on again. Unfortunately I (yes, it had to be me) failed to engage the locking mechanism properly and we had not been going long before the top flew up over our heads and landed in a crumpled state on the back of the car. Closer inspection revealed that the damage was not as bad as at first feared, but one of the metal spars to which the canvas was attached was bent. We were able to go on, if somewhat more slowly, and get to Fort Lauderdale. When we delivered the car to the garage next day, Christmas Eve, the people there were surprisingly understanding and did not make as much fuss as I would have done myself. I did not let on that I had only had a driving licence for a few weeks. I had taken the test in New Haven and it was not exactly demanding: drive round the block and if you come back safely you pass. Those were the days.

I saw Ted again years later, in 1992. A letter arrived out of the blue saying that he and his wife, Lucy, were coming to Britain and could we meet? Anne and I had them to stay and liked them very much. It was planned that we would follow it up with a visit to them in Cape Cod and perhaps they would rent our house in Collobrières some time. Sadly, however, Ted died suddenly of lung cancer the following year. We have seen Lucy since, during a visit to Emma and family in New England.

I carried on playing tennis and squash at Yale and was a member of the college teams. I also did rather well in the university's main Squash Tournament, though I do not remember the details. I do recall making use from time to time of the Turkish baths at the gym to lose some weight, either to perform better in the squash court or perhaps cut a finer figure with the girls.

In 1950 the Korean War broke out and a surprise was in store for me. When I was originally advised by the U.S. Embassy in London to apply for an immigrant visa they neglected to tell me that I would be liable to military service if need be. One might have supposed, and I am sure I did, that only American citizens could be drafted, but this was not so. Without much delay I received a notification from the Draft Board to the effect that as a bona fide resident and immigrant I was subject to the draft and should report for a preliminary "physical" examination. To sugar the pill they also explained that if I did military service it would accelerate my progress to becoming an American citizen. A number of other people must have been in a similar situation, because it became known that one or two had panicked and taken the "chicken run" to Canada. I did not have to go as far as that and my explanation that in a few months I would be returning home to undertake military service there did the trick (Britain was by then in the war too). In fact I sometimes feel I missed a trick: it would have been quite an adventure to become a GI and surely I would never have been sent to Korea.

I was becoming more and more attached to both the idea of staying in America and, in truth, to Charlotte. Compared with dreary old, exhausted Britain the USA was a land of opportunity for anyone young. With hard work and a bit of luck there seemed to be no limits to what one might achieve. I felt at home there. However, despite the fact that it had been a bit of an afterthought in the first place, the idea of joining the British Foreign Service continued to attract me and in the end I decided to go back home. I feel sure I had the comforting thought in the back of my mind that I could go back later to the USA, if things turned out that way.

First, however, in the long summer vacation I set out on a grand tour of the country, in accordance with the terms of the Fellowship. A South African colleague in the Graduate School, Bob de Waal, and I agreed to join forces, buy a second-hand car and drive round the country. We soon found a second-hand car, an ageing Chevrolet owned by two old ladies who ran an antique shop in New Haven and who had treated their auto with loving care and not put many miles on the clock. After that we sat down and mapped out a rough itinerary. This was dictated to some extent by the need to economise on our living expenses by staying as far as possible in university fraternities en route. On that basis it looked as if we would be covering some 9,000 miles in the nine weeks at our disposal. We had not reckoned on the detours occasioned by the snowball effects of spontaneous American hospitality. The further we drove the more we found ourselves being handed on to friends or friends of friends like the baton in a relay race. In the event we went some 14,000 miles and the car took quite a beating. I still have a diary recording our itinerary. It was quite a Cook's tour and by the time we got back to New York we had seen the sights from New Orleans to Houston, Dallas, Oklahoma, the Panhandle, New Mexico (including the home of Freda Lawrence, D.H.'s widow, at Taos), the Grand Canyon, Las Vegas, Los Angeles, San Francisco, Yosemite, Reno, Salt Lake City, Wyoming, Yellowstone, Minneapolis, Chicago and Pittsburgh, to name but a few. We had even crossed the Mojave Desert during the day, which was a silly thing to do and the car did not like it either. Poor thing, it had never been out of New England before.

Bob and I had (have) different temperaments and occasionally during our nine weeks on the road together we got on each other's nerves – the familiar driver/navigator type of spat for one thing – but in general we learned to live and let live and had no serious problems, except with the car, which had never before experienced the hard going to which we subjected it. Half way along the clutch and brakes had to be replaced.

Thanks to these and other unexpected expenses and the extra mileage we clocked up, I finished the trip badly out of pocket and owing Bob a tidy sum of money, with another ten days to go before catching the *Queen Mary* home. When I explained my plight to Paul Mellon's secretary in New York, the great man himself generously wrote me out a cheque for double the amount I had mentioned, accompanying it with a brief note in his own hand to the effect that he was sorry for the embarrassment I had been caused and he did not want to hear mention of it again.

I was even able to fit in a quick trip to Boston to say fond farewells to Charlotte and her family. Everyone had been so kind to me and I left those friendly shores with a lump in my throat and uncertain whether I was doing the right thing. Of course it would be nice to get home, but within a matter of days I would be facing an abrupt change of lifestyle as I ventured into two years of National Service in the RAF. Most of all I hated parting from Charlotte. We had grown very close and it was thanks to her I overcame the hesitancy I had sometimes felt in earlier years about making the running with girls.

RAF National Service

After a few weeks at home to see the family and readjust my bearings, I packed the few belongings I was allowed to take with me and set off, on 29 November 1950, for RAF Padgate to begin my National Service. I was given a railway warrant to go by train to Manchester and on arrival I lined up with other recruits and marched in bedraggled formation to the city outskirts where Padgate was situated. There we were met by the N.C.O. who was to oversee our induction, Flight-Sergeant Holmer, and allocated to huts. I remember his name for two reasons. First, because although he liked to tease and take the mickey out of us, he was not the overbearing, lick-em-into-shape sort of N.C.O. Second, as fate would have it, he came into my life again later, when he asked me, by then a Flying Officer at RAF Debden, to act as his "Friend" during his Court Martial for going A.W.O.L.

Before I even went to Padgate it had been decided that, as a university graduate, I was the right material for turning into an Education Officer. So as soon as my week of documentation, medical tests, injections, kitting out etc was completed I was destined to go off to an Officer Cadet Training Unit (OCTU) at RAF Spitalgate, near Grantham, where I would spend twelve weeks being licked into shape as an officer. I would have liked to fly, because that is the raison d'être of the RAF, but not many National Servicemen were given the chance to do so and, in any case, my mother, who had lost one son in the RAF, would not have wanted to risk losing another. Like any bunch of raw recruits, we came from all walks of life to Padgate and represented, I suppose, a rough cross-section of the population. Some were very rough, or so they seemed to me, and did not know one end of a toothbrush from the other. Others were experiencing being away from their families for the first time in their lives and were homesick. As for me, I could not help comparing my present lot to the life I had led so recently in the USA and pined to be back there. However, I kept that strictly to myself and generally made a conscious effort not to appear stand-offish. It was a long, eye-opening week, to say the least. As we left at the end of it, Flt-Sgt Holmer said words to the effect that if ever those of us destined to become officers bumped into him again he hoped we would remember how kind he had been to us. I for one thought he was joking.

There was plenty of spit and polish for us Officer Cadets at Spitalgate – shining of buttons and boots and blancoing of webbing, cleaning of rifles, kit inspections, hours of monotonous drill and some pretty boring class work on "staff duties", Queen's Regulations and administration. Last but not least, we were made to run the gauntlet of a fearsome battle (i.e. obstacle) course, in full kit plus rifle or Bren gun, at night as well as by day, to the deafening accompaniment of thunderflashes thrown by grinning instructors. It was mid-winter and the fact that the ground was as hard as iron and there was snow lying around made it all the more unpleasant. It was certainly not my best thing. On the other hand, thanks to what I had learnt in the J.T.C. at Tonbridge, things like parade ground drill and firing weapons on the shooting range – so useful for an Education Officer – I found relatively easy. My abiding memory of those three months is that we were kept hard at it and that all I felt like doing when evening came was to collapse in my "pit" and go to sleep. Some evenings we had formal mess dinners where we practised the etiquette of how to behave like officers. The theory may have been all right, but later on in my brief service career I discovered that RAF mess nights were usually marked by far less decorous behaviour. We did not have many opportunities to get off the Station and go down into Grantham, and when we did we were required to wear uniform. I recall one or two Saturday afternoon sorties to the cinema and high tea to follow. Some time before Christmas I did have a day off to go to London to sit the Civil Service qualifying exam again for entry into the Foreign Service, as it was still called then. More of that later.

To my surprise and, possibly the disgust of some of the old warriors from the regular ranks on the OCTU course, I passed out top and was awarded the Sword of Honour (a paper sword only, unfortunately) at the end of the twelve weeks. That meant leading the passing out parade and, in case anyone should doubt it, I have some official photographs to prove it. Admittedly they are not as clear as they might be, because the parade was enveloped in a thick fog and even the hardy bystanders did not always find it easy to make out what was happening.

From Spitalgate the newly-fledged, but forever wingless, Pilot Officer Leahy was posted first to the RAF Education HQ at Wellesbourne Mountford in Warwickshire for a brief "orientation course". Thence to RAF Debden, near Saffron Walden, where I was to instruct officers attending Signals Staff Courses, under the auspices of the RAF's Engineering College at Henlow, how to write the King's English and set down on paper the logical development of an argument. Not very demanding, you might think, but you would be wrong: with many of the course members it was a case of starting from scratch. However, it did not take too much out of me and left me plenty of time to enjoy other things that the Service had to offer.

My first approach to Debden was not encouraging: as I got off the train from Liverpool Street at Audley End to change for Saffron Walden, I heard a porter shouting "Deadly End, Deadly End, change here for Suffering Boredom"! The RAF station itself was large, with a number of hangars surrounding an airfield, a parade ground, Station Headquarters and several other office blocks, a substantial brick-built Officers Mess and a married quarters area. As a bachelor National Service officer I was given a bedroom on the first floor of the mess, and the rather rough and ready services of an old civilian batman, who amongst other things would wake me up in the morning with a cup of very strong, orange-coloured tea. There was a flying wing equipped with old Anson and Oxford aircraft, but their activities were subsidiary to the main signals training component of the Station. A bit of a comedown, perhaps, since during the war Debden had been an active fighter station. It is recorded that one day during the Battle of Britain a German Luftwaffe pilot had lost his bearings and landed there by mistake. Fortunately for him he realised his error in time and took off again before anyone on the ground could do anything about it.

Apart from my main job, I had various general duties to perform on the Station. Like other junior officers I had to take my turn at being Orderly Officer, which entailed making various tours of inspection round the place, including looking in on the "erks" (other ranks) eating their meals and asking them whether they had any complaints. This was intended to be a rhetorical question and was normally taken as such; I do not recall ever having to deal with any grumbles. One also had to visit the Guardroom, to see who, if anyone was in the clink and, if so, how he was. I say "he" without hesitation, because we had no WAAFs at Debden, which made it all the odder that our Medical Officer should be a gynaecological specialist. I think he spent quite a lot of his time doling out a rather painful ointment to idiots who had been careless enough to catch the clap.

The sports facilities were excellent – good tennis and squash courts, as well as pitches for the major team games – and we were encouraged to make full use of them. Wednesday afternoons were given over to R and R (rest and recreation) and in the season this meant for me playing in the tennis team against other Stations. More often than not we were flown in one of the Station's aircraft to away matches. One year Debden did well in an Inter-Station league and as a result my doubles partner and I found ourselves playing in the RAF Tournament at Wimbledon, which was quite a thrill, even if we were knocked out in the second round. At a less exalted level I won the Men's Singles and Doubles of the Saffron Walden Hospital Cup Competition in 1952 and still have the cup and a newspaper cutting to remind me of it. The same local newspaper also records me as playing the leading role in an amateur society production of "See How They Run", a farce by Philip King

I had not been long at Debden before I received the news that I had failed the written qualifying exam for the Foreign Service. This came as a blow to my pride, because it was the first time I could remember having failed an exam. On the other hand it was not the crushing disappointment it would have been had I had my heart set on a Foreign Service career. As explained earlier, it had been a fairly casual choice from the start, although as time went on I had become more attached to the idea. Anyway, it seemed that was that and I now had to put it behind me. Here I was wrong, because, unbeknown to me, my brother-in-law, Phil Green, who was Chairman of his local Conservative Party, took up my case with his Member of Parliament, Captain Henry Kerby. He in turn approached, whether directly or indirectly I do not know, the Civil Service Commissioners and put it to them that it seemed unfair that someone who had passed the qualifying exam once and had been obliged to take it again when he was undergoing strenuous training in the RAF should be eliminated from the further stages of the competition. Somewhat surprisingly, the Civil Service Commissioners agreed and informed me that I "had been deemed" to have passed the written exam. Apparently other candidates had been in the same boat, for it was decreed at the same time that in future no one who had passed the qualifying written exam once need sit it a second time.

A few months later I appeared before the Civil Service Selection Board. For a number of years it had been the custom to have the candidates stay at a country house in Stoke d'Abernon for the purpose and it was jokingly said that they were closely watched to see how they used their forks when eating peas. By the time my turn came round it took place in London and was not a residential affair. But it still involved three days of fast-moving tests of various kinds, both in groups and individually, and I found it a draining experience. If I had a sense of humour, I had lost it by the time I had my interview with the psychologist member of the examining staff. He asked me what I thought about the Selection Board process and whether I felt I had been able to give a fair account of myself in the tests.

Fools rush in where angels fear to tread. I could see that he had before him on his desk two five-minute self-assessments we had been asked to make, one as if written by a biased friend and the other by a penetrating critic. I told him that with hindsight I felt that I had not done myself justice in either of them, to which he replied with a wintry smile that he thought they were about right. I was not amused. One other thing I remember is that at the end we were required to rank the members of our group in two lists, first on merit and second as holiday companions, and that my two lists differed greatly. Not really surprising: if someone like Margaret Thatcher had been in my group she would have been top of one list and bottom of the other.

Not long after came the final interview. It was set up in classic, horse-shoe style and, apart from the Civil Service Commission Chairman and a senior member of the Foreign Office (FO), the five or so other interviewers were drawn from different walks of life. It was obviously a nerve-racking experience for the candidates – and was intended to be – but I do not recall any particularly hostile or tricky questions. The tittle-tattle among the candidates waiting their turn in the ante-room was that you were in serious contention if, on leaving the room at the end of the interview, you were asked by the Chairman to stay outside for five minutes in case they should want to call you back in for further questioning. No such request was made to me and I felt deflated. In fact I now know from my later experience sitting as one of the interviewers on the board that there is nothing in this, but of course I did not realise it at the time. In any event I was put out of my misery about two weeks later when I received an official notification to say that I had passed.

It would be some time yet, however, before I could enter the hallowed portals of the FO, because I had to finish my National Service first. In October 1951 I was sent to the RAF Hospital at Ely to have an operation on a hammer toe. Definitely not the most glamorous or deserving case in the orthopaedic ward, it has to be said. In one of the neighbouring beds, I remember, there was a pilot encased in splints and plaster and suspended on pulleys who had somehow been rescued from the wreck of his aircraft. On coming round from a long operation he found the Hospital Matron looking down at him over the top of the screen and, to her great surprise, he shouted at her "Matron, if you come one step nearer, I'll rape you". His spirit might have been willing, but sadly the flesh definitely was not. By comparison I felt a terrible fraud. The more so when, as tutored by the nurses, I lay back on my pillow looking pale and pitiable on one of the doctor's rounds and was prescribed a bottle of Guinness a day as a pick-me-up. This was an enviable perk, because alcohol was otherwise not allowed in the ward. The rule was also honoured in the breach on the night of the General Election, when the nurses connived at our holding a party in the ward by smuggling in some of the hard stuff. Every time a Conservative victory was announced on the radio we had another drink and as the overall result was a victory for the Tories those of us who were in bed got quite sozzled in a horizontal position.

The death of King George VI in February 1952 was keenly felt at Debden. We know now that he was already in a frail state of health when it happened. At the time, though, it came as a bolt from the blue to most people. Along with other Service establishments, Debden observed a long period of official mourning during which semi-official social activities, such as Mess Nights, were cancelled or curtailed. This, combined with a general injunction not to indulge in unseemly private behaviour like organising or going to parties and dances, meant that we young bachelor officers hung around the Mess at a bit of a loose end. The vacuum was partly filled by taking up playing snooker, mainly with a fellow Education Officer, John Myrnagh. Day after day he and I monopolised one of the tables and played a long series of very competitive games, which is euphemistic language for saying that neither of us liked losing. From that day to this I have hardly been near a snooker table.

Early that summer, Charlotte, with whom I had been keeping in regular touch by letter, came over to England. I took some leave and we went off on a tour of Devon and Cornwall in a car kindly provided by Phil Green from the transport section of his family firm at Portslade (I did not have a car of my own). We stayed for the most part in pubs and had a happy, relaxed time picking up the threads again since we last saw one another. Outwardly Charlotte seemed to be as warm as ever, but she let me know that she had acquired another steady boyfriend and I was not the only man in her life.

For my part I still felt much attached to her, but was not in a position financially to propose early marriage. So we held off from making any decisions about the future. I did not, of course, know it at the time, but this proved to be a blessing in disguise, because not long after that, in August, I met my future wife, Anne Pitchford, at the 21st birthday party of a mutual friend, Pat Fuente. I do not remember much about the party – nor does she – nor was it a case of love at first sight. But I was impressed enough to ask her out to the cinema in Brighton shortly afterwards. Her mother, however, was anything but impressed when she heard that after the show we had had fish and chips on the beach and I had walked her to the bus station instead of seeing her home to Rottingdean. After that we did not see each other for 18 months, by which time my boorish behaviour was forgiven, if not forgotten, and things began to move fast. More of that anon: I must first finish my National Service, which I duly did at the end of November 1952.

All in all I enjoyed my two years in the RAF. National Service officers were certainly not well paid. I think that at its best my monthly pay cheque came to something like £25, before tax and compulsory mess deductions, which left me about half that amount for out of pocket expenditure (which included some items of uniform). I got by somehow and cannot say that I suffered many deprivations. However, it never entered my head to stay on and make a career of it, certainly not in the Education Branch, and it was a bit of an embarrassment to be given the job of trying to persuade NS "erks" to do so. On the other hand, I did not feel my two years were by any means wasted years and rather saw them as a supplementary part of my own education. At the risk of sounding like an old blimp, I often wish that the young people of today had the opportunity to benefit in the same way, albeit in a non-military environment.

FO Central Department and Private Secretary

I presented myself, all bright-eyed and bushy-tailed, to the Personnel Department of the FO on the morning of 10 December. I am not sure they were expecting me then, because the first thing that happened was that I was asked to come back after lunch. Eventually I was ushered in to see the Head of Personnel Department, John Henniker-Major, who told me that early in the New Year I would be joining the Central Department as the "Desk Officer" dealing with the Soviet Zone of Germany ("East Germany"). The intervening period I was to spend brushing up my French as a paying guest with a French family recommended by the Embassy in Paris. This was not obviously relevant to East Germany, but apparently was the best thing Personnel Department could think up to keep me occupied until my desk became vacant. At that time there were no beginners' training courses – jump straight in at the deep end was the order of the day. Happily, my jump was from a low board. My joining pay, incidentally, was the princely sum of £450 a year.

A day or two later I went off to Tours to join the Dreux family. A very nice, kind family they were too, father and mother in their forties and two teenage children. He was a hard-working local businessman and I did not see much of him, except at weekends. Madame was jolly and vivacious. I am sure some of the family must have had some English, but they were careful not to speak it to me. They lived in a town house not far from the centre of Tours. I do not remember much about it, except that its plumbing was antiquated and there was that distinctive French aroma about the place that I met on my first visit to Paris.

I spent the mornings attending French classes at the Institut des Etrangers, an extra-mural department of the University of Poitiers. Much time was given up to correct pronunciation, which was fitting since Tours is reputed to be the place with the most "correct" accent in France. We looked in mirrors while we shaped our lips in the approved fashion to elicit unfamiliar vowel sounds until we had mouth fatigue. At the time it seemed very tediously, but it stood me in good stead later on: as Professor Higgins famously said in My Fair Lady, in France it does not matter what you do as long as you pronounce it right. The afternoons were for home study and for absorbing the sights and sounds of Tours in any way I chose. Madame Dreux was kind enough to show me round. Once or twice on Sundays Monsieur took his son and me shooting with his "chasse", of which he was a prominent member. I am not a field sports man and have never been keen on shooting animals. But it would have been churlish of me to refuse, so off I went with him, with a borrowed shotgun and, compared with the others, badly turned out for the occasion. I did not do much damage to the wildlife myself, but the display of hares, rabbits and pheasants laid out on the ground at the end of the day was impressive. I would not have been surprised to see the odd chasseur lying there too, given the disconcerting way in which they would form contracting circles round a copse or field and blaze away at anything that moved. But somehow we all survived to partake in mid-afternoon of a convivial late lunch cooked and served in the forest cabin where we had forgathered earlier in the day.

As luck would have it, I was just beginning to make real progress with my French and to feel that if this agreeable introduction to diplomatic life might be allowed to go on for a bit longer, I might become quite proficient, when I received a summons back to the FO. I was reluctant to leave, but of course a new boy does what he is told and I returned to the FO towards the end of January to take up my position in Central Department.

The department was housed in the old India Office side of the building. Like all departments, we had a "Third Room", which was shared by four or five "desk officers", each with one or two telephones. So one soon learnt to work amidst a constant buzz, even bedlam, of conversation and ringing of bells. Moreover the room was so crowded that visitors often had to be seen on a couch in the corridor outside. A coal fire burned away in an old-fashioned grate and added to the positively Dickensian atmosphere. Nowadays such conditions would surely not comply with the conditions of this or that Health & Safety Act, but we took them for granted. Central Department's area of responsibility was Germany and Austria and it rated as one of the more important political departments in the office. It was not a conventional one, in the diplomatic sense, because both countries were still occupied and were not yet independent. The British Control Commission for Germany, for example, was still formally the administering power in the British Occupied Zone, although in practice the German authorities had assumed responsibility for running many of their own affairs. The Austrian section of the department was small, consisting of two desk officers engaged in the long and tortuous negotiation of the "Austrian State Treaty". It almost seemed as if they had a job for life, so protracted was the negotiation (eventually the thing was signed, after my time in the department, and they moved on to pastures new). The German section was appreciably bigger. The desk officers were Michael Palliser, George Hall and Alan Brooke Turner, whom I was replacing on East Germany. There was also a more senior man, Fred Warner, who rated a room of his own. The Head of Department was Denis Allen, and the Assistant was Pat Hancock. Some of these were high-flyers who were to distinguish themselves in their later careers. Fred Warner was a colourful character who caught my attention by appearing one morning still attired in the tails he had donned the evening before for some society ball. He came to the attention of the Permanent Under-Secretary, Sir William Strang, for a different reason. Fred's main subject was the deconcentration of German industry and one day a submission he had put up about one particular industrial plant came back from the P.U.S. with the crisp comment that while he did not disagree with Mr Warner's action he should point out that decisions on such matters could only be taken by Ministers. Fred was later to come under a more serious cloud in the aftermath of the defection of Burgess and Maclean because it was felt that as he knew Burgess well he should have reported his errant life-style, especially his heavy drinking, to his superiors. In fairness to Fred it should be said that telling tales on one's colleagues was frowned on by most people in the Service at the time and only became part of the new security culture after the horses had bolted. Fred ended up as Ambassador to Japan and after taking early retirement became a member of the European Parliament. So he did all right.

As I mentioned earlier, in those days one learnt one's trade in the FO on the job. The departmental day did not start until 10am, at least not for lesser mortals like me, and finished somewhere around 7pm, depending on how much was going on. Leisurely, perhaps, by modern standards, but we did work Saturday mornings as well. Some people wore black coats and striped trousers, but most of us made do with dark suits, bowler hats or homburgs ("Anthony Edens") and, of course, we carried umbrellas. In other respects, however, the FO was neither as formal nor hierarchical as I had expected: mostly we addressed one another by Christian name, up and down the line, and "Sir" was reserved only for exalted people like the P.U.S., whom one rarely if ever met anyway. Stiff shirts were more in evidence physically than metaphorically.

My particular area of responsibility, the Soviet Zone of Germany, did not involve me in any conventional diplomatic activity. I was concerned almost entirely with collating information from various sources about the East German political and economic scene. Quite a lot of this came from the intelligence agencies, including the British Military Mission (BRIXMIS) accredited to the Soviet military authorities. Like their Soviet counterpart (SOXMIS) in the three occupied zones of Western Germany, BRIXMIS ran cloak and dagger patrols in fast cars across the countryside, taking illegal photographs of strategic installations, counting parked aircraft, assessing the load-carrying capacity of bridges etc, often hotly pursued by the security police. It was obviously considered important to maintain this activity – and I am sure those involved enjoyed it – but I cannot now recall how valuable in political terms we found the information it produced. I do remember that the volume of intelligence documentation generally that came my way was such that my "press" (cupboard) was soon bursting at the seams and I quickly learnt to give only the most cursory of glances to the lower grade material. After the first excitement of exposure to the espionage scene had passed, it was quite humdrum stuff and the regular summaries I produced for my seniors rarely induced any reaction.

It was, therefore, all the more surprising when after only a few months I was summoned to the office of the Minster of State, Selwyn Lloyd, for an interview as a candidate to be his Assistant Private Secretary. Even more surprising that I got the job, particularly as I thought I had given a rather inept answer to his provocative question of why on earth I wanted to do it. It did not make me feel any better when he added that he would not want to do it himself! Anyway, get it I did and I suppose it was something of a feather in my cap. I was now (July 1953) in a much more exposed position, still knowing very little about the organisation of the FO and the people at the top of it with whom I would henceforth be in daily contact. Luckily for me I had a splendid mentor in Tony Duff, the senior Private Secretary, who sat at a desk opposite me and observed everything I was doing or not doing. (Actually he did not always sit, because he also liked to stand and work at one of those high clerk's desks so familiar in the Victorian era.) Tony was a man of great experience and strength of character who was not afraid to speak his mind to whomsoever, including the Minister himself. He had been at Dartmouth before the war and served in the RN throughout the war, in which he distinguished himself as a submarine commander, winning both the DSO and DSC. He acted as the channel of communication on all matters of substance between Selwyn Lloyd and the FO Departments concerned and also as the Minister's sounding board and personal adviser.

My job was principally concerned with making the minister's appointments, arranging his papers, liaising with his constituency secretary in the House of Commons, arranging his "pairs" in collaboration with his Parliamentary Private Secretary, David Ormsby Gore, and doing other fairly mundane, but still quite important, things. How important I found out to my cost on one occasion when I sent him off to a big dinner where he was the guest of honour and principal speaker dressed in his dinner jacket, while all the rest of the assembled company were in tails. I heard about that next day all right.

Two of my other functions required delicate handling. One was to keep in touch with his wife, Bae, to make sure that any social engagements she wanted to make did not clash with his official commitments. Bae was twenty years or so younger than him and liked London society life; she was not much interested in his Wirral constituency, to which he often had to go at weekends. He was more attached to a quiet home life and doted on their small daughter, Joanna. I remember once meeting him at Euston on a Sunday night with his red work boxes and as he looked over his programme for the coming week in the car he groaned at the prospect of two or three late night sorties which Bae had arranged. "Never", he said, "marry a woman twenty years younger than you!" They were later divorced.

The other, somewhat strange, responsibility I inherited from my predecessor, Jimmy Reeve, was to dictate Selwyn's "personal" diary every day to Beatrice Flynn, his formidable Personal Assistant, who typed it up on quarto sheets. I assume it was intended to be a sort of aide memoire for the time when he came to write his memoirs. Moreover, it was not just a case of recording events, I was also expected to reflect his own reactions to them and how he felt about problems and people he was dealing with. What I never found out is whether any use was ever made of them; all I knew is that they were put away in big red file boxes on a shelf in the outer office.

At first, I found working for Selwyn Lloyd unsettling. Until I got to know him better, I did not appreciate his quirky sense of humour. One day early on he asked me to decypher something he had scrawled in his execrable hand on a document which had now come back to him for the second time. When I had to admit defeat, he said, without a hint of a smile, "that is what you are paid to do, I am not". I remember on another occasion answering a summons to his room, only to be told "What the hell are you doing here? Get out". It later transpired that he had wanted Tony Duff and had pressed the buzzer the wrong number of times. According to

Tony, Selwyn asked him why I could not get the hang of things. To which Tony claimed to have replied that he supposed I would soon learn to treat him with the contempt that Private Secretaries often developed for their Ministers. He was quite capable of saying that, but I doubt that he did.

In retrospect it is clear that I joined the Minister's team at a time when he was under especially severe pressure and, for that reason, he may have been unusually tetchy. The Foreign Secretary, Anthony Eden, had been ill for some time and had had two operations on his gall bladder the year before. Shortly after the Coronation in June, which because of his illness he was unable to attend, he went to Boston for a third operation. In Eden's three absences, the Prime Minister, Winston Churchill, assumed formal responsibility for the FO, whilst in theory leaving Selwyn Lloyd to run the day-to-day affairs of the office. In practice, however, Churchill could not forbear to intervene in matters he would normally have left to Anthony Eden, and this was very frustrating for Selwyn. But at the end of June the Prime Minister had a stroke and had to retire from the fray. It must have been even more irritating for Selwyn that in this situation, with Churchill off his back, he now had another overlord to contend with in the person of Lord Salisbury ("Bobbety"), who was put in temporary charge of the office.

The extent of Churchill's illness was disguised from all but a restricted inner circle. Outwardly at least he made a speedier recovery than expected and before long resumed his supervision of the FO. Missives on matters great and small came tumbling out of No.10 again. Many of them passed through my hands for further distribution in the FO One I have never forgotten read "I have frequently noticed in FO papers the use of the word 'prepared' when what is meant is 'willing'. In my experience the Foreign Office is often willing, but never prepared". To this day, I try not to confuse the two. Recovery or not, Churchill's physical stamina was now clearly diminished and Ministers found it increasingly difficult to get him to focus properly on the agenda of Cabinet meetings. More and more he was apt to waste time on personal reminiscences, and yet his colleagues were so much in awe of the old man that they held back from calling him to order. Several times I recall waiting for Selwyn outside the Cabinet Room to pick up his papers at the end of the meeting and to hear how he had got on with a particular item on which we were anxiously awaiting a decision; and when he emerged he would pull a long face and say there had been no time to discuss it.

Eden himself returned at the end of September. If his operation had provided some relief of his gall bladder problem it did not appear to have done much for his bile, because he could still have a filthy temper (the famous suave exterior was reserved for the cameramen and the Party faithful). One Saturday morning when I was alone in the office and Selwyn was in his constituency, Eden rang from No.1 Carlton Gardens to speak to him. I started to explain that I could not put him through when he exploded "Don't waste my time, put him on the line". Again I started to say that Selwyn was not there and the best I could do was to get a message to him to ring him at No. 1 Carlton Gardens, when he became even angrier with me for "prevaricating". Just before slamming the phone down he asked who the hell I thought I was. Happily my name did not mean anything to him.

Amongst other subjects, U.N. affairs came under Selwyn's wing in the FO and throughout the autumn of 1953 he was much preoccupied with the General Assembly. He went to New York on two, possibly three, occasions during this period and on one of these he took me with him as well as Tony Duff, to help lighten the load of arranging the unending round of calls, meetings, interviews, lunches and dinners which were an inherent part of the General Assembly scene. I stayed for about ten days and when I had the chance wandered around the U.N. building familiarising myself with what was going on in the various committees. I was fascinated by both the theatre of it and the actors themselves, prominent amongst whom I remember the notorious head of the Soviet delegation, Andrei Vyshinsky, and the wily, mercurial Indian, Krishna Menon. Our own representative, Gladwyn Jebb (later to be my boss in Paris) was one of the star performers.

Charlotte Sears came to New York for a few days during this time and I saw her whenever I could get away. There was no doubting we still felt warm and affectionate and physically attracted, but somehow our attempts to rekindle the old flame lacked the vital spark. The absences had been too long. Eventually Charlotte confided that she was now unofficially engaged to a young American Foreign Service officer. This hit me rather hard at the time and I remember feeling pretty miserable on the flight back to London. We lost touch, but in 1955 I heard that she and her husband were in the American Embassy in Phnom Penh. By then I was happily married too and Anne and I were en poste not that far away, in Singapore. Some time later I received a letter from Charlotte's father, Mason Sears, telling me the sad news that she had died from a severe attack of polio in Cambodia. As fate would have it, Anne too subsequently contracted polio, on 9 May 1957, but mercifully she pulled through and survived.

On Monday 15 March 1954, Anne and I renewed our acquaintance, by chance, on a train from Worthing to Victoria. We had both been spending the weekend at home, she in Durrington where the family had moved from Rottingdean, and I with Ma and Pete at "Bruff". In fact I think we merely glimpsed one another on the train (I noticed she was wearing a funny little hat with a big feather) and it was only when we reached Victoria that we had a brief moment to talk. Two days later Peter and Ricky Hall, an old school friend from Tonbridge, and I were throwing a party on St. Patrick's Day in the flat we shared at St. Andrew's Mansions, West Kensington, and, thinking Anne would be a great asset, I invited her to come. To my pleasant surprise she agreed, despite the short notice. On the evening in question, she arrived late because she had just been to the Ideal Home Exhibition at Olympia with her mother and had had to rush home to change. I wonder if the latter warned her to get me to organize a taxi back for her, because otherwise I was liable to put her on a bus? I do not recall, but I do know that I was very excited by her and arranged to see her again soon.

We went out a lot in the next few weeks and many early mornings I spent wending my weary way back across London from Anne's flat in Russell Square to St. Andrew's Mansions. I must have presented a bleary-eyed picture in the office. Some time towards the end of May I took her out to dinner at Veeraswamy's, a favourite place of my father's in days gone by, and fired up by the curry proposed to her later in the evening. She seemed pleased but said she would have to think about it. Happily for me she did not take too long about it and next day said yes. But before we could make it official, in time-honoured fashion it was agreed I should ask her father for his consent, which I did at Durrington Manor the next weekend. That was quite a pantomime, as he was even more nervous about his lines than I was. As for Anne, she was in a state of high old excitement and had to be calmed by her mother in another room. Jack Pitchford and I first fortified ourselves with a drink and talked about a number of things before we got to the point. Even then the point was a bit blunted because I don't think he asked me the traditional questions of what I was earning and what my prospects were. Nor, thank heavens, did he ask me what I knew about motor cars. It was only later that he, a distinguished automobile engineer and the Manager (subsequently Chairman and finally President) of Ricardo Engineers at Shoreham, discovered that his future son-in-law could not distinguish the sound of a diesel engine under the bonnet. Anyway, he signified his approval and we both heaved a sigh of relief that it was over.

Wedding day, August 1954

From that moment things gathered pace. The official announcement appeared on 10 June and after consultation with all concerned it was agreed we would be married on Saturday 14 August at Durrington Parish Church (St. Symphorians). Nowadays one would not choose August for a wedding because so many would-be guests would be away on holiday, but at that time holidays were taken in shorter bursts and more spread out. I cannot pretend that I was much involved in the detailed wedding preparations, but I was kept pretty busy at weekends with meeting Anne's relations and introducing her to mine. I also had to plan our honeymoon and, more important still, find somewhere for us to live.

As luck would have it, both things fell into our laps. René and Geneviève Wisner, long-standing family friends of the Pitchfords, generously offered us as a wedding present the use of their house at Pramousquier in the South of France for a fortnight, including the services of their bonne-à-tout-faire. Soon after I learnt that Julian Bullard, a fellow new FO entrant, had been posted to Vienna and he and his wife were vacating a flat they had been renting in Orange Street, just off the Haymarket. It sounded too good to be true, first and second floors over an old-fashioned "wholesale purveyor of caviar"; weekly rent £4, easy walking distance from the office. The caviar merchants, Whites, were the landlords and they seemed only too pleased for us to take over the flat from the Bullards.

Other things soon fell into place. My brother, Peter, agreed to be my Best Man and I was able to get on with more mundane matters like fixing our travel to France and arranging a new passport for Anne in her married name. The days seemed to fly by and 14 August was upon us almost before I realised it. I had a month's leave from the office, including the week before, during which, amongst other things, a stag party was arranged for me in a pub at Burpham, near Arundel. In time-honoured fashion I cannot say I remember much about it.

It rained a lot in the days running up to August 14 and we were all getting quite anxious, as the plan was for the bridal party to walk to and from the church. Happily, the sun shone on the day itself and all was well. The wedding was set for 2.30pm and I remember taking a long walk along the beach with Peter in the morning, ending up with one or two fairly stiff drinks with Uncle "G", who was known for his heavy hand with the bottle. I suppose he thought I needed some Dutch courage. Anyway, like Mr Doolittle, I made it to the church on time. After the service conducted by the Vicar, Rev. Nathaniel Evans, we processed back to Durrington Manor, where a marquee had been set up on the lawn. There were some one hundred guests in morning coats, colourful dresses and big hats, the champagne flowed, the pictures were taken, the cake was cut, the speeches made, all as it should be, and before too many people could become tired and emotional Annie and I made our getaway. The family Land Rover was waiting outside the front door, with Smooker, the Ricardo Works' driver/handyman at the wheel, as we emerged dressed to the nines in our going away outfits, including hats for both of us. It was clear from the number of tin cans, kippers etc tied to the back and the shaving foam smeared on the windscreen that it was not going to get us very far. But this had been foreseen by Jack Pitchford and the Land Rover only had to go a short way from the house, before we abandoned it and transferred to another car which had been parked out of sight. With even greater foresight someone had left us a bottle of champagne and two glasses, presumably thinking that we should keep ourselves topped up. Perhaps for that reason we made an unscheduled stop in the middle of Horsham to relieve the pressure a bit, only to bump into Tony Duff doing the same thing – he had brought his small daughter to the wedding. Then on to the Richmond Hill Hotel, where we were to spend the night before catching an early flight to Marseilles next morning. (For the record, the wedding reception was captured on ciné-film and later transferred to videotape. Once or twice it has give our children a good laugh: what our grandchildren would make of it I hate to think].)

Our flight was uneventful until the last ten minutes, when I became very queasy as we circled the airport in bumpy air. I held a sickbag close to my mouth, while Anne, bless her, put a comforting arm around me, and between us we saw the crisis off. She now had her first inkling of what "in sickness and in health" might mean. I am sorry to say she had the message brought home even more forcefully when on one or two nights during the next fortnight I had bouts of migraine and paced around the room holding my head.

I had arranged to hire a Renault 4 in Marseilles and we had to find our way to the garage to pick it up – nothing so simple then as doing it at the airport. Having done all that we eventually got going in the heat of the day and on reaching Toulon decided to quench our thirst in a café. When we got back to the car I could not persuade it to start, indeed I could not even get the ignition key to turn. After a fruitless struggle, we flagged down the first Renault 4 that came by and asked the driver to help us. He quickly explained that the anti-theft locking device had to be released and that one did this by turning the driving wheel at the same time as the ignition key. Commonplace nowadays, I know, but I had never seen one like it before. Jack Pitchford, of course, just loved it when we told him about it later! No more adventures, I am pleased to say, before we arrived at "Le Cisampo" in Pramousquier.

It was an idyllic spot for a honeymoon. Perched on the rocks with a crescent-shaped balcony looking down on the clear blue water below. From the garden, stone steps led down to the rocky shoreline and, although the place where we swam was theoretically open to the public, in practice access to it was not easy from either side and not many people made the effort. The maid seemed anxious to please and looked after us well. She was also anxious about the two Briard hounds the Wisners had left behind in her care, because they were of different sexes and the bitch was on heat. An appropriate honeymoon problem it might be said, but it was no joking matter to keep them apart all the time, as instructed. One day towards the end of our stay they did get together. We never heard whether anything came of it, so to speak, and were too afraid to raise the matter with the Wisners.

We spent our time lazing and swimming and did not venture very far afield. The odd meal out, but even in those days the beaches were crowded in August and compared with swimming off the rocks below the house they held little attraction. I said earlier that the maid looked after us well. Too well, I fear, because by the time I had settled our account with her at the end of our stay I had precious few francs left. So it was that on our last day we were practically on the breadline and instead of rounding things off with a final dinner in Nice before catching our late night flight from there, we made do with a bowl of soup and spent the rest of the time sitting on the beach in our going-away suits and with our luggage all around us. Anne found it difficult to believe that the £10 traveller's cheque I later found in my wallet was a genuine oversight, but I swear it was. With the franc exchange rate as it was then, £10 would indeed have bought us a good dinner. Anyway, we arrived back safe and sound at Heathrow in the early hours of the morning, to be met, very sportingly, by our two mothers.

We moved into the Orange Street flat soon after. The Bullards had told us that when they took up residence there they found a tin of caviar and a welcoming message on a table. We looked for ours in vain; sadly Whites must have decided once was enough. I said earlier that they were an old-fashioned establishment. An indication of this was the stand-up clerk's desk in their office, and another the old-fashioned ice-box in our kitchen, instead of an electric refrigerator. Twice a week, at about 7am, the iceman came carrying a big block of ice on his shoulder, which he placed in the box. It worked more or less all right most of the time, but when we came back after a weekend away we would find that melted ice-water had overflowed on to the floor. Never mind, the flat suited us well and we were lucky to have it. The building was later pulled down to make way for a multi-storey car park.

Back in the office, a number of changes occurred. First Tony Duff left on posting to Paris and was replaced by Richard Sykes (later assassinated by the I.R.A. when he was Ambassador to the Hague). I liked Tony very much and our paths were to cross again during the course of our careers. Then, in a ministerial reshuffle in October, Selwyn Lloyd was moved to become Minister of Supply and was replaced by Anthony Nutting. I had got used to Selwyn and, I think, he to me. I did not have time to get to know his successor in the same way, because early in November I was told by Personnel Department that I was being moved myself, on posting as Third Secretary in the Commissioner-General's Office in Singapore, where I was expected early in the New Year.

We had to get our skates on. The first thing was to have official medical examinations to make sure we were physically fit enough for the tropics. That done, the next thing was to book our passage on a boat, which we did in the old P&O offices a stone's throw from the flat in Cockspur Street. To this day I can never pass that spot without recalling some of the excitement we felt as we looked at a deck plan and chose a cabin on the S.S.

Chusan leaving Tilbury on 21 December. Booking an airline ticket pales by comparison. There were all sorts of other things to get done: ordering a car (a Morris Minor), arranging tenders from three removals firms for packing up and sending off our goods and chattels, and buying tropical clothing. We also had to study the "post report" to find out about conditions in Singapore – having a baby, in particular, for Anne was expectant. At the same time I had to find out more about my job there, as well as hand over my present one to my successor. Last but not least, I had to write in time-honoured fashion to the Head of Chancery and ask him whether there was anything I could bring out for him in our baggage. Imagine my surprise when he wrote back to say he would much appreciate it if I could bring him a minnow-catcher from the Army & Navy Stores. I wondered whether he was teasing me, but along I went to the old emporium and got one for him. It looked like a metal tube with chicken wire set into one end, but there must have been more to it than that.

December 21 was dank, dark and overcast, as befits the shortest day of the year, and Tilbury was hardly at its best, if it ever was. I am not sure what the family, including Ma, felt as they came to see us off, but they all put on a smile for the camera. Annie and I could hardly wait to get going. As we were getting ready to go aboard, I bumped into George Jellicoe, a fellow member of the FO, who was seeing off his mother, the widow of the famous Admiral, and he asked me to keep an eye on her during the voyage – she was doing the round-trip to Hong Kong and back. She looked a pretty formidable old biddy to me, with a brooch of her husband's flagship, the *Iron Duke,* adorning her ample upper deck, and quite capable of looking after herself. As things turned out, the main thing she wanted me to do was to act as a sort of bridge matchmaker, i.e. finding people to make up her bridge fours. The first time I did this, I reported to her, all bright-eyed and bushy-tailed, that I had found three suitable players and told them where to find her and how to recognise her. "And I suppose you described me, young man, as looking like an old battleaxe?" she said looking me straight in the eye. As these were more or less the words I had used, I retreated in some confusion; and I was more circumspect the next time.

Soon after we set sail, we met Stuart and Dorothy Hills, with whom we quickly struck up a close and lasting friendship. Very sadly Stuart died two years ago (2004) at the age of 80. He was some two to three years older than me and was a senior boy at Tonbridge when I arrived there in 1941. When he left the next year to join the army he would not have known of my existence, though he remembers my two elder brothers, Roly and Peter. I certainly knew of his, all the more so when a year or two later he returned to the school sporting the MC ribbon on his subaltern's uniform and looking every inch the glamorous war hero. Some time after the war he joined the Malayan Civil Service and was now returning to Ipoh, where he was Deputy Labour Commissioner, after a spell of home leave. We got on well from the start and found we had a lot in common, quite apart from the old school tie. Notably the same sense of humour and views on some of our more comic, and tiresome, fellow passengers, about whom Stuart would make funny comments in all too audible stage whispers, which made us all giggle

What a lovely girl!

(there were quite a few old cruise types on board doing the round trip to Hong Kong who made ready butts for his wisecracks). Stuart and I played a lot of deck games, while Anne and Dorothy, both being pregnant, preferred less strenuous pursuits. We had quite rough seas most of the way to Port Said, including Christmas Day, when the lurching and slithering that accompanied dinner made it difficult to get the turkey and Christmas pudding down, and keep it there.

It was still very chilly when the four of us went ashore at Port Said and made our way, like many a traveller over the years, to that exciting Aladdin's Cave, Simonartz. Unlike our forebears, we did not equip ourselves with solar topees, but Anne bought a pair of gold sandals to mark the occasion. As we later walked back to the ship, we inhaled those never-to-be-forgotten aromas of the East, compounded of spices, perfumes, donkeys and drains, to name just the mentionable elements. On going back on board we found two "Gully Gully" men entertaining the passengers with their baby chicks and sleight of hand, another traditional part of the Port Said scene; as also the men stretching up in their flowing white jellabas from their small boats to sell their wares, and take the money, by hauling up small baskets over the side of the ship. The next day the *Chusan* made her stately way down the Suez Canal, reaching Suez itself in the early evening. On New Year's Day we stopped at Aden, where it was warmer – I imagine it always is there – and we threw pennies over the side for small boys to dive down and retrieve in the rather oily-looking water. Thence to Bombay, and Stuart thought fit to record in his diary the exciting news that en route I had been defeated in the finals of the men's ping pong competition. We spent the day by the swimming pool in a well-known local club and made the mistake of eating cold meat and salad, which unfortunately made Anne feel very sick next day. We should have known better.

Next stop Colombo, on a very hot day. The four of us went to Mount Lavinia and did some swimming in the surf before, and after, lunch at the hotel. Another leisurely interlude in a leisurely journey. How I feel sorry for those younger people who missed the era of sea travel and now have to rush everywhere and back by air. On 11 January, two weeks after leaving Tilbury, we arrived at our penultimate stop, Penang. For the Hills it was the end of the voyage and we bade each other fond farewells as they disembarked. We had had a lot of fun together. An old school friend of Anne's, Anne (Brucie) Crawford, was on the quayside with her husband, Hunter Crawford, to take us off for the day. He was the manager of a rubber estate not far away and an old Malaya hand. They gave us our first experience of trishaw travel and our first taste of that delicious Malay dish, nasi goreng; and probably a lot of good advice as well. The next day we made our way down the Malacca Straits to Singapore, accompanied for part of the way by some flying fish, and reached our final destination the following morning.

Singapore

We were met by the Administration Officer from the Commissioner-General's Office at Phoenix Park, Bill Bates, and his very efficient "fixer", Colin Elloy, a locally-employed Anglo-Indian, who dealt with the formalities and whisked us and our cabin luggage off in no time. He also ensured that our car and heavier baggage were unloaded, while we were driven to the Cockpit Hotel, where we were to stay until an official house became available in a week or two. The hotel was quite small and consisted of a central reception and dining area and a number of separate bedroom annexes connected to it by covered pathways. The roofing was made of tin and when the rain came down, as it did every day and/or night, it made a very loud drumming noise. The only other memorable thing about the Cockpit was the Indonesian rijstafel served at lunch on Saturdays. Otherwise it seemed to us rather a dreary place and after a few days we were impatient to get away from it. A semi-detached house at 75 Holland Road had been earmarked for us, but it was occupied by Brian Shepherd, a bachelor, who was apparently in no hurry to up sticks. Eventually it was agreed that we would move in with him for the time being and this we did early in February. Shortly after this I was sent off to Bangkok to join the UK Delegation as a record taker at the first Ministerial Meeting of the South East Asia Treaty Organization (SEATO). At this point Anne put her foot down and insisted that Brian should leave forthwith, which he did. The house was quite modest, in accordance with my lowly place in the hierarchy, but we were pleased to have it to ourselves and, with it, the services of an excellent Chinese "boy", Ah Wong, and family.

As we had been warned, the climate took a bit of getting used to – 80/80/80, i.e. average temperature, rainfall and percentage humidity. There was no air-conditioning, either at home or in the office, and having to sleep under a mosquito net made for hot and sweaty nights, even with the ceiling fans whirring round. It was difficult to stay dry at any time and even the slightest exertion, such as getting out of the car to wipe the windscreen, brought out beads of perspiration. Like other recent arrivals, and perhaps nearly all the Europeans, we found ourselves changing our clothes two or three times a day. They were, however, all washable and we were lucky to have Ah Wong and his family to wash them. Office wear was very informal, white short-sleeved shirt, shorts and long socks, but later, when there was a change of Commissioner-General, the dress code also changed to ties and long trousers. We started work early and finished in time for a late lunch, followed by a siesta.

Phoenix Park also housed the HQ of the Admiral C-in-C (Far East) and representatives of various intelligence agencies. All told, the staff numbered more than a hundred. In essence it was a regional outstation of HMG with a coordinating role for promoting British interests in the whole of South-East Asia. The Governors of such colonies as Singapore, Malaya and Borneo, and our diplomatic representatives in the independent countries of the region, continued to do their own things, but the Commissioner-General, who at the time was Malcolm MacDonald, the son of Ramsay, exerted his influence behind the scenes and through his direct line to No. 10. No doubt there were clashes of personality and a crossing of wires between him and the others at times, as also between him and the three Cs-in-C, but that was all above my head. Malcolm MacDonald was unusual in more ways than one. He got on well with influential local people in Singapore itself, but paid scant attention to the expatriates. In this I think he had his priorities right. But it was frustrating that, apart from his Deputy, Alan Dudley and his Private Secretary, Lt. Col. (Ret'd) Pat McKay, members of his staff saw very little of him. Anne and I were once invited to lunch, when I had the excruciating experience of sitting next to a Chinese lady who spoke not one word of English, but that was about the extent of our contact with him. He liked to work on his papers at night and would leave them, with his comments and instructions, in a safe, to be picked up and distributed by McKay in the morning, while he himself caught up on his sleep. It was commonly said that he had other reasons too for being a night bird, but if so he was discreet about it (his wife was not with him).

I had an interesting job myself, as one of the two civilian members of the Joint Intelligence Staff (Far East), along with three military members, one from each of the Services. Our role was to provide assessments of the political and economic situations and prospects in the countries of the region for the more senior Joint Intelligence Committee (Far East), which in turn reported to the Commissioner-General and the Cs-in-C, as well as to the Joint Intelligence Committee in London. The JIC (FE) was chaired by Andrew Gilchrist, a colourful Scot who later made a name for himself when, as Ambassador, first in Djakarta and subsequently in Reykjavik and

Dublin, he contemptuously defied ugly mobs of hostile demonstrators. I quickly learnt a lesson from my Service colleagues, which I never forgot in my later career: that it is often more useful to come to a view and be found wrong than to avoid making a mistake by hedging one's bets. The occasion was a plan by the RN to send a warship to Saigon on a goodwill visit in a few months' time. The situation in Vietnam was already highly volatile and the naval planners needed to know soon whether to go ahead with the visit or cancel it. I studied all the information available to me and came up with the sort of on the one hand, on the other, advice for which the FO, rightly or wrongly, had a reputation. At which, David Conn, my naval colleague, blew his top and said "Dammit, John, we need a decision now, so which is it to be, go or no go?" I never forgot this and there were many occasions in my later career when I found that under pressure I had to come to a quick conclusion without the benefit of having all the facts of a situation at my finger tips.

Anne's mother and father came to stay with us at the end of April, travelling on the Dutch liner, *Willem Ruys*. Anne, who has an inconvenient (no pun intended) memory for such unimportant things, reminds me that in honour of their arrival I applied some fresh paint to a lavatory seat, but so thickly that they were in danger of sticking to it. Of course, she exaggerated and they didn't. Betty was to stay until after the baby was born, due in June, but Jack had to fly back to England before that. As it happened, he had some difficulty in getting a seat on a BOAC flight and in some irritation he eventually told the booking clerk that she should know he was a personal friend of the Chairman, Sir Miles Thomas, thinking, of course, that this would clinch matters. To which she responded with the perfect put-down "I am sure Sir Miles would be delighted to hear how booked up we are!" He got a seat all the same.

Emma Jane was born early in the morning of 10 June in the Singapore Nursing Home. Anne lost quite a lot of blood in the process and had to have a transfusion – she was to have similar problems when the other children were born and one of our daughters, Alice, has had the same experience. That apart, everything went well, although I have to confess that I was not present to witness the great event myself. The doctor, a smooth type called Laidlaw-Thompson, clearly thought that I would either pass out or get in the way, or both, and suggested I go home. Betty and I were summoned at about six o'clock to greet the new member of the family. When later we returned to the house and gave the good news to Ah Wong, he did what any self-respecting Chinese would do on learning that his first-born was a daughter, he turned on his heels without saying a word. He was probably even more startled when Betty and I announced that in celebration we were going to go on a diet of bananas and milk for a bit – something we had planned beforehand. Ah Wong probably thought we were doing penance. Anyway it made a change from the bacon and eggs which we otherwise had for breakfast every day of the week. Emma took some time to settle down and cried a lot at night. Many a time I can remember picking her up and walking her round and round in my arms to get her to go back to sleep, only to have to start all over again as soon as I put her down. I can understand how some people lose their patience altogether in such situations and resort to violence to shut the baby up. There but for the grace of God went Emma.

At the end of August we moved to a house in one of the official compounds, Braddell Hill, where we stayed until we went on home leave in September 1956. It was a three-bedroom bungalow, rather more spacious than the house in Holland Road, with a better garden. There was no swimming pool in the compound, so we joined the Singapore Swimming Club. The pool was excellent, but the club was not very conveniently situated for us, and in due course we did what most people did and applied to join the Tanglin Club, which apart from a pool had tennis and squash courts and quite a good dining room. It had a whites-only membership policy and new applicants were scrutinised very carefully to ensure that they conformed. Malcolm MacDonald was so disgusted by this that he refused to join and went off and founded a multiracial club, the Island Club, together with the then up-and-coming young politician, Lee Kuan Yew. Lee, a prominent member of the opposition Peoples Action Party (PAP) – in opposition, that was, to the Chief Minister, David Marshall – was quite a firebrand who narrowly escaped arrest on a number of occasions for his rabble-rousing activities. What saved him was his friendship with a number of leading members of the Labour Party in Britain, who would have created a stink on his behalf if he had been put inside. But when he was not stirring people up in the streets Lee liked to play golf and the Island Club soon had a good course.

We also joined the RAF Tengah Sailing Club and made some use of the club boats there. One particular day Anne stayed too long out in the open at the back of a boat and, despite the fact that the sun was hidden behind clouds most of the time, was badly burnt and had to stay in bed next day. On several occasions we hired a motor sampan with our friends Rhoddy and Rosemary Warren and others to take us out to one of the surrounding islands for a Sunday picnic. Our social life was more or less confined to members of the expatriate community. We did not get to know many

Chinese and my job was not concerned with them. We entertained quite a lot, but mostly members of the Consular Corps and visitors.

I travelled to Thailand and other countries in the region, including Cambodia and the Philippines, mainly on Economic Commission for Asia and the Far East (ECAFE) business, which occupied a little of my time in addition to my JIC (FE) job, but Anne was not able to accompany me. She, I am afraid, had to be content with a week at the guest house at Telok Paku on the island or the odd trip across the causeway into Johore. We could not go very far there either because much of the State was designated a black area in terms of the Malayan emergency. The police searched the boot of each car at the end of the causeway and if they found any tins of food they punctured them so that the contents would have to be consumed without delay and not be of any use to the terrorists, led by the notorious and elusive figure, Chin Peng, if by some mischance they fell into their hands.

Malcolm MacDonald was succeeded by Sir Robert (Rob) Scott as Commissioner-General in October 1955. He had been captured by the Japanese shortly after the fall of Singapore in 1942 and thrown into Changi gaol. He had been very badly treated there and condemned to death for having a clandestine radio set. But he survived and the extraordinary thing was that he seemed to bear no ill will towards the Japanese generally. This was noted when he later gave evidence against some of the camp guards at the so-called "Double Tenth" (i.e. 10 October) war crimes trial in Singapore. He made a special point of distinguishing between the lesser ranks among the offenders and those in positions of greater responsibility. So it caused him no embarrassment when the first member of the Consular Corps standing in line to shake his hand when he arrived at the airport to take up his appointment was Japanese. He was also tactful enough to arrive on 11, rather than 10, October!

Stuart and Dorothy Hills and their baby daughter, Susan, came down from Malaya to spend Christmas with us. On Christmas Eve we went with them and two friends from the CGO, the Cranmer-Byngs, to a dinner-dance at the Tanglin Club. The band played some very old tunes like "I'm for ever blowing bubbles" and we all wore paper hats. Christmas Day was spent in traditional style: morning service at the Garrison Church, drinks for about 20 people before a light lunch, presents round the tree, and a full Christmas dinner – turkey, plum pudding etc. Finally, we rounded off the day listening to the Queen's radio broadcast at about 10.30pm.

A few weeks later, we drove up to Muar (North Johore), where Stuart was Deputy Labour Commissioner, and stayed the night with them. Next day we went with them in convoy to Port Dickson, where Stuart had booked us all into a small hotel, close to the beach. One evening we dressed up in our best bib and tucker and went, as the guests of a colleague of Stuart's, the elegantly named Adrian Alabaster, to the Seremban Club for a Rotary International Dinner. The Ruler of Negri Sembilan, the Yang de Pertuan Besar, was there and his daughter sat at our table. When the dancing began the men took it in turn to dance with her. I was the last and not long after I took her on to the floor, I realised that we were the only couple dancing. I was acutely embarrassed, but she seemed to think it was very funny. It transpired that the Ruler had decided to go on home and the band was playing the State anthem!

Adrian, who was Secretary for Chinese Affairs in Negri Sembilan, also arranged for an Army spotter pilot to take me up in his Auster aircraft to look for "bandit" campsites. As we flew low over the jungle he pointed out suspicious clearings etc in the jungle and would then do a steep banking turn to get a better view. It was all I could do to hang on and avoid being sick. I was later shown round the local counter-terrorist operations room.

In September 1956 we set off on home leave in the SS *Oranje*, a Dutch boat. The Suez crisis was coming to a head at that point and Egyptian pilots had already assumed responsibility for navigation through the canal. The received wisdom in London was that they were not competent to do the job properly and P&O were already diverting their ships round the Cape. On the *Oranje* the passengers were told that if the situation deteriorated further we might have to do the same, and a decision would be made when we reached Colombo. There we were informed that the company had retained the services of a senior Egyptian pilot to take us through, and through we went. There were a number of British service personnel on board and they were instructed by the Captain to stay out of the sight of the thin line of Egyptian soldiers who were bivouacked on the West bank of the Canal – and a pretty miserable bunch they looked shivering under blankets in the chill night air. The passage went off without incident, but as things turned out we were the last big liner to pass through the canal before the Anglo-French military action began at the beginning of November. Needless to say, we did not disembark at Port Said, but we did have an interesting stop in Naples on the final leg of the voyage. On arrival in Southampton we were met by Jack and Betty, Ma and other members of the family and driven back to Durrington.

The Suez crisis dominated the news and regrettably overshadowed the simultaneous Soviet invasion of Hungary. It also divided the country from top to bottom. There was so much uproar during a debate in the House of Commons that the sitting had to be suspended. Outside parliament the clash of opinions, for and against military action to enforce our will on Egypt, went across traditional class loyalties: the views of the milkman and the factory worker could be quite the opposite of what one expected, likewise those of the Company Director and retired Brigadier. The argument raged in the press and on television and generated more heat than light. I myself thought the whole thing was a terrible mistake and was glad that I was not back in Singapore having fierce arguments about it with all and sundry. None of the shifting, and shifty, explanations put forward by the government for the action they had taken in collusion with the French and Israelis held water. In addition, colleagues in the FO felt bitter at having been bypassed and kept in the dark. One or two resigned in protest. The French Government, on the other hand, acting on the principle of "qui s'excuse, s'accuse", made no bones about the fact that its main objective in sending its soldiers to Egypt was to get hold of Nasser and string him up from a lamp-post in Port Said in revenge for the active support he had given the insurgents in Algeria. During a brief visit to Paris, Anne and I found a much greater air of calm and unanimity of view than in London.

None of this was allowed to cast a shadow over our leave or the enjoyment of Christmas at home. But it complicated our return journey, as the canal was now blocked by sunken ships. It might be thought that we should have flown back to Singapore, but the "approved route" was still by sea, even if that meant going round the Cape. The FO booked a cabin for us on the SS *Laos* (Messageries Maritimes) and we joined her at Marseilles after an overnight train journey across France. The trip was to take us nearly a month and twice across the equator. First stop was the Canary Islands, where we basked in some warm sunshine, and the second Cape Town, where we were met and taken ashore by Uncle "G's" brother, Teddy Trimming, and his family. They took us home and then out to lunch at the Kelvin Grove Club. It was our first contact with South Africa and our immediate reaction was that it would be an attractive place to live. But we knew next to nothing about its problems. In any case the country was still in the Commonwealth then (it left four years later) and naturally it never entered my head that one day I would return there as Ambassador.

When we returned to the ship after our outing we carried with us, amongst other things, some "mielies" (the local name for sweet corn) and passed a message to the kitchen asking if we could have them for dinner. To our surprise the message came back to the effect that the chef would do his best but he was not used to cooking corn cobs since in France they were mainly used for pig food! Happily for us and the other passengers, the Captain of the *Laos* showed himself to be more flexible than the chef, so that when we hit a bad storm off Madagascar, which was forecast to continue for another twenty-four hours or more, he allowed us some respite from the rough seas by taking us into the lee of Réunion and anchoring there. Eventually, at the end of January 1957, we arrived back in Singapore, where we had been allocated a staff flat in Balmoral, not far from the Tanglin Club. This was a bit of a come down from the house and garden we had had before. How long we would have stayed there in the normal course of events I do not know, because members of the staff seemed to be moved around fairly often, but as fate would have it we were to be there only a short time.

At the beginning of May, the 9th to be precise, Anne had the great misfortune to contract poliomyelitis. At the time there was an epidemic of Asian flu in Singapore and she began by showing all the usual symptoms – aches and pains in the joints, headache, temperature etc. I consulted our doctor, who advised keeping her in bed and giving her disprin every two hours. Despite this she had a wretched night and could not get to sleep, so next morning I asked the doctor to call. Having examined her he confirmed that she had flu and gave her some sleeping pills. By that evening most of the aches and pains had eased and she had a reasonable night's sleep, although she experienced some twitching of her legs. Next morning, however, it quickly became apparent that she was feeling very weak and I had to help her to the bathroom because her legs, particularly the left one, would not support her. This time when the doctor came he at once diagnosed polio and took her off to the British Military Hospital (B.M.H.). The immediate aftermath is described in some detail in a letter I wrote to Anne's parents the following day (Appendix I).

The fact that Anne was given a private room and generally received V.I.P. attention at B.M.H. was reassuring, but I was anxious lest this would give her the impression she was at death's door. I need not have worried: she told me later that she was not really aware of her surroundings at first. It is not possible to say for certain how she contracted it: there was some polio about in Singapore at the time, but by no means an epidemic. Indeed nothing like the proportions of the outbreak that had been reported in Colchester not long before. A close friend of ours in Singapore also went down with it at more or less the same time and since they both frequented the same swimming pool it is possible that they picked up the infection there. Swimming pools were commonly thought to be likely breeding grounds, but nobody knew for certain. Not long afterwards I myself began to feel some stiffness in my neck, which is one of the symptoms of polio, but it was a false alarm. I was told that there was no specific treatment, i.e. no drugs to contain the spreading of the paralysis from one part of the body to another. While the fever continued, nothing could stop the disease from running its course and the only way of countering it was to try to bring Anne's temperature down as quickly as possible with ice-cold drinks and disprin. As soon as this returned to normal, the disease stopped of its own accord and at least we knew that things would not get worse. They might indeed have been much worse, in particular if the paralysis had reached Anne's chest and she had needed an iron lung, like some victims. Things were bad enough, but not as bad as they might have been and we now knew what we had to cope with. Easy words to say, but in reality Anne was faced with a long period of rehabilitation to help compensate for the loss of muscle power because of the irreversible damage to her nervous system; and this was going to require the exercise of superhuman determination and patience on her part. She also had to cope with giving birth to our second child, expected in three months' time. While the doctors at B.M.H. had assured her from the start that the foetus would not be affected, the fact that her pelvic muscles had been weakened was bound to complicate her labour. The medical advice was that she should return to England as soon as she was fit enough to travel. On hearing this, the FO Personnel Department immediately decided to post me home as well. Throughout this entire crisis they showed themselves to be kind and considerate employers.

Towards the end of June, Anne was moved to RAF Changi for her flight as a stretcher case on a Comet "casevac" aircraft. Emma and I were to travel a day or two earlier on a commercial flight in order to make last minute arrangements for her arrival and be there to greet her. Although the nurses on her flight were apparently prepared for the possibility that they might have to cope with a premature birth en route, Anne's journey went off without incident. Which is more than could be said for Emma's and my journey. Our BOAC aircraft, not being jet-engined like the Comet, took more than 26 hours and several stops to do the trip. Things looked ominous even before we set off. On the morning of our departure, Emma had bad diarrhoea and in desperation I took her to a chemist in Orchard Road and asked them to give her something to stop the flow. Which, as things turned out – no pun intended – they did very effectively. As soon as we got on the aircraft she threw a tantrum because I stopped her from taking the whole tray of sweets being handed round by the stewardess, and in the process she slipped out of her seat on to the floor. By now I was conscious of sternly disapproving looks from other passengers, who had already been on the flight for some hours and were no doubt wondering if this was going to continue all the way to London. Mercifully the combination of the medicine she had been given and the amount of effort she had put into raising the roof had the effect of making her feel rather drowsy – she was after all just two years old – and before long she lapsed into a long sleep. The stewardesses soon got the message that here was a helpless father travelling with a fractious child and we received every attention during the rest of the flight.

A further problem arose, this time at Zurich airport, the last stop before London. During the hour we had on the ground I took Emma off to the nursery area in the transit lounge and asked one of the by then only-too-anxious-to-please stewardesses to change her into some warmer clothing I had brought with us, while I did the same thing in a men's room nearby. When I returned I found Emma playing happily with some dolls in a pram provided by the nursery and in no hurry to move. This seemed to her to be a particularly good stop and she made it clear that for her at least it was the last one. She was not going to take any more and was not impressed to hear that the next stop would be London. Where was that anyway? As the last call was made for transit passengers to reboard the aircraft the stand-off continued, and it was only resolved when one of the stewardesses cleverly suggested taking dolly for a walk in her pram. She readily consented to this and the three of us made our way to the aircraft, where at the foot of the steps the stewardess released Emma's grip on the handle of the pram and I swept her up and carried her protesting back to our seats. Just over an hour later we arrived at Heathrow to be met by Jack and Betty Pitchford and were driven down to Durrington Manor.

Anne arrived a day or two later at RAF Lyneham in Wiltshire and was taken briefly to nearby RAF Hospital Wroughton. She had weathered the journey well and greeted everyone with a big smile. From there an ambulance took her, with me sitting beside her and the Pitchfords following in their car, to the maternity wing of Worthing Hospital, where she was to come under the care of Mrs Beynon, a consultant obstetrician and friend of the family, and Dr Donald Wilson. A few weeks later, on 10 August, Peter was born. As forecast he arrived hale and hearty, and weighing over eight pounds.

Western Department

As soon as Anne had recovered and was fit enough, we moved from Durrington into a rented house in Ditchling, Little Shirleys. For a month or so we had the services of a children's nurse to help us settle in. Anne now had a long stint of rehabilitation and physiotherapy ahead of her. She started off in a wheelchair, progressing from there to first shoulder, and then elbow, crutches, and, after a stint with a cumbersome calliper on her left leg, to two walking sticks. Easily said in one sentence, but what an unrelenting struggle it was for her over many months, indeed years, and how bravely she persevered with it. She never grumbled or indulged in self-pity. It certainly brought home to me the mettle of the woman I had married. She was never going to be able to recover full use of her left leg, but she was gradually learning how to compensate for the muscles that had wasted.

Meanwhile I joined Western Department as a Desk Officer dealing with Western European Union (WEU). It was a rather humdrum job, but I was lucky to have a good Head of Department in Pat Hancock. He was an amusing, unconventional man, whom I had previously come across in my first posting to Central Department. One of his endearing habits was to come round the office early in the evening and tell us young men to stop shuffling papers around, get some fresh air in our lungs and go home. He and I used to play squash once or twice a week at his club during the lunch hour. He was no fitness fanatic, but he firmly believed, sensible chap, that there were more things to life than sitting at a desk.

Over the next few months, Anne made slow, but steady, progress and in May of the following year, 1958, the FO Medical Adviser decided that she was now fit enough to accompany me on an overseas posting, provided it was to a country not too far away and having good health facilities.

Paris

Thus it came about that I was sent as Second Secretary (Commercial) to Paris in August. John Robinson, whom I was succeeding, was not at all pleased to be leaving and even suggested, tongue in cheek, that I must have conspired to get him out. He explained that his flat would not be suitable for us and we would have to set about finding one of our own, with the help of the Embassy's Administration Section. In the meantime, the Minister at the Embassy, Gerry Young, who was on mid-term leave, kindly put his flat in Auteuil at our disposal. I went ahead in our new Hillman Minx and, to my agreeable surprise, on arrival in Paris found the streets deserted. It was 15 August, the Feast of the Assumption, a day on which those inhabitants of Paris who have not already started their annual holiday get out of town. Anne, still on walking sticks, arrived a week or so later with Emma and Peter and Cynthia, our new children's minder. Before long we found, and moved into, a first-floor furnished flat at 10bis Rue Anatole de la Forge, a small street which runs between the Avenue de la Grande Armée and the Avenue Carnot in the 17th arrondissement, a short distance from the Arc de Triomphe. We were to stay there four years, the longest time we had under one roof in any of our overseas posts. Dark and not very comfortably furnished, without a garage, it nevertheless suited us well, being in a congenial, but not too fashionable, area and well placed both for getting to the Embassy and, at weekends, out of Paris.

It was a fascinating time to be in France, coinciding as it did with the recall of General de Gaulle from his retreat at Colombey-Les-Deux-Eglises and the transition under his leadership from the Fourth to the Fifth Republic. My particular job in the Embassy was anything but fascinating; in fact it was distinctly humdrum. A major part of it was the compiling of long monthly reports on the state of the French economy for the benefit of the Treasury and Board of Trade. I was not sure whether anybody ever read them, because I received little, if any, feedback from its intended recipients and began to wonder after a time whether its usual destination was a wastepaper basket rather than anybody's desk. In strictly financial terms the French economy was in a fragile state and another of my more interesting duties was the daily monitoring of the official gold and foreign exchange reserves.

The Ambassador for the first half of our stay was Sir Gladwyn Jebb. He and his wife, Cynthia, were a formidable couple. As I mentioned earlier, his previous post had been as Head of our UN Mission in New York, where he had made a reputation for himself in the Security Council and in the American media as the most effective Western protagonist in the cut and thrust of Cold War infighting. To me he came over as an old style grand seigneur of an ambassador who looked down his patrician nose at most of his staff, while expending his main energies on alternatively cultivating, and crossing swords with, the leaders of French political and social life. On the few occasions we had any direct dealings I remember how nervous he made me feel. Awe would not be too strong a word to describe my reaction to him and I was not alone in this.

Cynthia Jebb had much the same effect on Anne. Shortly after she arrived she was to be taken by Margie Isaacson, the wife of my boss, the Minister (Commercial), to call on the great lady. She was told in advance that she would have to wear hat and gloves, which she did not have, as they were still in our heavy luggage, which had not yet arrived. Consternation all round. Eventually the compromise solution was found of transferring the call to the Embassy garden, where apparently hats and gloves were not de rigueur. Those were the days.

We saw the Jebbs from time to time on big Embassy occasions when all members of staff were enlisted to help entertain the guests, but tucked away in the Commercial Section I was at some distance from the centre of things. Other more senior and grander people, like the Beiths, the Pallisers and James Murray revolved in close orbit around them. It was, therefore, somewhat out of the blue when Anne and I received an invitation to drive out into the countryside one Sunday morning to have lunch in a restaurant with them. Out we went in the Rolls, flag flying, Gladwyn reading papers in the front seat next to the driver, Cynthia and Anne on the back seat, and me on a jump seat looking out of the window at the passing scene, which at odd moments was enlivened by mocking gestures from the local village lads standing by the side of the road. Eventually we stopped at a restaurant in a small town and went into lunch. Gladwyn did not wait for anyone else to be served before getting stuck into his food, which he downed quickly without making much effort at conversation. At the end of the meal, when it came to paying the bill he confessed that he had left his wallet behind and I settled it instead. A day or two later

Cynthia repaid me by sending the money round in an envelope. Apparently it was not the first time this had happened.

In May 1960 we had the drama of the aborted Summit Conference in Paris between Eisenhower, Khrushchev, de Gaulle and Macmillan. There was much coming and going between the great men, some of it in our Embassy, where Macmillan was staying, but the conference as such never got off the ground as a result of what became known as the Gary Powers U-2 Affair, which had happened just beforehand. As a condition for sitting down with Eisenhower, Khrushchev insisted that he should first apologize publicly for the incursion into Soviet airspace, something which Ike was clearly unwilling to do. Meanwhile we Embassy underlings hung out of the windows to watch the spectacle of Khrushchev sweeping into the courtyard in an enormous Russian imitation of an American convertible, with bodyguards clinging to the sides, to call on Macmillan. There were other, more mundane, diversions too, such as the arrest by a British military policeman of Gravitt, Gladwyn's crusty old butler, as he walked Jasper, Cynthia's dachshund, in the ambassadorial garden. From the ridiculous to the ridiculous, I suppose, but we all enjoyed the welcome break from routine.

James, our third child, was born on 26 November that year, 1960. As in the case of his elder brother, Peter, there was some drama in events leading up to his birth. Blood tests Anne had during the pregnancy indicated an abnormality in the development of the foetus and there was said to be a serious risk of having a less than fully-developed, or "puny" (chétif), baby. The Embassy doctor, Dr Réveillaud, who was attending her, seemed to be in two minds about what to do. On the one hand, he suggested that termination of the pregnancy would be the best course, on the other he explained that legally he could not agree to an abortion except in exceptional circumstances. For us it was an agonising decision anyway, but after consultation with the gynaecologist, Dr Grandjean, it was eventually agreed that Anne should have a termination operation in a private clinic, where a bed had been reserved. Fate now took a hand, because when we arrived at the clinic we were told that there must have been a mistake because there was not a spare bed in the place. In some distress we turned on our heels and went home. What to do now? Having talked it over we agreed that we would go away on holiday in La Baule, as planned, and let nature take its course. Which it did. A few months later James came into the world at the American Hospital in Neuilly. A healthy, bouncing baby he was too, even though Anne herself, not for the first time, suffered a lot of bleeding. After this experience I can only say that I have been in two minds about the rights and wrongs of abortion. I would like to think that medical science has now advanced to a point where the mistaken prognosis that so nearly deprived James of his life would not be made today. Or is that wishful thinking?

The holiday in La Baule had its lighter moments. The Mayor had generously offered Princess Margaret the use of a large house owned by the Commune for her honeymoon. When she declined his offer in favour of the Royal Yacht, he put it at the disposal of the Embassy for two months and several of us, including the Jebbs, stayed there in relays. We went with Michael Hadow, the Head of Chancery, and his wife Lolita. With the use of the house went the services of a cook-general and it soon became apparent that she had a weakness for the bottle. As a result of his earlier years in India, Michael fancied himself as a dab hand at making curry, and to go with the meal he had put quite a few large bottles of beer in the refrigerator, only to find when the time came that the cook had been there first and the cupboard was bare. As for me, I am no cook, but I do have a reputation in the family for dealing with troublesome drains and things of that ilk. So it was only natural that I was the one deputed to stop water overflowing from an overhead lavatory cistern. The Jebbs were following us and the mind boggled at the thought of him standing on the loo seat to fix it.

Not long after this Gladwyn retired and was succeeded by Sir Piers (Bob) Dixon, who like him had come from being the Head of the UK Mission to the UN in New York. But there the likeness ended, as they were quite different people, Bob being the quiet, academic type without Gladwyn's undoubted flair and charisma. His wife, Ismene, was Greek, very much a family person and I cannot say we got to know her well.

April the following year, 1961, saw the threatened military coup led by General Raoul Salan and three of his colleagues in Algeria. It was all very dramatic, banana republic stuff: "Les Paras" (dissident parachutist soldiers) loaded on to military transport aircraft in Algiers and threatening to land at Le Bourget and take over the government in protest at what they saw as de Gaulle's betrayal of France's Algerian destiny. Old snout-nosed Paris buses were taken out of mothballs by the Gendarmerie, the only armed force the government felt it could fully rely on to obey its orders, and parked across the ends of the bridges over the Seine so as to block the paras' path. I witnessed all this from the conveniently placed flat of our friends, John and Lalage Shakespeare (he was the Ambassador's Private Secretary). Anne was away in England at the time and so missed the excitement.

Le Clos, Collobrières

What followed was both tense and melodramatic. First, a clearly rattled Prime Minister, Michel Debré, appeared on television and exhorted the good people of Paris to drive out to Le Bourget in order to dissuade the paras from attempting to overthrow the government. An hour or two later, de Gaulle himself appeared on the screen in uniform and in cold, calm terms proceeded to pour scorn on the would-be insurrectionists. In contrast to Debré's pathetic effort, it was a masterly performance that turned the tide and quickly brought the rebellion to an end.

Life in Paris was certainly not dull: when we arrived in 1958 tongues were still wagging about a bizarre incident in which a certain François Mitterrand had appeared to stage an assassination attempt against himself in the Jardin du Luxembourg; and there had also been the notorious Ballet Rose scandal in which the President of the Senate had been implicated. Sadly, I cannot remember the details. Life was not as exciting in the more mundane circles in which the Leahys moved, but we continued to enjoy ourselves and Anne made steady progress with her "re-education", graduating to one stick for walking and generally playing a full part in everything. In the summer of 1961, we went on holiday to Antibes with John and Lalage. We hired a caravan on a camping site and the Shakespeares occupied a tent close by. It was a squash in the caravan with Anne and me, three children and our nanny. Apart from going down to the nearby beach we went out and about a bit in the car and in the course of one expedition we had a picnic in the garden of a ruined house that was apparently up for sale. It was a nice spot and both families were soon involved in day-dreaming about buying the place and doing it up as our holiday home. We came down to earth when we discovered that the ownership of the place was in dispute – and that was that.

However, a seed had been sown in our minds and when we got back to Paris we mentioned to other Embassy friends, Robin and Joan Farquharson, who were themselves about to go on holiday in the South, that we had had this romantic idea of acquiring a dilapidated house and doing it up. They said they were going to do some looking themselves. It still came as a surprise when shortly afterwards they telephoned to say that they had found a two-roomed hut, or "cabanon", with some three acres of land, including a small vineyard, outside a village called Collobrières in the Var, about 15 miles from the sea. It was, they said, something that could be easily extended and converted and was going for a song. They intended to buy it and wanted to know whether we would like to go halves with them. As this would only set us back the equivalent of some £250, we immediately said yes, sight unseen.

So it was that we became part-owners of a holiday home that was to figure prominently in the life of our family over more than thirty years. We subsequently acquired as well a small neighbouring vineyard and brought in a third partner, Christopher and Anne Wake-Walker (he was Naval Attaché in Paris after our time). Le Clos, as it was called, was an idyllic spot, about two miles from the village near the bottom of a quiet valley, with a splendid outlook towards the surrounding wooded hills, and approached by a long, narrow path that led from an unmade-up road across a rickety bridge up to the lower terrace. No electricity, no telephone, spring water only, more than an acre of wine-producing vines and plenty of cork and chestnut trees. The hut itself had apparently been used by its owners as an overnight lodging when they were working on the vines and it had stone walls no less than a metre thick, providing excellent insulation against both heat and cold.

We hired the services of a young, newly trained builder in the village, Loulou Mura, to help us plan and build a substantial extension. Robin took charge of organising the building, while I entered into negotiations with the people who owned small plots of land bordering the path ("riverains"), to let us widen the path so as to take a four-wheeled vehicle and also to get them to contribute towards the cost of building a proper bridge. This all took time and in the process I drank more pastis than I had ever done before. I still do not like it much.

The village itself was somewhat run down, having a population of 1,200–1,300 people, compared with 3,000 before the Second World War. It was tucked away in an unfashionable part of the country far from the madding crowds and had retained much of its original character and charm. For its size of population it was overstocked with butchers, bakers and groceries; it also had two thriving bars and a pissoir, outside which the old men sat in order of seniority, doing nothing in particular. We were practically the first foreigners to buy property there and the locals tended to look upon us as somewhat picturesque oddities who posed no threat to their way of life and brought some welcome new business to their community. In other words they were friendly and not a little curious.

Over the next three years we gradually built what was virtually a new house, doing quite a lot of the unskilled labour ourselves as and when we could tear ourselves away from Paris. We also organised working parties of young able-bodied friends to join us in return for free board and occasional visits to the local beaches. It was hard work and a fascinating experience about which we should have written a book. Had one of us done so Peter Mayle would not have got a look in later on. During the 35 or more years that we had Le Clos it became an integral part of our family life and it was a sad moment when we eventually sold it in 1997.

On one of our visits to Collobrières we set off from Paris by car at midnight, having just attended a memorable dinner party in the Ritz, given by Lord (Harry) Tennyson, great-grandson of the poet. He worked for J. Walter Thompson, the advertising company, in Paris. We knew him quite well, but he was not a close friend. More to the point, he was well acquainted with the Duke and Duchess of Windsor, and the dinner party was for them. We numbered eight in all: Anne sat next to the Duke and I next to the Duchess. I can't say that the conversation reached any great heights, except of decibels – the Duke had a great booming voice, which despite his wife's entreaties to tone it down, reverberated round the Grill Room and meant that at other tables they were hanging on every word. He could be quite funny at times, but was apt to embark on rather tedious monologues on one of his favourite subjects, such as South Africa, the Royal Navy and golf. I remember as well his saying in a loud voice, and a distinctly American accent, that he felt more at ease speaking German than French, which made the rest of us squirm a bit. The Duchess, I should add, looked younger and nicer than her photographs and was easy enough to talk to; and throughout the meal she kept a close eye on her husband. When the coffee came, she produced a peppermint cream from her handbag and handed it to him across the table in a teaspoon; he in turn took out a pocket knife from his waistcoat pocket, cut the chocolate in half and handed back her share. We were clearly witnessing an intimate, if rather banal, domestic routine.

Enough said. In September 1962 we were posted back to the FO and we had to concentrate on settling into a small, semi-detached house we had bought in Ditchling – No. 1 Dymocks Manor in East End Lane.

Permanent Under-Secretary's Department

This is a rather bland name for intelligence assessment and liaison work and the provision of political advice to the military planners in the Ministry of Defence. Once again I was appointed to the inter-service Joint Intelligence Staff. As in Singapore, the essence of the job was the production of agreed assessments of the situation and prospects in various parts of the world as required by the Joint Intelligence Committee, but this time it was all on a much larger scale. We had two teams covering separate regions. The team I was in dealt with the Warsaw Pact threat to NATO and the Western world, while my colleague, Bryan White, and his team covered the rest. My role was to feed in political and economic contributions from FO Departments and to canvas their opinions of the contributions made by the Ministry of Defence and the Joint Intelligence Bureau. In the process of hammering out an agreed text with my military colleagues a lot of argument and bargaining took place. Before long the team spirit and sense of common purpose that grew up between us began to prevail over our separate departmental loyalties and we found ourselves not infrequently taking issue with those who provided our briefs.

About a month after I joined the team, the Cuban missile crisis landed on our desks, and it gave us plenty of work to do. The US Government sent special emissaries to the major allies carrying copies of the photo-reconnaissance evidence of the presence of the missiles and other supporting intelligence. Hal Sonnenfeld of the CIA came to London and gave various presentations. It was certainly a dramatic time and the nation held its breath for fear that another world war was about to start.

In general there was very close intelligence cooperation with the Americans and we paid a number of visits to the Pentagon in Washington to draw up agreed assessments of Soviet military capabilities with members of the DIA (Defense Intelligence Agency) and CIA. These meetings always seemed to coincide with something else. Alice was born during the first one, in March 1963, and to this day she is apt to remind me that I did not stick around for her birth. The second, in November the same year, coincided with the assassination of President Kennedy. We arrived on Saturday, the day after it happened and the funeral took place on the Monday. My colleagues and I were among the throng of people who lined the route, and before leaving Washington a few days later I queued up at Arlington Cemetery to visit his grave.

Another visit in this series, in March 1964, coincided with the wedding of Anne's brother, John, with Betty Bass in Charlotte, North Carolina. I flew out first to attend the meeting in Washington; Anne travelled separately to New York and stayed for a week or so with an old school friend, Angie Kenedy, in New Jersey, who then drove her down to meet me in Washington. From there we took a long-distance bus to Charlotte for the wedding. We were put up in a local motel, where amongst other things we were introduced to hominy grits, a sort of coarse porridge made from ground maize of which for some reason the locals seemed to be proud. In other respects it was a most enjoyable occasion.

Dymocks Manor did us well for a time, but when there were seven of us, including a resident mother's help, under the same roof it was bursting at the seams. Being on three floors, it was not an easy place for Anne to run and the garden was very small for the children to play in. We were clearly going to have to look for something bigger before long. Moreover, commuting by train from Haywards Heath became a bit of a drag, particularly in the winter months, for Anne as well as me – she and Elizabeth Rose, whose husband, Clive, also worked in PUSD, shared the chore of driving us to and from the station. Deliverance, in the form of another overseas posting, came in September 1965, and we were able to let the house to some friends of Anne's family, Nicholas and Pat Neve, and put off the business of selling it until our return.

Tehran

I was posted to Tehran as Head of Chancery. In giving me the news, Geoffrey Arthur, my Head of Department, said that I was a "lucky sod", he would love to be going there himself. It also came as a complete surprise to me. Geoffrey was right; it turned out to be a very happy posting, one that we think of nostalgically forty years on. The journey was an adventure, for a start. In succession to our seven-year old Hillman Minx, which we sold to a car knacker's-yard in Brighton for the insulting sum of £50, we had bought a short-wheelbase Land Rover, specially adapted for Anne with a lighter clutch. There were five of us in it for the first part of the trip – the two of us, James and Alice, and Ann Richardson, who was coming to Tehran to look after them. Emma and Peter had just started their second terms at boarding school.

We drove first to Collobrières, where we spent a week or two recovering from the exertions of packing up and saying our goodbyes. From there we drove through the night to Venice and, after doing a bit of sight-seeing, boarded the SS *Achilleus*, a Greek passenger ship bound for Beirut. The Land Rover was hoisted on to the foredeck and parked there with other vehicles. Then off we went on a leisurely Mediterranean cruise. First stop Piraeus/Athens, via the dramatic, steep-sided Corinth Canal, and then Rhodes and Alexandria, where two-year-old Alice wandered off on her own along the quayside and was found holding hands with a swarthy Egyptian docker. Finally Beirut. The plan was for Anne and me to drive to Tehran, via Baghdad, while the children and Ann Richardson flew on ahead, to be looked after until our arrival by Charles and Maria Wiggin – he was the Embassy Counsellor. Having seen them off at Beirut airport and spent the night in a hotel, we set off next morning, in company with John and Mary Caines. John was the regional Civil Air Attaché, based in Beirut, and was paying a visit to Baghdad. (He ended his Civil Service career as Permanent Secretary in the Ministry of Education.)

It is sometimes difficult to remember these days that there was a time when you could get in a car and drive through Syria, Jordan and Iraq all the way to Iran. It took us the inside of four days. On the first day we managed to get through the various frontier posts without undue delays and drove, for part of the way, along a sandy track beside the oil pipeline linking Haifa to the Persian Gulf. We stopped for the night at the oil company guesthouse at the H4 pumping station in Jordan, where we were treated to toast and Chivers marmalade for breakfast and could look at old copies of *Country Life* magazine. Next day we left the pipeline behind and struck out on a lonely road across the desert to Baghdad, some 450 miles away. We had been warned that there were no petrol stations on this section of the route and had fitted reserve jerrycans to the front of the car. The Iraqi frontier guard made a point of examining our passports from every angle and recording all our details; whether he was acting out of concern for our welfare or suspicion of what we might be up to we could not tell. When eventually we arrived in Baghdad we made for the Embassy to find Alex Birch, the Commercial Counsellor and an old friend from our Paris days, who had invited us to stay the night. He guided us to his house, where we were greeted by his wife, Joan, and had a very convivial evening catching up with our news. Refreshed by a good night's sleep, we moved on next morning to Iran, where the scenery changed dramatically.

We now had to climb up through the Zagros Mountains and make our way, via Kermanshah, to Hamadan, where we stopped for the night in a hotel. It seemed to us fairly basic, but was in fact the best in town. Our education began when we asked at the reception desk if we could use their telephone to ring the Embassy and confirm the time of our arrival next day. We kept being told that it would take another half an hour and eventually we lost patience and gave up, only to find out next morning that the line had been out of order for some days and had not been repaired. After an early start we eventually reached Tehran in the late afternoon and made our way to the Ferdowsi Avenue compound of the Embassy. Our new house – actually it was a very old one with mud and wattle walls – was close to the entrance and no sooner had we parked outside than Abbas, the cook we were inheriting from our predecessors, appeared to take us in hand. He had the car unpacked in no time at all and, after giving us a reviving drink, served supper. Meanwhile, Jack Burridge, the Embassy's Transport Supervisor, arrived to take the car away and give it the once over after its arduous journey. We began to feel quite cosseted already.

I could devote a whole book to the three years we were to spend in Tehran. They certainly lived up to the expectations Geoffrey Arthur had aroused and to this day Anne and I look back on them with a great sense of nostalgia. By the time we left I had begun to harbour a secret ambition to return there one day as Ambassador. In the event it was fortunate that I did keep it a secret and never told Personnel Department, because about the time it might have come to fruition the revolution occurred and in the ensuing upheaval the Ambassador was recalled to London and Sweden took charge of British interests.

What was it that made our time in Iran so attractive to us? For starters, the Embassy itself. It was just the right size, not too big and not too small, and because of the long history of Britain's relations with Persia it was still very much at the centre of things. It might be fairer to say that the Ambassador was very much at the centre of things. Sir Denis Wright was already an old Iran hand, having been sent there originally as Chargé d'Affaires on the resumption of diplomatic relations after the ousting of Mossadegh in 1953. He got to know the Shah well and was one of the few people in Tehran who could speak to him frankly and tell him things that his own Ministers and courtiers dared not tell him. I did not meet the Shah myself until after we left Tehran, when as Head of News Department I accompanied the Foreign Secretary, Sir Alec Douglas-Home, on a visit to Iran. He and Farah Diba, the Shahbanu, gave us a fabulous lunch, gold plates and all, I recall.

The Shah was certainly a good host, in the tradition of Iran and the Middle East generally, as was made clear when the Duke of Edinburgh came on a three-day visit to Tehran, after attending an international meeting of the World Wildlife Fund. The FO referred to it as a private visit, but from the amount of work it caused us I cannot think that it differed much from an official one. We received in advance from Buckingham Palace a folder explaining in minute detail what the Duke's likes and dislikes were, what sort of whisky and mineral water should be in his bedroom, and other things of that kind. As the Shah had invited Prince Philip to be his guest, the Ambassador turned a blind eye to these pernickety instructions and we did no more than respond to such requests for guidance as the Iranian protocol people put to us. As it turned out, Prince Philip showed himself to be much more flexible and the visit passed off well. A tricky problem did, however, arise at one stage, when the Shah decided to take his guest to the Caspian, piloting his own aircraft. There were clear rules that members of the royal family could only travel in British aircraft flown by British pilots. To have to explain to the Shah, who ever since we had deposed his father during the Second World War was extremely sensitive about any perceived slight emanating from the British, that Prince Philip could not go with him, would be extremely difficult, to say the least. How exactly the question was resolved I am not entirely sure these many years later, but I seem to recall it was agreed that it would be easier to accommodate both entourages if both aircraft were used.

Denis Wright was one of the most intellectually, and morally, honest men I have ever met and his integrity came across in a number of ways. He was warm and generous to his friends and to people who enjoyed his confidence. At the same time he expected the highest standards of performance and behaviour from those around him and could come down hard on those who for some reason had forfeited his trust. Nor did he forgive or forget. He did not believe in trimming his views in order to ingratiate himself with his listener, be it the Shah or anyone else. I myself looked up to him and learnt a great deal from him. Indeed I came to regard him as my mentor. His wife, Iona, was a quietly spoken, gentle person whose softer personality complemented and offset his in a most effective way. He was aided and abetted by Charles Wiggin, the Embassy Counsellor, who was not one to suffer fools gladly but was also a lot of fun beneath a somewhat rugged demeanour. His wife, Maria, is shy, like Iona, but it would be wrong to give the impression that either of them was a shrinking violet.

When I began to write the above about Denis I was using the present tense, because he was still alive. Sadly he died last year (2005) at the ripe old age of 94. He remained a good friend until the end. Iona died, also at the age of 94, on 1 April 2006.

If Denis had a fault, it was that he was such an indefatigable traveller around the country that the rest of us had to take our turns in between his frequent journeying. I cannot really complain: we did manage to get out of Tehran from time to time and traversed quite a lot of the country in our Land Rover. The memories come flooding back of crossing deserts on dirt roads to visit magical places like Isfahan and Shiraz, driving up into the Elborz mountains to get to the Caspian, and camping in the Lar Valley, where Denis showed me how to fish for trout. Even a duty visit by train to deliver the diplomatic bag to our Consulate at Khorramshahr in the height of summer, when the temperature was way over 100°F, was an experience not to be missed – once. We also undertook an exciting car journey to Kabul, by way of Meshed, Herat and Kandahar and drove up the Khyber Pass towards the Pakistan frontier. We were lucky: only intrepid journalists can do that sort of thing now.

Speaking of luck, I was fortunate not to lose my life during another outing. One Sunday Denis Wright had invited Peter and me to go country walking with him. At one particular point our path led up quite a steep hillside and we left Peter, who was about ten years old at the time, to walk along the river bank below, while we traversed the hill. At a crucial point the path divided into a higher and lower course across the scree and Denis went one way and I the other. I definitely chose the wrong one, because after a time it petered out altogether and when I tried to turn round to go back I fell on the scree, which was anything but stable. The more I moved the more it did too and I was soon spread-eagled, hardly daring to breathe for fear of falling straight down into the valley many hundreds of feet below. I was precariously poised and paralysed with fright. Happily Denis, who had gone on ahead, turned round and quickly sized up the situation. He managed to edge his way back and held out his walking stick for me to grasp and slowly hauled me in. I was not really hurt, just a few minor cuts on my chest, but badly shaken. Later in the Land Rover on the way home Denis expressed his own relief by saying that it had occurred to him I would have been a very heavy corpse to carry back.

Tehran and Iran were two different worlds. The milieu in which we lived and worked was full of well-heeled, sophisticated people, educated in Europe or America, much-travelled, English-speaking and enjoying an active social life uninhibited by the need to pay much attention to Islamic religious observance. Few, if any, women wore the veil (chador), except in the poorer districts of the city in and around the bazaar. Outside Tehran, in the countryside, the opposite was true and people felt estranged from what was happening in the capital. This was one of the factors that led to the undoing of the Shah: he allowed himself to believe that he was loved and revered throughout the land – his sycophantic press and cow-towing courtiers told him so – but he made little effort to show himself to his people in the remoter regions and associate himself with their daily lives. Moreover he offended many of the devout Muslims amongst them by his apparent indifference to the traditional observances of their religion.

Like others who served in the Tehran Embassy about that time, and subsequently, I have often been asked why we did not foresee the overthrow of the Shah in 1979. When I was there, that is more than ten years beforehand, we did take into account, and report to the FO, the possibility that the Shah would be assassinated by a lonely fanatic. We also speculated what would happen in the aftermath of such an event. But we never gave serious thought to the possibility of a coup or a revolution, for the simple reason that at that time the Shah's all-pervasive security organisation, Savak, appeared to have things well under control and those opposed to the regime were both weak and divided. Indeed some of the more militant activists like Khomeini and various student leaders were forced to give voice to their opposition from abroad. In other words the writing was not then on the wall. If Savak had no inkling of what was to happen ten years later, it is hardly surprising that we did not either.

What eventually led to the Shah's downfall – and this is an irony of history – was his success in mobilising the members of OPEC to introduce huge increases in the price of crude oil, in the aftermath of the Yom Kippur War of 1973. It went to his head. He tore up Iran's existing economic plans overnight and with a stroke of his pen decreed that Iran was to embark on a great leap forward that would enable it to catch up the West in a decade. This was manifestly an absurd dream. In no time there was a queue of foreign contractors beating a path to Tehran to sell their wares and a dramatic upsurge in the flow of goods, including large quantities of modern military equipment, coming into the country. Inevitably the existing port infrastructure lacked the capacity to deal with the sudden influx, and as a result ships were kept waiting for months offshore in the Persian Gulf to unload their cargoes. Meanwhile, people poured into Tehran from the countryside in search of work that was not there, and, forced to live in overcrowded slums, were soon seething with discontent. The Shah should have been, but was not, aware of the way in which all this was having the effect of persuading the disparate opposition groups, i.e. the mullahs, the merchants, the underground pro-communist Tudeh Party, and the students, to put aside their differences and work together to overthrow his regime.

During the three or so years we were in Iran the country was relatively peaceful, on the surface at least, and we were able to enjoy it to the full, as I have already made clear. For the first half of our stay we had just the two younger children, James and Alice, with us, Emma and Peter having been left behind at boarding school in the UK. But Peter, who was still seven when he first went to Ashdown House, found it difficult to settle down there and on our return from home leave in the autumn of 1967 he came with us and joined James in the British School in Gulhak (which operated in the so-called "summer compound" of the Embassy).

The year 1967 was memorable for another reason – the "June War" between Israel and its neighbours, and its aftermath. Following the breaking of diplomatic relations with Iraq there was a sudden exodus of the British community to Tehran. The Ambassador there, Sir Richard Beaumont, led a convoy of cars from Baghdad and others made their way as best they could. With hardly any notice we had to arrange for the reception and temporary lodging of hundreds of refugees, as well as their onward travel to the UK. Anne took charge of this with a small group of other Embassy wives. They set up an office in the Embassy Library and began ringing round members of the British community to solicit beds for the night. Many, but by no means all, were found places in Embassy houses. Members of the Consular Section stood by to give consular help of other kinds and British Airways had someone permanently available in the Embassy to arrange onward travel. So it continued, day and night, for several days. Given that our contingency plans were more geared to an evacuation from Iran than to this specific situation, it all worked pretty well. But it was a tiring experience for all concerned, especially for Anne and her colleagues. When it was all over, Denis thanked them warmly for their efforts and told Anne that if he could have done so he would have recommended her for an MBE. As it was, we both felt we had earned our mid-tour home leave by the time we got on our flight a few days later. In fact when we arrived in Istanbul, our first stop on the way, and reached our hotel we crashed out and slept round the clock, despite the raucous noises in the street below our bedroom window.

We could not use Dymocks Manor during our leave because the Neves were still there, but they kindly arranged for us to rent another house in the village belonging to Canadian friends of theirs who were themselves going on leave. No. 5 Beacon Road was a comfortable house and there was the added advantage that we had the use of a big American car that went with it. I have no particular memories of what we did during our leave, except of course seeing a lot of our families. On our way back to Tehran we stopped off for a week or two in Collobrières, and after that for a few days in Tel Aviv, where Michael Hadow, who was Ambassador at the time, had kindly asked us to stay. The Israelis were cockahoop after their crushing victory in the June War and I recall Michael pointing out to us huge concentrations of virtually new Egyptian military trucks that had been captured intact without a fight. He also took us on a tour of Israel and the West Bank. Apart from the familiar holy places, I have a clear imprint in my mind of the great flat-topped hill of Masada, where the Zealots were besieged by the Romans and committed mass suicide by throwing themselves off the steep-sided top.

Not long after we had returned to Tehran, on 8 December, Ma died. I thought she had been showing her age on the number of occasions we had seen her during our leave, but her death came as a shock. I would have liked very much to go back for her funeral, but sadly for various reasons it was not to be. She was a remarkable person.

There is not much more to say about our time in Tehran, particularly as the second half of our tour was cut short in September 1968, when I was posted back to London to take charge of the Establishments and Organization Department (E&OD) on the administration side of the office. As this involved promotion to Counsellor, I could not complain, but we were very sorry to be leaving. Just as we had at the beginning of our posting, we did part of our return trip by sea, from Beirut to Genoa, with stops at Syracuse in Sicily and at Naples (including Pompeii) en route. From Genoa we did the last leg by train.

Administration

Our first priority on our return was to find a new house. As I have already explained, No.1 Dymocks Manor was now too small for our enlarged family. Moreover I had had enough of commuting by train from Haywards Heath. We therefore looked further afield and before long found what we wanted in Wimbledon. No.15 Ernle Road was a five-bedroom family house with a fair-sized lawn (originally a tennis court) in the back garden, not far from the Common. It had been built some time in the 1920s and, although showing its age, suited us well. What suited us less well was the difficulty we had in selling the old house and the fact that we had to take a bridging loan to tide us over until we could, which turned out to be a few months later. James and Alice were soon found places in the local Primary School, I went to work either by car or the District Line, and we all adapted quickly to suburban life.

Before taking over E&OD I had a few months' stint as a Postings Officer in Personnel Department in order to give me a broad view of what the administration of the Service involved. Shortly after I joined E&OD, its somewhat forbidding name was changed to Personnel Services Department (PSD), which better described what it was about, namely the conditions of service, pay and allowances of Diplomatic Service staff. It was not exciting work in the broad scheme of things, but more often than not it involved the taking of decisions that greatly affected individuals, in particular family hardship problems or disciplinary cases. The files that crossed the Head of Department's desk tended to be the difficult ones and the decisions I had to make could even determine whether a person remained in, or had to leave, the Service. The easiest thing was to go by the book and follow the regulations, but I soon came to understand that there was more to it than that and it was sometimes necessary to bend the rules or find a way round them. In the process I learnt a lot about the vicissitudes of life and the saying "there but for the grace of God go I" often came to mind. I also came to realise how misplaced were the "we and they" attitudes which often infected relations between those involved in the administration and operational sides of the Service and how valuable it was to have experience of both types of work. We were, after all, interchangeable members of the same organisation. A fact that was brought vividly home to me when in January 1971 I was moved, to my great surprise, to be Head of News Department.

News Department

Two more different jobs could hardly be imagined, one essentially an HQ staff appointment, the other very much in the front line. As things turned out, the two and a half years I was to have in News Department were amongst the most enjoyable of my whole career. I soon discovered how exhilarating it was to be near the centre of what was going on and right in the thick of things. It was anything but a safe, backroom job; there were plenty of banana skins around to slip on and the adrenalin often flowed. It was a time when what Britain did and said counted for more in the world than it does today. The press gave more column inches and air time to what the FO had to say than now, and even the tabloids had full-time diplomatic correspondents. Including the wire services and others, for example leader writers and specialist reporters, they must have numbered sixty or seventy. There was also a large foreign press corps in London. A day or two after my appointment I was to shake hands with them all at a big reception at Lancaster House given by the Secretary of State, Sir Alec Douglas-Home, to mark the changeover from my predecessor, Robin Haydon, to me. There had been nothing in my previous career to prepare me for that – and I was excited.

The following afternoon things began in earnest and I was nervous as I began my first press briefing, a one-to-one affair in my office with Sandy Rendel of *The Times*. I started diffidently by saying that I was not quite sure what he was expecting of me. At which he smiled and explained that the easiest thing would be for me to tell him everything and then he would let me know what I should not have divulged. A lovely man, and because he was so nice and trustworthy there were times when he was indeed given more information than he should have been. On one occasion, so the story goes, on a visit to Bucharest or some other East European capital, he found to his horror that he had copies of several FO telegrams in his brief case. So he rushed round to the British Embassy to hand them over for safe keeping. True or not, it could have been.

News Department had a complement of about a dozen people, including two secretaries. Most, like me, were generalist members of the

Service on a home posting, but continuity and expertise were provided by two specialist information professionals, Eleanor Booker and John Burgoyne. Every weekday morning the Head of Department held an on-the-record news conference at which he made formal announcements about ministerial travels and speeches, ambassadorial appointments and other forthcoming events, and answered questions. It was not a large affair and I found that it was attended mainly by representatives of the Press Association and the other wire services. The main business of the day, the off-the-record briefing of small groups of accredited British diplomatic correspondents and, less frequently, London-based representatives of foreign newspapers, took place in the afternoon. By tradition the Reuters diplomatic correspondent, and those of *The Times*, *Sunday Times*, *Daily Telegraph* and the *Observer*, received individual briefings. We also handled requests for press interviews with the Secretary of State or one of the other FCO Ministers. A Duty Officer was available to deal with matters that arose outside normal hours. He or she would go into the office at times during the week-end and could be reached on the telephone in the evenings. By comparison with how the press side of the FCO is now run, we provided a Rolls-Royce service to our "customers".

Not all of them were as cosy as Sandy Rendel. They were a mixed bunch, ranging from the out-and-out news hacks looking for scoops – and trouble – to the serious columnists and pensive leader writers. What I had not expected was that I would grow to like and respect so many of them. I suppose before my appointment I had shared the apprehension of the press and distrust of journalists that was felt by all too many members of the Service, whose preferred reaction to any journalistic enquiry was "no comment". However, the more I came to know the correspondents as individuals and to understand the demands of their profession the more comfortable I felt in their company. It was very much a two-way relationship that could be beneficial to us both, the essence of it being that if I was to trust them they had to trust me. If I misled them or gave them a bad steer I would forfeit their trust. If on the other hand I told them frankly that I could not answer a question because, for example, negotiations had reached a delicate stage, most of them would accept that, albeit reluctantly. Sometimes correspondents had information that we did not have from our own sources or received breaking news more quickly than we did. Occasionally someone would decide not to risk spoiling a good story gleaned from another source by checking its accuracy with us. I thought that was unprofessional and would let the offender know. In general, however, I can number on the fingers of one hand cases where I felt a journalist had really let me down. In this general context it has to be borne in mind that however good relations between the press and News Department may have been, we were not on the same side of the fence: they had their job to do and we had ours. It was only natural that they would not take everything we said at its face value and would probe further than we wanted them to go. It was only natural that we, for our part, did not want to expose too much surface: it is a truism that diplomacy is often best conducted behind closed doors.

Not all of the on-the-record press conferences were routine. There was one moment of high drama in September 1971, when we announced the expulsion of 105 Russian spies. It had been a long-running sore point with Sir Alec that despite several unpublicised requests he had made to his Soviet opposite number, Andrei Gromyko, to scale down Russian spying activities in London, nothing had happened. Indeed Gromyko had not even deigned to reply. Sir Alec's patience finally ran out and he decided to use a show of force to demonstrate that we meant business. Detailed planning for the expulsions, including the preparation of dossiers of background information for public dissemination in explanation of this action, was put in hand. There was a worrying moment when, following the defection of a Soviet intelligence officer, it was feared that the Russians might get wind of what was in hand, and so the preparations were speeded up, with relays of typists staying up late into the night to complete the dossiers. Eventually everything was ready and the Permanent Under-Secretary, Sir Denis Greenhill, summoned the Soviet Chargé d'Affaires, Ivan Ippolitov, to the FO on the afternoon of Friday 24 September to give him the names of ninety Russians who were being expelled from Britain and of a further fifteen who were out of the country and would not be allowed back. Meanwhile there was flurry of activity in News Department, as we telephoned round to all our regular contacts to invite them to an immediate press conference. Sensing something dramatic afoot they came in large numbers and packed out our conference room. The timing was acute if the news was to make the last editions of the evening newspapers (there were still two in London then) and the early evening TV and radio bulletins. So without delay I delivered the bombshell and there was an audible intake of air round the room. Someone shouted out "Did you say 19?" "No", I said, "Nine O" and there was a rush for the door towards the row of telephones in the corridor outside. We had anticipated this and had locked the door, so that we could at least make sure that they took with them the folders of background documents we wanted them to have.

It was pure theatre, and a journalistic sensation. All the papers and news bulletins had to scrap their leads and start again. Remarkably, it seems to have taken the Russians completely by surprise, despite our earlier forebodings, and they were temporarily knocked off balance. There were no immediate reprisals of the usual kind, and when they were eventually announced they amounted to less than we expected. Moreover, Gromyko did not try to snub Sir Alec by cancelling a previously arranged meeting for the following Monday in New York, where both would be attending the UN General Assembly. I was one of those present and can testify that it was a frosty occasion. Gromyko left Sir Alec in no doubt how angry he was, but he remained icily cold and did not raise his voice. He left it to his experienced interpreter, Sukodrov, to lay on the theatrics. Sir Alec was his usual calm self and he infuriated Grom (as we nicknamed him) even more by saying that he realised the spies concerned worked for the KGB and were therefore not under his control. At the end of these exchanges Sir Alec said that there was a crowd of journalists waiting outside (we were in the Soviet UN Mission building) and he wondered whether Gromyko had any views on what he might say to them. Grom gave him a stony look and said he did not care, he could say what he liked. Which he did. Game, set and match to Sir Alec.

The relationship between a Cabinet Minister and the head of his press office is a critical one and I was terribly lucky to have Sir Alec as my boss. My predecessor, poor fellow, had had George Brown as his. Amongst other things, he had been fired several times, normally late at night, only to find that when George woke up next morning he had forgotten all about it. Alec had no interest in self-publicity and was never on the look out for a journalist to talk to, but when he did have dealings with them he was his natural self. There were times at press conferences when he could not remember some detail he ought to have had at his finger tips, but he would say so out loud and ask someone to help him out. Happily the journalists had such affection for him that they did not report it; and when he told a BBC reporter at the foot of the aircraft steps in Tunis how glad he was to be in Rabat he was merely asked to record the piece again.

Some of the slip-ups were mine. I remember on one occasion overseas handing out to the press advance copies of a speech Alec would be making at an official dinner given by his opposite number that evening, only to be told at the dinner that he had agreed with a suggestion made by his host that they should not have any speeches after all. I sent a note up to the top table telling Alec what I had done and suggesting that he should at least say something. To which he replied "You can tell them to take it as read!"

Arrival in Salisbury, 1971

Which brings me to our travels. The Head of News Department was a regular member of the Secretary of State's entourage wherever he went abroad. I have not totted up how many trips I did with Sir Alec in the two and a half years I was with him. Suffice it to say there were a lot, both near in Europe and further afield in the USA, Middle East, Africa, Asia and Australasia. The only areas I did not go to were Latin America and Eastern Europe. As early as 14 January 1971, when I had only been in the job about a week, I accompanied him to the Commonwealth Heads of Government Meeting (CHOGM) in Singapore. The meeting was dominated by the fierce opposition of many member countries to the Heath government's decision to resume supplying arms to South Africa. Heath himself became so fed up with it that he was in half a mind to walk out of the conference and the story goes that it was Alec who dissuaded him. I myself played second fiddle to Donald Maitland, the Prime Minister's Press Secretary, himself a former Head of News Department, and I was able to pick up from him some useful tips for dealing with journalists.

When Alec travelled overseas he was invariably accompanied by his Private Secretary, one or two senior advisers, the Head of News Department, Private Office secretarial staff, and one or two Special Branch protection officers. Sometimes his wife, Elizabeth, and Miles Hudson, his Political Adviser, would join the team. I would have my Personal Assistant, first Pat Noble and later Anthea Perry, with me. For security reasons we nearly always used RAF Transport Command aircraft, either an HS125 for short journeys or a comfortable "ministerial" VC10 for longer trips. In the VC10 we often took journalists with us, as John Dickie of the *Daily Mail* has narrated in *The Boys in the Bongo Bus* (University of Luton Press, 1997). On arrival in a foreign capital the Secretary of State would be met at the airport by his opposite number and the British Head of Mission, and usually he would be asked to make a statement for the benefit of waiting journalists and answer a few questions. It was my job to stick by him when that happened. Alec and his Private Secretary and one or two others would be lodged in the ambassadorial residence and the rest of us in a hotel. I would always be allocated a suite for use as a press briefing room and we usually brought with us ample quantities of alcohol to assuage the thirsts of the hacks as they waited for our briefings. This is where Pat Noble and Anthea Perry came into their own – they had to be barmaids as well as secretaries and keep the drinks flowing.

At this distance in time there is nothing particularly memorable about some of the trips we made and I have not made a chronological list of them. I have already mentioned taking part in an early trip to Singapore for CHOGM, and visits to Tehran and New York for the UN General Assembly. There were moments of high drama, or low farce, on other occasions. In the latter category was one that occurred during a tour of countries Alec made to the Middle East, amongst them Egypt, in September 1971. While there he took time off to visit the pyramids. On emerging from inside he was confronted by Peter Snow of ITN, along with a camera crew and a camel. Peter invited him to pose by the side of the camel, which he duly did. Peter then tried his luck by asking him to have his picture taken on the camel's back and to don an Arab kefiya headdress he had thoughtfully brought with him. Alec again consented and the next day his photo was all over the British newspapers. Some thought it was funny, but several criticised him for making himself a laughing stock and demeaning the serious conduct of diplomacy. I felt very contrite, because I had been forewarned in general terms that Peter would be waiting outside with a camel, but I had failed to warn Alec. When I owned up, he did not utter a word of blame and just shrugged it off as a matter of little importance. The milk was spilt and there was no point in crying over it. I hate to think what George Brown would have done.

Never out of earshot

Two months later, in November 1971, Alec flew to Salisbury to see if he could negotiate a settlement of the Rhodesia problem with Ian Smith and his colleagues. He took with him the Attorney-General, Sir Peter Rawlinson, and Lord Goodman, who had made earlier reconnaissance visits to Salisbury, and a team of FCO advisers led by Sir Denis Greenhill, the Permanent Under-Secretary and including, as usual, myself. Most of the party stayed in Mirimba House, the old residence of the British High Commissioner, which had been closed since UDI and had been taken out of mothballs for the occasion. I had a suite in the Meikles Hotel. Details of the agreement that was eventually reached after prolonged negotiations, and its subsequent disavowal in the course of the soundings of Rhodesian opinion taken by the Pearce Commission (Lord Pearce, incidentally, was a member of the Skinners' Company), are matters of public record and do not need repeating here. However, two particular episodes are worth a passing mention, because they convey some idea of the atmosphere in which the talks took place.

First, Alec had made it clear in advance that while he was in Salisbury he wanted to have access to members of different political groups and amongst those was Joshua Nkomo, an African opposition leader who had been held in detention since 1964. Nkomo was duly brought to Mirimba

House by security police in a closed van. As he emerged blinking into the sunlight, the van hardly seemed big enough to accommodate his huge figure. Since it was assumed that the Rhodesians would have planted listening devices in the house, Alec sat him down under a jacaranda tree in the garden for their talk and I joined the small circle of people present. Despite being out of circulation for so long, Nkomo showed himself to be well-informed about what was going on in the country and beyond, and he did not hesitate to criticise the actions of the British government. When the time came for him to leave he went up the garden steps to the waiting van and before climbing into it asked if he could use the lavatory. Ten minutes later, when he had still not reappeared, we began to get worried about what might have happened to him. He was far too bulky to have escaped through the window, but had he had a stroke or something? When to our relief he eventually reappeared he said with a broad smile on his face that he had just been prolonging his last few moments of freedom.

The Rhodesian Intelligence people could be very clumsy. One day while the talks were going on, Pat Noble went back to the hotel to fetch something from my room. As she opened the door she saw a man leaning over the dismantled telephone, screwdriver in hand. With a look of acute anxiety on his face he rushed past her out of the room. When she returned she told me what had happened and I let Denis Greenhill know. His immediate reaction was that it was hardly surprising and I should not say any more about it. It was probably in his mind that as the room was principally used for briefing the British journalists there was little risk of sensitive information being given an airing there. In a funny sort of way the boot was in fact on the other foot. It was widely known that the crew of our VC10 was on standby to leave at any time if the negotiations looked like grinding to a halt and one of the journalists had the bright idea of asking me one day whether I had sent my washing to the hotel laundry. I said I had and this was repeated each day, until for a bit of a tease I let it be known one morning that I had not done so. This was at once taken as a sign that our departure was imminent and was reported in a diary piece sent back to London. It would be nice to think that my dirty socks and pants helped to concentrate Rhodesian minds at a critical moment, but that would perhaps be presuming too much.

In January 1972 I accompanied Alec on a visit to the Far East. Our first stop was in India, which had just achieved a decisive victory over Pakistan in the Bangladesh war of independence. Alec decided that no time should be lost in demonstrating HMG's support for the new Bangladesh

Visit to Pakistan, 1972

Prime Minister, Mujibur Rahman. He therefore decided to detach two of us from the next part of his tour, a visit to Thailand, and to send us off instead to Dacca to pay his respects to Mujib. Iain Sutherland, the Head of South Asia Department, was an obvious choice and I went with him to take care of the PR side of things. We made our way via Calcutta and eventually ended up at Mujib's house in Dacca, where we found long lines of people camped outside and on his balcony. They were petitioners who had come to pay homage and solicit his help and it took a little time for us to make our way through the throng. When we finally got to Mujib, he gave us a warm welcome and Iain said his piece.

We rejoined the aerial caravan in Bangkok and flew on to South Korea with the others. The final stop was to be Japan, but before we could go there Alec received a telegram from London summoning him home to take part in a critical vote in the House of Commons. So we turned on our heels and flew back post haste. One reads of such things still happening today, but do the demands of parliamentary democracy really have to be so inflexible, I wonder?

Dacca in January is a nice sunny place, but the next time I went there it was in June, when the monsoon was in full swing and the streets were flooded. Alec was on another tour, this time to Australia for a ministerial meeting of the South East Asia Treaty Organization (SEATO), New Zealand, Indonesia, Bangladesh and Afghanistan. Miles Hudson has given an amusing account of this trip in his book, *Two Lives 1892–1992* (Wilton 65, 1992), and I cannot improve on that. As he says, we were exhausted by the time we got back.

At the end of October we were back in the Far East, this time on a ground-breaking visit to China. Alec was the first British Foreign Secretary to go there since the People's Republic was established in 1949. As usual, we went in a VC10, but what was unusual was that we took the polar route and all but three of the 27 hours' journey took place in darkness. Alec and his wife joined the flight at Prestwick late at night and our first refuelling stop, roughly nine hours later, was at a U.S. Air Force base in Alaska. We ordered our daily routine on the aircraft by GMT and had just had breakfast when we were invited to visit the officers' mess. There it was still the previous evening local time and we were offered all kinds of alcoholic refreshment. Of course, it would have been churlish to refuse such hospitality and so it was that I made the acquaintance, for the first and last time, of a very powerful concoction called a Harvey Wallbanger.

There was much press interest in the visit and, unusually, a party of London-based journalists had received permission from the Chinese authorities to go on a three-day conducted tour before we arrived. But as soon as the talks started it became apparent that the Chinese had a very different approach from us to briefing the press. My opposite number, Mr Ma, was used to making the most anodyne and uninformative statements, whereas the British journalists expected me to give them a good deal more than that and to reply to questions. Knowing something of Chinese sensitivities I was in fact more cautious than usual in what I said, to the point where some of my News Department regulars complained about my reticence. But that was nothing compared with the complaints heaped on me by the Chinese when they saw what was reported in the wire services. At the beginning of the second plenary meeting the Prime Minister, Chou En-lai, was clearly very angry. Pointing across the room at me, he asked Alec what his Press Officer was up to, since he seemed to be giving the press a full account of their discussions. It was no use, he went on, having private discussions of this kind if their content was made public; perhaps he should invite Chinese journalists in to witness them. It was a fierce onslaught and I wanted to sink down in my chair, as in a Bateman cartoon. But once again Alec's light touch and gentle humour saved the day. He turned to Chou and said words to the effect "Oh, don't take any notice of what John Leahy says, none of us do". Denis Greenhill added a few soothing words of his own and the tension relaxed. After the meeting he told me not to worry about it.

Take no notice of Leahy, Peking 1972

The rest of the trip took place without incident. We did the usual tourist things like visiting the Forbidden City, the Great Wall and the Ming Tombs. We were also taken out into the countryside to see a collective farm. Perhaps the highlight of the visit was the large banquet in the Great Hall of the People in Tiananmen Square. As Alec and Elizabeth processed into dinner with their hosts the Central Band of the Peoples' Liberation Army played the Eton Boating Song, an unforgettable moment. The rest of us sat at round tables with our individual Chinese hosts, who spent much of the meal transferring the delicacies from the serving dishes on to our plates with the deft use of their chopsticks. They also saw to it that we knocked back the Maotai wine, which reminded me of old boots. I sat next to the Vice-Minister of Health, who, like most people we came across, smoked a great deal, following no doubt the example of Chairman Mao Tse-tung. Packets of cigarettes – and spittoons – were much in evidence in every room we used. At one stage during the dinner I asked him through an interpreter why there was no warning on the packets about the potential health hazards. He looked straight at me and said that in China more people died of obesity than inhaling nicotine. Touché, although he was not exactly a sylph-like figure himself.

This topped the chart of the travels I made with the Foreign Secretary. But before leaving this section, I will just mention the numerous trips we made to meetings of the European Council of Ministers after the UK entered the EEC on 1 January 1973. Alec was not really European-minded and the arcane procedures of the meetings often bored him. There was, however, one hilarious occasion when either through oversight or inattention he voted in completely the opposite sense to the recommendation in his brief. As the UK had been in a minority of one throughout the preceding debate, this turn of events was greeted with delight by all the other Ministers. A quick huddle then took place behind Alec's chair, and Sir Michael Palliser, the UK Permanent Council Representative, gently pointed out the error of his ways. Alec was not in the slightest bit put out. He tapped his microphone and said that for the benefit of his colleagues he would just like to "clarify" his position. He then proceeded to go smartly in reverse, to the chagrin of the others round the table. Only he could get away with that sort of thing, because, as politicians went, he was seen to be a straightforward, honest man who did not play devious games but occasionally got his lines wrong.

One other European trip is worthy of mention. Alec was invited by his Spanish opposite number to pay a visit to Madrid at a time when tension was fairly high over Gibraltar. We flew there in an HS125 and as we drove away from the airport to make our way to the Embassy our convoy of cars was stopped by a large crowd of gesticulating, banner-waving demonstrators. It was obvious that Franco's government had stage-managed the whole thing, because a strong force of police had also been drafted in and for a time they stood by as the mob started rocking our cars from side to side. It was certainly anxious-making, but the police finally called a halt before things got right out of hand and we continued on our way. On entering the Embassy we were greeted at the door by flunkies in full livery offering us glasses of champagne. The Ambassador, John Russell, who had himself been Head of News Department, was living up to his reputation as a master showman.

On a more modest plane, I received a CMG in the June 1973 Birthday Honours List. At about the same time, I was also informed of a posting back to Paris, this time as Head of Chancery. Both developments were of course gratifying, but I could not help feeling sad about leaving News Department. It was a great job and I would have liked to continue doing it, but I had now been five years in London and it was time to move on.

There was one last service to perform for Alec. BBC Panorama was preparing a special programme to mark his 70th birthday in early July and wanted to include a sequence of him at home at The Hirsel. It was agreed that a crew would spend a couple of days filming on the spot and Alec asked me to look after them. He accordingly invited Anne and me to stay with him and Elizabeth at the Hirsel. In the event we arrived nearly an hour late after a long drive, but they greeted us warmly despite that. Alec even insisted on carrying in our suitcases himself and taking us to our room. Shortly after, we went down to the kitchen to join them for a cup of tea, only to catch Alec on his hands and knees clearing up some cake crumbs from the floor with his handkerchief as we entered the room. He explained that one of the dogs had managed to steal the cake from the table. Anne was a bit reluctant to accept a piece when it was offered, but felt it would be impolite to refuse. Mercifully, the film crew were not around.

During our stay two rather different crises were going on. First, the so-called "cod war" with Iceland was at its height and had reached the point where Joseph Luns, the NATO Secretary-General, was using his good offices to resolve the conflict. Alec was of course being kept closely in touch with events. The second crisis was closer to home. No pun intended, it was in fact right at home. I forget the details, but the essence of it was that a gardener had run off with a game-keeper's wife, or vice versa, and Alec's daughter, Caroline, who acted as the Estate Factor, was pressing him to knock their heads together and restore peace and harmony to the household. He for his part was most reluctant to become involved. One morning I took a telephone call for him and went to find him. He asked me who was on the line and when I told him the Prime Minister was waiting to speak to him, he laughed and said "Thank God for that, I thought it might be Caroline"!

Before we left for Paris, the two of them gave us a farewell party at No.1 Carlton Gardens. Nor did we forget one another. Whenever our paths crossed later they always had a friendly word and they were meticulous about writing letters and sending us Christmas cards.

Paris Again

I was not given much time after leaving News Department to get ready for Paris. It did not matter all that much because we were going back to a familiar scene and a house we knew. But it was a rush all the same and when I drove off in our new, gleaming white Triumph Stag on the last day of July to catch the ferry at Newhaven, Anne had to stay behind to supervise the packing up and despatch of the family belongings, organise the letting of the house (to an American family called Godkin), and undertake all the hundred and one other chores associated with a diplomatic move. A long sentence, I know, but so was the list of things she had to do.

I moved into the Gate House and camped there for a week or so until Anne drove over with the children and our Cairn Terrier, Milly, in our little Renault 4. Emma, meanwhile, had gone off to Spain with her Spanish boyfriend, Juan Robles. The rest of us drove down to Collobrières in the two cars – before leaving London I had managed to arrange that we would not have to forgo our long-planned holiday. After two or three weeks we returned to Paris and Anne took the children back to Wimbledon, leaving Milly with me in the Gate House. She did not finally join me *in situ* until October, having seen the children back to school.

The Gate House gives directly on to the Rue du Faubourg St. Honoré in the most prestigious area of Paris. The Presidential Elysée Palace is just up the road, the American Embassy and the Cercle InterAlliée are neighbours, Hermès is close by and Maxims is round the corner in the Rue Royale. So it is not, or at least it was not then, the sort of place where Embassy staff could be seen taking their ease in scruffy old weekend clothes or looking anything but their best. Living as we did right on the Ambassador's doorstep, we had to take care not to let the side down. In short, it was not a relaxing place to live. It was not merely a matter of clothes either. In the entertainment field we had to do more, in terms both of quantity and quality, than on our previous tour. The house served as a free hotel for English friends we did not know we had, and of course for members of the family. For one special occasion, Betty Pitchford's 70 birthday, the family came over in force and filled every available space, but of course nobody minded that. Less enjoyably, the Gate House also became an overflow annexe of the ambassadorial residence for visiting delegations. We also had to take care when we gave dinner parties to ensure that the French guests we invited were all on speaking terms – franco-franco bad blood round the Paris dinner tables could cause more trouble than notional Anglo-French ill feeling. We did not find our Parisian guests unfriendly, but they seemed to be more interested in one another than in us and we made few real friends among them. For these various reasons Anne did not enjoy our second tour in Paris as much as she had hoped. So much so that when some ten years later I heard that the Prime Minister, Margaret Thatcher, had overruled a tentative proposal to send me back to Paris as Ambassador, in favour of John Fretwell, a specialist in European affairs, Anne breathed a sigh of relief; for my part, I can truthfully say that I had been half hoping, but not expecting.

The Ambassador was Sir Edward (Eddie) Tomkins. Much quieter and less flamboyant than his predecessor, Christopher Soames, but with excellent credentials of his own. Half French and a wartime liaison officer with the Free French Forces. Nice enough, but slow to make up his mind and not very inspiring. His wife, Gillian (Jill), a family member of the Benson half of the Kleinwort Benson merchant bank, was an altogether tougher character and made her views known loud and clear. She did not, for example, hide her dislike of Jane Ewart-Biggs, the Minister's ambitious wife. Christopher Ewart-Biggs himself was a fascinating, unconventional character who, if anything, came from a pre-war mould. Tall, willowy, languid, black patch over one eye, with literary interests and talents, and political attitudes somewhat left of centre. He enjoyed the company of les bien-pensants of the Paris upper crust and was a dedicated networker. He could spend hours polishing and repolishing draft despatches; but when necessary could galvanise himself and the rest of us into action. All, that is, except the Ambassador, who liked to chew the cud, thereby causing Christopher much frustration. He in turn caused much frustration for the Minister (Economic & Commercial), the equally ambitious Ronald Arculus, who did not like the thought that Christopher was primus inter pares and competed with him for the Ambassador's ear. Christopher, I should add, had a well-developed sense of humour and was apt to poke fun at Ronald behind his back.

At first I too had my frustrations as Head of Chancery, resulting from a sort of turf war I had inherited. Chancery was full of bright young men, all with restless energy and champing at the bit, and displaying a marked tendency to think that I was there just to run the machine while they dealt direct with Christopher on important matters of substance. So I had to make a special effort to insert myself in the chain and, for good measure, reserve one or two political subjects to myself. It worked out all right and I was not aware of any resulting friction. One of my rather more boring duties was to give regular briefings to my E.C. colleagues on such things as visits by British ministers to Paris. If they could not all come at the same time, I might find myself having to repeat the exercise two or three times in the course of the same day. On one occasion I just stopped myself from nodding off to sleep in mid-sentence.

The reader may derive the impression from the above that it was an unhappy Embassy. I would not say it was. But more generally and in the nature of things, large diplomatic missions, with a number of separate sections and a big local staff, rarely have the same cohesion as smaller ones and Paris was no different. Despite a quite active Embassy club, most people did not mix after work or at weekends. In general junior members of the staff found they had an unexpectedly restricted social life. Perhaps as Head of Chancery I should have done more to correct this; but there were heavy calls on my time and opportunities for pastoral work were limited.

While the other children continued at boarding school at home, Emma, who had left Roedean at the end of the 1973 summer term and gone off to Spain for a time, joined us in Paris and managed to get a place at the renowned Institut des Sciences Politiques ("Science Po"). Like most French educational establishments, it is a highly competitive institution and as a foreigner she did very well not only to survive the three years there but to graduate with honours. By this time she was more or less tri-lingual, English/French/Spanish, and a few years later she got a good job working for French television, at first in London and then in Paris.

A short time after our arrival in Paris stirring events occurred elsewhere in the world, notably the Yom Kippur war in the Middle East and with it an economic crisis for the West caused by a sharp increase in the price of oil. In Britain a prolonged and bitter coal miners' strike led to widespread electricity cuts, the introduction of a three-day working week, and the holding, in February 1974, of a general election, which brought Harold Wilson and the Labour Party back to power. From the not so sublime to the ridiculous, one of the main consequences of the economic crisis in Britain was that people became caught up in a hoarding frenzy and, as a result, some things disappeared from the shelves, including lavatory paper. We became a source of supply of this fundamental product for visitors from the old country.

In March a terrible event occurred close to hand. Soon after take-off from Paris, a Turkish Airlines DC10 crashed in a forest between Senlis and Compiègne, killing all on board. Among the passengers had been many British rugby fans who had been attending the France–England rugby match at the Parc des Princes the day before and who had had to transfer to this flight because the British Airways flight on which they were booked had been seriously delayed as a result of engine trouble. It quickly became apparent that not only were there no survivors, but hardly any of the physical remains were recognisable. To aid the process of identification the Gendarmerie collected the personal belongings they found on the ground, or in one or two cases in the trees, and brought them to a deconsecrated chapel nearby, where the relatives could inspect them. A few were taken to a morgue to identify such recognisable body parts as there were. It was a harrowing business and the Embassy naturally became deeply involved in assisting the British families. In particular Anne organised a team of wives to accompany them on their distressing visits to the chapel and help them in their dealings with the French authorities. An additional complication, which had to be handled with great care, was the discovery from perusal of the passenger list that one or two people had been travelling with girl friends rather than their wives. The Embassy also helped to organise and look after the families at a big outdoor memorial service held in Thiais cemetery at the beginning of May.

In April President Pompidou, who had been in failing health for some time, died. The British delegation to his funeral at Notre Dame Cathedral was headed by Prince Philip and included the Prime Minister, Harold Wilson, the Leader of the Opposition, Edward Heath, and the leader of the Liberal Party, Jeremy Thorpe. As the cars arrived from the airport a small crowd of spectators gathered outside the Embassy gates spotted Wilson and booed him; Heath on the other hand they cheered, presumably because he had brought about the entry of the UK into the European Community a year earlier, in the face of opposition from Wilson and the Labour Party. After lunch in the Residence the Prime Minister had various official appointments, but the others were at a loose end before their flight back to London. So I took Heath out for a walk in the Tuileries Gardens, accompanied by Emma and James, and Milly, our Cairn terrier. Heath seemed pathetically pleased when passers-by recognised him and asked him to pose for a photograph – the bitterness of his recent electoral defeat clearly rankled still, all the more so because he could see at close hand his victor in the recent election getting all the official attentions he once enjoyed from the very same officials.

The Presidential Election took place the following month and in the run-off on 19 May Valéry Giscard d'Estaing, the Gaullist candidate, narrowly defeated François Mitterand, his Socialist opponent. Back home Wilson called another election for October, when he secured a slender majority. During the rest of that year and the first part of the next Anglo-French relations were dominated by the efforts of the Labour Government to "renegotiate" the terms of Britain's entry into the EEC, as pledged in its election manifesto, and the determination of the French Government to frustrate them. There were a number of ministerial visits to Paris, including one by the Prime Minister, and when necessary the Gate House served as the overflow annexe for the entourage. The "renegotiation" did not in fact achieve very much, but was enough for Wilson to paper over the deep divisions in the Labour Party on the subject. The ensuing national referendum in June resulted in a resounding yes in confirmation of the UK's membership of the EEC. As we all know by now, that was by no means the end of the story and to this day Europe remains a deeply divisive issue in British politics.

Early in 1975 a minor bombshell descended on us from a clear blue sky, in the form of a posting on secondment to the Northern Ireland Office in Belfast. This was to take place in June, less than two years after our arrival. My first reaction was one of dismay. I, at least, was enjoying Paris and did not want to leave so soon. More importantly, I was concerned about the safety implications of taking the family to Northern Ireland at a time when the security situation seemed to be as bad as ever. I also wondered whether my Co. Limerick family connections would not be a handicap in Northern Ireland. On the contrary, Personnel Department said, off the top of their heads I feel sure, that would be an advantage. They also went through the motions of pretending that it was open to me to decline the move. This was coupled with the suggestion that I should take into consideration the early promotion to Assistant Under-Secretary; I had been specially picked out for this job and there was no telling when a similar opportunity might come along, if I turned it down. They also offered to let me go over to Belfast for a preliminary visit to see what was involved and assess the situation for myself. Which I did – I could hardly refuse without appearing to be bloody-minded. But they knew, and I knew, that from that point there could be no turning back, the die was cast. The one saving grace was that it did look like being an interesting job, Head of Public Relations and Political Affairs.

We decided to treat ourselves to a good night out before leaving Paris in early June. Although Maxims was very near we had never set foot in it.

So, throwing caution to the winds, we went and had dinner there. A very good dinner it was too and afterwards we made our way home in a happy frame of mind. But that soon evaporated when we were met by the embassy's Duty Officer to be told that earlier in the evening British football supporters had caused serious trouble at the European Cup Final in Paris between Leeds United and Bayern Munich.

The main incidents had apparently occurred outside the ground, when some drunken idiots had gone on the rampage and smashed shop windows. Several were being held in police custody. Worse still, it soon became known that one of those who had been arrested was an Embassy registry clerk, who was seen picking up a moped by the side of the road and hurling it through a shop window. The police had released him without charge, presumably because he was a member of the Embassy, although in fact he only had qualified diplomatic immunity, i.e. in relation to acts committed while he was on duty. It was quickly decided that the Ambassador should issue a public apology for the loutish behaviour of the English troublemakers; and that our Embassy offender should agree to pay for the damage he had caused and be sent back to London at once to face disciplinary punishment. This turned out to be a farce: to my chagrin, he was transferred to the Home Civil Service and promoted to a higher rank not much later.

Northern Ireland Office

The job was a new one and its origin was as follows. The Secretary of State for Northern Ireland, Merlyn Rees, had decided to bring under the central direction of the NIO the Army's press and information office at HQ Lisburn, which up to then had acted independently with some highly embarrassing results. He had been particularly upset when reports appeared in the press of various "dirty tricks" and disinformation operations being run, without his knowledge, by the so-called "Information Policy" section at Lisburn . These had clearly got out of hand and Rees was determined to bring those concerned to heel. I was to be his instrument for doing this, as a sort of press and information overlord. The local Northern Ireland departmental information office (as distinct from the London-based NIO press office) also came under my control. The Political Affairs part of my job description mainly concerned getting to know, and establishing a rapport with, local politicians. Of course a number of other people, starting with the Minister himself, were engaged in that as well, so it was hardly an exclusive responsibility.

As a Department of State the NIO was *sui generis*. For a start it was split between Belfast and London and, while the junior members of staff were mainly static in one place or the other, more senior people were constantly travelling between the two. I was based in Belfast and was provided with an official house and car there, but found myself frequently flying to London for consultations, meetings etc. The family home was still in Wimbledon and while the children did not spend much time in the province Anne divided her time between our two houses. This of course made it difficult to have a settled life-style. The Northern Ireland security situation at that time was not good, but it was not as bad as it was made to appear in the press on this side of the Irish Sea. Before we went friends and family were apt to express concern about our safety. In fact there was only one occasion in the next eighteen months (which I will revert to later) when I myself was made to feel in any kind of danger. Obviously we had to take some everyday precautions. We had, for example, bright security lights in the garden of our house and my official car was painted an unofficial-looking colour. For good measure its number plates were changed every so often in the vain hope of fooling would-be attackers. Also I was advised to vary my routes to and from the office, although from our seaside house at Craigavad on Belfast Loch the first half mile or so of the route consisted of a narrow tree-lined road which would have made an ideal place to stage a hold-up. Such things apart, we were able to lead reasonably normal lives without looking over our shoulders. We even got used to the idea that some guests who came to the house would hang up their personal firearms with their overcoats before entering the main room. Anne remembers well one particular occasion when she found Gerry (later Lord) Fitt, a brave and charismatic nationalist politician, out in the hall demonstrating the workings of his revolver to our young daughter, Alice.

What made the NIO even more unusual was that as a result of its ad hoc creation it did not have a career staff of its own, but comprised a mixed bunch of people, relatively few in number, seconded from the Home Office, Ministry of Defence and FCO. In contrast to the orderly and predictable ways of these parent Ministries, it soon improvised its own style of operating. The Permanent Secretary, Sir Frank Cooper, was the key figure here. He was a buccaneering character and most unconventional civil servant who combined a subtle knack of ensuring that his Minister took the right policy decisions with an energetic hands-on approach to carrying them out himself. He had come from the MOD and the story goes that when he was a Squadron Leader in the RAF during the war he had had at one stage a certain Flight Lieutenant Merlyn Rees under his command. Perhaps Merlyn never forgot it, because he certainly allowed Frank a lot of leeway. The latter manipulated the senior members of his staff with great dexterity. If for example he thought you were good at writing speeches, you wrote speeches, no matter whether that came within your remit or not. Conversely if in his view you were not doing something well, he might cease to ask your advice on it and let someone else have a go at it. All very stimulating, perhaps, but confusing too. One particular activity he kept really close to his chest was the conduct of the highly confidential back-stairs contacts that were taking place at that time with the Provisional IRA in an attempt to achieve a ceasefire. I was not directly involved in these meetings myself, but was kept, more or less, in the picture.

I enjoyed being one of Merlyn Rees' senior advisers. First of all, he was clearly a very nice, decent man. Secondly, he took us into his confidence and sought our advice. There were frequent discussions and brain-storming sessions with fellow Ministers and senior officials in Stormont Castle, often over a whisky, or two, late into the night. On such occasions I would not get home until the early hours. He cared deeply about Northern Ireland and what he wanted to achieve there, but he did not come over as a strong character. He tended to wring his hands in public over the latest murderous attack and was not as crisply decisive as he might have been. His successor, Roy Mason, was just the opposite. He came direct from being Minister of Defence and was a pugnacious little man who made a show of taking decisions with a snap of his fingers. Shortly after his arrival in the middle of 1976 Mason called us senior officials in and said words to the effect that when he pressed buttons in the MOD things happened fast and he expected the same in the NIO; he was more interested in having things happen than in listening to what we thought about them. Fair enough, I suppose, but I did not welcome the change. Fortunately it was not long before the end of my tour and return to the FCO.

A few weeks after my arrival in Northern Ireland in June 1975 it was suggested that I should witness at first hand how the army conducted its patrolling activities in Belfast. Soldiers had been criticised for reacting in a heavy-handed way when faced with hostile demonstrators in nationalist areas and Merlyn Rees was anxious to be in a position to rebut such allegations. So it was arranged that I should accompany a foot patrol of the Scots Guards into the Lower Falls area on the evening of 27 June. I was in civilian clothes and walked beside the Section Commander, the rest of the Section being strung out in formation on both sides of the street. It was still quite light when, to quote the official army report, "at 2231 hours 4 shots were fired by a gunman at the junction of Leeson Street and McDonnell Street, Lower Falls". At the time all I knew was that there were some loud bangs, and I did not realise they were from gunshots. I was, however, all too quickly aware that the reflex action of the soldiers had been to disperse into doorways and other hiding places, leaving me standing alone and bemused on the street corner. Not for long, because I was quickly scooped up from behind by a couple of soldiers and practically carried to an armoured vehicle not far away, which drove off in a hurry to the Hastings Street police station, where we had started from. My escorts treated it all quite lightly and one remarked that I was lucky to see some action so soon after my arrival in Northern Ireland, whereas they had had rather a dull time recently. Follow-up investigations next day revealed "4 strike marks 12 feet above street level" on a nearby building and local people gave it as their opinion that the shots had been fired over my head as a warning to the patrol against taking a Special Branch man round the area. The next time I went out on a similar exercise I was attired in a flak jacket and beret and nothing untoward happened. I cannot say that I learnt very much of immediate use from these first-hand experiences, but as time went on I came to admire the discipline and self-control of the "squaddies" as they coped, for example, with foul-mouthed harpies spitting in their faces and shrieking abuse from street corners or with the taunts of stone-throwing youths. It was a well-trained force and I doubt whether any other army in the world would have behaved as well.

I am not so sure about the undercover activities of the SAS. None of us, including, I suspect, Merlyn Rees, knew the details of how they operated. Eventually, however, part of the veil of secrecy was removed when a small group of SAS soldiers involved in a surveillance operation were caught and detained by the Irish Army on the wrong side of the border with the Republic. By and large units of the two armies cooperated well with one another and if the matter had been left in their hands it could probably have been sorted out quickly and quietly on the spot. Unfortunately, the Gardai appeared on the scene and the men were handed over to them. From there things escalated fast and the press had a field day. The men were charged with unlawful incursion, or some such, and released on bail to return for trial later. At this point Merlyn Rees flew down to the army base near Forkhill to debrief the team himself and I went with him. Up to that point the excuse had been advanced that the men had made a mistake in their map-reading and the border was not clearly marked (which was true). I do not remember exactly how those concerned explained themselves to us, but I believe what emerged was that the quarry they were pursuing had done a bunk across the border and they had followed. I do clearly recall the chilling answer given by one Sergeant Rees when his namesake asked him how he would react if ever he found himself in the same position again: "We would rub them out, Sir"! In due course the men pleaded guilty to the charge and, with a little behind the scenes help from the two governments, the court case was got over without much further fuss.

A major advance that was made during my time in the province was the ending of detention without trial. This had been introduced a few years earlier at the instigation of the security forces because of the difficulty they were experiencing in getting the necessary evidence to bring known members of the Provisional IRA to trial in the normal way. It was anathema to the nationalist community at large, who closed ranks behind the fighting men and did all they could to help them avoid arrest. By 1976 the situation on the ground had improved enough to persuade the security forces to bring it to an end. A the same time, and as a sort of counterweight, the status of "political prisoner" in the Maze and other prisons, which had long stuck in the throats of the army and police, was abolished: henceforth all prisoners were to be treated the same whatever their crimes and no one would be treated as if he were a prisoner of war. As the saying went, they would all be "ordinary decent criminals".

In the immediate aftermath of one particularly bloody atrocity, Graham Greene wrote a letter to Merlyn Rees from his home in Antibes to say how shocked he was and how he felt moved to offer whatever help he could. He thought there must be something he, as a converted Catholic, could do. Merlyn handed me the letter in a rather weary way and asked me to get in touch with GG. Accordingly I invited him to lunch next time he was in London. He accepted and I booked a table at Lockets in Marsham Street, a restaurant frequented by MPs, which for that reason had itself been subjected to an IRA bomb attack. I was fascinated by the prospect of meeting GG and also dreading it, because I felt sure he would be altogether too self-important and demanding. As it turned out, he was polite and somewhat reserved and the conversation took some time to warm up. I asked him when he had last been to Northern Ireland. He said he had only been there once, during the Second World War. He had sailed on a convoy from Liverpool to West Africa, where he was to undertake Secret Service work. The convoy made a preliminary stop at Belfast to pick up more ships and he was allowed ashore for a few hours. As it was a Sunday and the voyage ahead was potentially dangerous, he decided to find a priest to whom he could make his confession. "I am a converted Catholic, you know", he said, a phrase he repeated several times in our discussion. By the time he found the right place and knocked on the door it was lunchtime. After a long wait "a slatternly woman" opened the door, but refused to let him in – "not on your life, not in the dinner hour". However, before she could close it on him, the priest appeared behind her and let him in. Having heard what GG had to say, Father Murphy, or whatever his name was, agreed to hear his confession in the front parlour, instead of going over to the church. Apparently it began in the conventional way, but it was not long before GG began to think that the man of God by his side was asking some rather pointed and detailed questions about the size and make-up of the convoy, the number of ships, their speed etc and the penny quickly dropped. So without more ado GG got to his feet and saw himself out of the house. "That's my only experience of Northern Ireland", he said. He then began to expound his bright idea for bringing a bit of sanity to bear on the present conflict. He felt it was necessary to extract the poison from traditional popular prejudices and one way of helping to bring this about might be to have a sort of travelling brains-trust debating the issues in a civilised way up and down the province. The people he had in mind for the job were himself, the converted Catholic (once more), John Betjeman as a notable Protestant, and Sean O'Faolain, well-known Irish writer and republican activist. I thought this sounded a crackpot idea, but being a trained diplomat forbore to say so. Instead I suggested that before he made up his mind about how best he could make his contribution he should pay a second visit to Northern Ireland, and if he wished we could help to arrange this for him. He sounded quite attracted by the idea and said he would think about it more and let me know his decision.

A few days later he confirmed that he would like to take up my suggestion, but he added that he would not want it to be obvious that he was going under our auspices. As "cover" – a harking back, no doubt, to his wartime Secret Service days – he was proposing, with the help of his old friend, Bill Deedes, to write an article on Northern Ireland for the *Sunday Telegraph* magazine. I was to make all the necessary arrangements for a three-day visit to various parts of the province, including the provision of a car, but was to keep strictly in the background. He would come to dinner at our house on his return to Belfast and report his reactions. In the event hardly anything went according to plan, at least not to my plan. As requested, I did not go to meet him on his arrival at Aldergrove, but someone else did, namely Gerry Fitt. Whether this happened by accident or was pre-arranged between the two of them I do not know, although I have my suspicions. Anyway, the upshot was that we lost contact with him altogether for 48 hours, When he finally turned up again at our house he was looking greener than Greene and confessed that he had been taken on what amounted to a two-day pub crawl across the province by Gerry, who was a notorious drinker. GG was clearly a wiser and sadder man following this experience and went away shaking his no doubt aching head. We continued to correspond, but he no longer had any illusions about the impact he personally could make upon the scene or about the usefulness of literary debates in solving deep-seated political problems. Eventually I received a signing-off letter from him, starting with the delightful greeting "Dear Leahy (can't we drop the Mr?)". Sadly I did not keep copies of these letters, but I hope they remain somewhere in the archives of the Northern Ireland Office.

I did not own up to the converted Catholic that my Catholic grandfather had become a converted Protestant. As explained earlier, there is no doubt that my great-grandfather, Daniel, was a Catholic, but when Anne and I paid a brief visit to Bruff in Co. Limerick to see the family birthplace we found no trace of him or any other Leahy in either the Catholic or the Church of Ireland graveyards. Indeed the only Leahy in evidence was on the nameplate above the door of the local "turf accountant", or bookie, and for the record Anne took a photo of me standing underneath it. The small town of Bruff obviously has good republican credentials, as was demonstrated by an impressive monument commemorating, in Gaelic, the glorious martyrs of the 1916 Post Office uprising in Dublin. Not perhaps the best place to hang around in at that time when driving a car with Northern Ireland number-plates – and not wishing to overstay our welcome, we didn't.

In July 1976 our old friend, Christopher Ewart-Biggs was appointed to Dublin as Ambassador. As part of their preliminary briefing he and Jane paid a brief visit to Belfast and came to stay with us. They were obviously excited by their first ambassadorial job, even if it was not quite what they had expected. A few weeks later, and a very short time after his arrival in Dublin, Christopher was assassinated by the IRA. The details of what happened have been well recorded elsewhere and I will not rehearse them here. Knowing the family so well, I hurried down to Dublin to offer any help I could. Not surprisingly, they were in a state of shock, made even worse by the fact that when the blow fell Jane was in England and heard the news on her car radio. There was not much I could do, in fact, except offer a friendly shoulder to lean on and after a day or so there I returned to Belfast. Richard Sykes, now a senior under-secretary in the FCO, was sent out to Dublin to give support to the Chargé d'Affaires, John Hickman, and liaise with the Irish Government in its investigations. Richard himself was assassinated in The Hague by the IRA three years later.

People who do not know Northern Ireland are apt to have some misconceptions about the true nature of its problems. I often hear it said, for example, that it is primarily a question of religious intolerance. It may have been once, but it is not the case today, except in the minds of extreme bigots like Ian Paisley and his cronies, who maintain their virulently anti-Papist stance. "No Pope here", as one graffiti artist put it, only to be trumped by the scrawl below of "Lucky old Pope". It is much more a conflict of tribal loyalties, between those who wave the Union Jack/Red Hand flag and those who hold aloft the Irish tricolour, those who want to remain part of the UK and those who wish to be reintegrated with the rest of Ireland. It is not unlike the situation in Cyprus today, with its partitioning. The larger part of that island is in the hands of Greek-speakers who look to Greece to protect their interests. The North is inhabited by largely Turkish-speakers who look to Turkey as their champion. It is true that on one side of the line they are Orthodox Christians and on the other Muslims, but that is not the root of the problem. As in Northern Ireland, the main source of the antagonism between the two communities is to be found in the conflicting attractions of two bigger countries with a long history of nationalist struggle. The two cases are not, of course, entirely similar: in Cyprus, for example, both Greece and Turkey are geographically separate from the island, and in Ireland there is one *lingua franca*. For all that the points of similarity are quite instructive.

In the country districts of Northern Ireland members of the two communities have lived together without too much difficulty in recent times. It is in towns like Belfast and Londonderry, where ghettos have grown up over the years in which the two communities live separate lives behind high walls, that the worst violence has occurred. In these ghettos children have been brought up from an early age to think of the people on the other side of the wall as dirty, wicked people, devils incarnate and sworn enemies. In fact they grow up in total ignorance of what the other boys and girls of a similar age are doing and thinking. From such ignorance there is a straight progression to fear and from fear to hatred: what you do not know you fear and what you fear you hate. Within their own communities people can treat each other with warmth and kindness and can act quite normally, but all this changes in relation to people from "the other side", against whom their hearts are more often than not permanently hardened and all decent feelings frozen. A case in point was Mrs Simms, our cleaning lady. She and her husband were god-fearing, church-going Protestants, pillars of respectable society, warm and friendly people. One day when she was in the house it was announced on the radio that a prominent republican supporter of the IRA, Maire Drumm, had been murdered by Protestant paramilitaries while she lay gravely ill in her hospital bed. In any ordinary society this would have been seen by everybody as a shocking event, but the upright Mrs Simms rubbed her hands with glee and practically shouted "They've got her!"

I hope and believe that the above picture, which was all too familiar to me in the 1970s, is now out of date and that following the Good Friday Agreement and the virtual cessation of major acts of paramilitary violence the old physical and psychological barriers are breaking down. An essential ingredient in this process must be the widespread extension of integrated schooling from the kindergarten upwards in the public education sector. In my time at Stormont Castle we tried to get this going, but could not make any headway in the face of strong opposition, especially from the hierarchy of Catholic bishops. I believe things are better on that score today; they need to be, because until it happens the old prejudices will continue to poison the atmosphere and hold back the chances of lasting reconciliation.

I am convinced that the ultimate solution must be the ending of partition and the reintegration of Northern Ireland with the rest of the island. Easily stated, of course, but fiendishly difficult to imagine how we get to that point in the foreseeable future. If only Northern Ireland could produce political leaders like Nelson Mandela and F.W. De Klerk, who were able to bury the hatchet and bring an end to years of bitter struggle in South Africa, but sadly there is no one of that calibre on the horizon in Northern Ireland.

Like it or not, Northern Ireland was a real challenge and, though I was not keen to go there in the first place and never became reconciled to the constant cruelty and violence that became part of my daily life, I would not have missed it. Our stay there certainly marked me and to this day I feel strongly about what goes on there and about the prospects of achieving a lasting settlement. I should add that Anne enjoyed it more than I did and thought the people were so much nicer than some of the hard-nosed Parisians she had had to deal with. She even volunteered to teach art in the Crumlin Road prison to some of the young paramilitary thugs awaiting trial for this or that violent crime. She insists she found it an interesting experience. Which confirms that there is no accounting for tastes.

Assistant Under-Secretary

On 17 January 1977, I took up my new appointment as Assistant Under-Secretary for Information and Cultural Affairs in the FCO. Not long before our return from Belfast we had sold our house in Wimbledon and moved into the middle of London, to a town house at 50 Stanford Road, between Kensington High Street and the Cromwell Road. I say "we" had moved, but in fact the main burden of arranging the move fell on Anne. We decided to make it, partly because the social life of the elder children was gravitating more and more towards the big city ("that's where our friends are") and they were no longer impressed by the advantages of a large garden and other traditional features of suburban living. For me, the fact that it would be quicker and easier to get to work was also an important consideration. The 10 o'clock start of the working day during my early years in the FO had long since given way to a more austere regime and, the more senior I became, the earlier it seemed I had to be at my desk. It was relatively easy to get there by underground or by car. In due course I found that the surest, if not the quickest, way was by bicycle, because that meant I did not get held up in traffic jams. I bought a second- or third-hand bike from a rather dodgy roadside dealer at Bethnal Green market, which was an experience in itself. When I said that I wanted to take it on a brief test ride round the green, he agreed on the understanding that I left Anne behind as a form of surety. Even then it was not all plain pedalling, because hardly had the deal been done and I started on my wobbly way back to Kensington, when the chain broke. However, he put it right without any argument. I would not pretend that I cycled to Whitehall every day, but often enough to be able to boast about it. In reality I was essentially a fair-weather cyclist: not when rain was about, not in the dark days of winter, nor for that matter in the warm days of summer (one could not arrive in a muck sweat). The ideal times were the spring and autumn.

50 Stanford Road was a narrow three-storey Victorian terrace house, with a minute front garden and a slightly bigger open space behind. A large sitting/dining room, a reasonable kitchen, and four bedrooms on

the two floors above. One unusual feature that took a bit of getting used to was the District Line running in a tunnel directly underneath: it was not only the rumble of the train passing below but the tinkling of the glasses in the corner cupboard that stopped the conversation. However, after a time we ourselves hardly paid any attention to it – until some years later when we came to sell the house. The best time for doing this would have been Christmas Day, the one day of the year when the Underground did not run, but of course there were not too many buyers about then.

After Belfast the job seemed unexciting, at least to start with. The information part was not, as the News Department job had been, directly concerned with handling the press. Much of it was taken up with overseeing the various information activities of our overseas missions, definitely not something to stimulate the adrenalin. Nor was the supervision of Cultural Relations Department quite my scene, philistine as I am. More interestingly, I was the senior point of contact with the BBC Overseas Service and with the British Council. Here I found myself in a quite a lot of strife with the Foreign Secretary, David Owen, who was intent on cutting back the budgets of both institutions.

I first came across Owen when he was a young MP visiting Tehran in a parliamentary delegation, but I did not get to know him then. Since that time he had moved swiftly up the ranks and was now a Minister of State in the FCO. When on 19 February 1977 the Foreign Secretary, Tony Crosland, suddenly died, Owen, still only in his thirties, was catapulted upwards to take his place. From the start he was a man in a hurry. He clearly felt the need to establish his authority as quickly as possible and decided that the best way to show who was boss was to give the FO machine a good shaking. There could be no doubting his intelligence and appetite for hard work, but his preoccupation with advancing new ideas left no time to spare for man management. His impatience and abrasive manner upset a lot of people, even his government car pool chauffeurs. But he was at his worst with senior staff. He was too ready to believe we were working against him and trying to frustrate his efforts. Misunderstandings occurred when we thought we were doing what he wanted but he, on further reflection, had changed his mind about what that was. There were faults in communication on both sides and it took his Private Office some time to get used to his working methods and to anticipate potential points of friction.

In June 1977, I became involved, at long distance, in negotiations taking place at Gleneagles in Scotland on the subject of sporting links with South Africa. Over that particular weekend I was the duty Under-Secretary in the

FCO. The subject matter was not then part of my normal portfolio, and little did I know that in two years' time it would be part of my daily round. At the Singapore Commonwealth Heads of Government Meeting in 1971 there had been an abortive attempt to raise the issue of banning sports fixtures with South African teams. The arguments had continued unabated since then and had now reached a critical point at this meeting. The majority of Commonwealth countries felt strongly that as long as apartheid remained the official policy of the South African Government there could not be "normal sport in an abnormal society" and all sporting contacts should be severed. The so-called old Commonwealth countries, Britain, Australia, and New Zealand, felt equally strongly that this was the wrong approach and we should be encouraging individual sporting bodies in South Africa to open their ranks to people of all races and rewarding them if and when they did. In other words, contacts with some sports, rather than a complete ban. The problem was to reconcile these two quite different approaches and as the British were in the chair it fell to Prime Minister Jim Callaghan to broker a solution. So it was that Sir Clive Rose, the Deputy Secretary in the Cabinet Office, and I became involved in offering advice from London on successive forms of words which might form the basis of a compromise acceptable to all the participants in Gleneagles. Back and forth we played the game of semantics on the telephone until agreement was eventually reached and the Commonwealth Statement on Apartheid in Sport, better known as the Gleneagles Agreement, saw the light of day. It contained high-sounding language about the unity of purpose of all the participants, but the price of such unity was the inclusion of some equivocal phrases that left the door open to individual member countries to pursue their own line. In plain language it was a fudge.

In pursuit of his aim to streamline the conduct of British diplomacy and at the same time achieve significant economies, Owen brought in the Central Policy Review Staff (CPRS), headed by Sir Kenneth Berrill and based in the Cabinet Office, to undertake a fundamental review of Britain's overseas representation. It did just that, and one or two of its members, notably an intellectual rottweiler called Tessa Blackstone (later to become Master of Birkbeck College and Minister of Higher Education in the Labour Government), made clear their intention of severely circumscribing the primacy of the FCO in the conduct of national diplomacy, by involving other government departments more directly in it, and at the same time drastically cutting back our overseas missions. It was not the first time in the post-war years that the FCO had been subjected to this sort of thing, the most recent being the Duncan Enquiry in the late 1960s.

So it knew how to defend itself ("cet animal est très méchant, quand on l'attaque il se défend") and by the time the final report appeared the CPRS had discarded its more radical ideas.

Owen himself continued to put pressure on the BBC Overseas Service and the British Council, both of which were funded through the FCO vote, to make economies and I was his instrument for doing this. For the BBC what was at stake was a substantial reduction of the so-called vernacular (as distinct from English language) services, coupled with savings in capital investment in its overseas transmitter and relay stations. They naturally resisted this and in so doing were beginning to drum up public support and lobby MPs. I had discussions with Gerry Mansell, the Director-General of the Overseas Service, in the course of which it became clear that the only sensible way out was to negotiate some sort of compromise. Which we duly did: some programmes would be abolished, some would stay. This in no way satisfied David Owen and I was summoned to see him in his room in the House of Commons. He was in a very bad temper and proceeded to berate me in a very aggressive way. I had never before been subjected by anyone in the office, not even the dyspeptic Anthony Eden, to such a torrent of abuse and I almost looked behind me to see if he was addressing someone else. He accused me of being lily-livered, disobeying his instructions, and betraying him. When finally I could get a word in to ask if he wanted me to go back to the negotiating table, he retorted that he was fed up with the whole business and did not care what I did. He then turned on his heels and stomped out of the room, followed by George Walden, his Private Secretary. I went back to the FCO with my tail very much between my legs and not knowing what to do next. I tried to telephone George, but it was not until well into the evening that he was free to talk. He laughed and said that he thought the upshot of the meeting had been quite good. I told him he had a mawkish sense of humour. He explained that he was only doing a brief note of it and would record at the end that the S of S had given me discretion to do what I felt best. Either David Owen had a short memory, which I doubt, or he forgave me, because subsequently he chose me to be Ambassador to South Africa, and when he came to stay with us there later he could not have been nicer. As for Gerry Mansell, he and I had a good laugh about it when we met in later years in the Franco-British Council, of which we were both members.

During the course of 1978 I became closely involved with another issue concerning the BBC. The Shah of Iran had long taken a jaundiced view of the BBC in general and its Persian Service in particular, not least because he knew how many people listened to it. As his own position in the country began to weaken as a result of a combination of factors, not least the strident verbal onslaughts of Ayatollah Khomeini from his refuge in France, his paranoia increased. He felt sure that the BBC had become the main instrument for disseminating the views of a man who was openly preaching the violent overthrow of the legally constituted government of Iran. He even believed that the Persian Service was sending coded messages from Khomeini to his followers in the country, in the manner of the wartime BBC broadcasts to resistance groups in German-occupied Europe. Instructions from Tehran to the hapless Ambassador, Parviz Radji, to make formal protests about these broadcasts proliferated. Parviz was someone I knew well from our time in Tehran, when he was the Private Secretary of the Prime Minister, Amir Abbas Hoveyda. He realised, as well as I did, that there was virtually nothing the FO or HMG generally could do to influence the BBC, whose programmes were produced entirely independently of government, but to satisfy the Shah he had to go through the motions. He did so partly by direct representations to the BBC management, where he was given a polite brush-off, partly by seeking the help of sympathetic Conservative politicians, who made the right noises but could not do much, and partly by tackling the relevant people in the FO, including myself. It was a hopeless quest and he never could satisfy the Shah, who until his dying day remained convinced that the BBC had played a leading role in his undoing and that the British Government could have called it to heel had it chosen to do so.

As events unfolded in Iran immediately after the revolution, news began to trickle through of the arrest and execution of people we knew or, in the case of the luckier ones, of their hurried and sometimes hazardous escapes to Britain, France and the USA. The Shah and his family did not find refuge in any of these countries and became wandering exiles. He owned a large estate in Surrey and although he made no formal application himself a number of friends, including ex-King Constantine of Greece, discreetly approached HMG to see whether he could settle here. The Labour Government prevaricated, but the Leader of the Opposition, Margaret Thatcher, told one of the intermediaries privately that when she came to power after the forthcoming General Election the Shah would be allowed to have asylum here. After the event in May 1979, she changed her mind on the advice of the FO. Various reasons of security and economic interest were advanced for keeping him away, the most cogent being that, following the example of the attack on the American Embassy, the British Embassy in Tehran would be seized and the staff held hostage. My old and much respected boss, Denis Wright, was brought out of retirement to fly to the Bahamas and break the bad news to the Shah. When asked about this later, Denis was reported to have said he did not mind doing it as he was himself against allowing the Shah to come here. Notwithstanding such arguments, I feel that we acted dishonourably and it leaves a nasty taste in my mouth to this day. President Sadat of Egypt did give the Shah refuge and later paid with his life for doing the honourable thing, when he was assassinated by the extremist Moslem Brotherhood

The election directly affected my own future as well. A month or so previously I had received the good, if unexpected, news that my name was being put forward to No. 10 as Ambassador to South Africa. However, as soon as the date for the election was announced, this and some ten other ambassadorial nominations were put on hold. The election on 9 May over, the other ten were quickly agreed, but mine was left in limbo. I was naturally anxious to know what was happening, but I only found out later what the complication was. Margaret Thatcher had had the bright idea of offering her troublesome Conservative predecessor, Ted Heath, the job of Ambassador in Washington, and of sending at the same time another political appointee to Pretoria. Happily for me Ted was not having any of this and turned her down. At which point it was considered too embarrassing to have the only political appointment in apartheid South Africa and, *faute de mieux*, I was given the job.

South Africa

It was by now near the end of May and I was told that I should aim to be at my desk in Pretoria towards the end of July, when the Lusaka Commonwealth Heads of Government Meeting, which would have the future of Rhodesia at the top of its agenda, was due to take place. There was much to do by way of preparation and no time to be lost. The usual wide-ranging briefing programme was lined up for me by the Heads of Mission Section of Personnel Department, and in addition a number of influential South Africans passing through London introduced themselves and bent my ear in different directions. There were also many long-distance consultations with the Embassy about such things as the arrangements for our arrival at Johannesburg airport and the programme for our first few days in Pretoria. No details were left to chance. Even the measurement of my head came into it, because I did not own a top hat and needed one for the presentation of credentials ceremony. Like all the Leahy males in our family, I have a big head, and as a last resort the Embassy was having to hire one from theatrical costumiers in Johannesburg. As if all that was not enough to keep us busy, Anne and I started to learn Afrikaans and had some preliminary lessons from the South African wife of a FO colleague.

One particular episode from this time is etched on my mind. Pik Botha, the South African Foreign Minister, visited London to pay his respects to the new Secretary of State and I was invited to the meeting. Pik held forth at some length on the issues of the moment as he saw them, especially the disadvantages of trying to negotiate a constitutional settlement involving new elections in Rhodesia. He did not draw breath. This was a characteristic I came to know well later on, but it clearly took Lord Carrington by surprise. Even more, Ian Gilmour, the Lord Privy Seal and Carrington's No. 2, who at one point slipped a note across the table to me saying "I feel sorry for you". It was perhaps not surprising, therefore, that Carrington's final words to me on the eve of my departure were to the effect that as my immediate task I should concentrate on trying to find out what the South Africans were up to in

Rhodesia and to head them off from undermining his efforts to bring about a settlement through a constitutional conference in London. They hated the whole idea, he said, and feared the repercussions on their own domestic scene if we succeeded.

Anne and I had our formal audience to "kiss hands" with the Queen on 12 July. It was a new experience to have twenty minutes alone with the Sovereign, but not at all a daunting one. In fact the conversation flowed easily and at times she was quite light-hearted, even indiscreet. She also showed what a good mimic she is. Which led me, after our arrival in South Africa, to send her via Susan Hussey, her Lady-in-Waiting, a copy of *Ah Big Yaws?* (David Philip, Cape Town, 1978), a spoof on South African English. Susan Hussey wrote back to say she had passed "this hilarious book" to the Queen and "we have already had one happy evening chortling over it and I am sure it is going to provide many hours of amusement in the future".

My head was still too big, Pretoria 1979

In the hectic run-up to our departure many things were happening on the family front, over and above the usual rigmarole of getting the packers in, ordering a new car, buying clothes, getting invitation cards printed and numerous other small details. At least we did not have to let the house, as it was to serve as a base for our children while we were away. Anne and I stole a week's R&R at Collobrières, the last we expected to have for some time. Emma and Juan Robles, her Spanish classical guitarist boy friend, got married. James left Tonbridge at the end of the summer term and had to be fetched with all his impedimenta. Last but not least Anne and I gave a big family lunch at Robin Green's pub, the White Swan, at Arundel to celebrate our coming silver wedding anniversary. The last three things, including a small but lively wedding party at 50 Stanford Road, all took place over our last weekend. No wonder then that by the time we boarded the BA flight to Johannesburg four days later, on the evening of Thursday 26 July, we practically collapsed into our seats. Indeed it took at least two glasses of champagne to revive us. The adrenalin was still running and we were keyed up by the excitement of having our first ambassadorial post – and nervous about what sort of fist we would make of it. I remember spending some of the time rehearsing what I was going to say at the airport press conference, before dozing off (I never sleep properly when flying).

Senior members of the Embassy and Protocol Department of the MFA were lined up at the foot of the aircraft steps to greet us on our arrival at Jan Smuts Airport, Johannesburg next morning. We were escorted to the VIP lounge and from there to the press conference room. There was a respectable turn-out of mainly South African journalists and I gave some bland answers to some bland questions. Early confirmation, perhaps, of the local convention that journalists did not subject public figures to aggressive questioning, unlike the British press. We then drove off in the Embassy Rolls Royce, accompanied by Joanna Lowis, my PA, to the residence in Pretoria. Because our arrival en poste had been brought forward to coincide with the Commonwealth Heads of Government Meeting (CHOGM) in Lusaka some of the residence staff, including the Social Secretary, Mary Rayner, had not yet returned from leave and the house had a slightly unlived-in feel about it, but the others greeted us warmly enough.

The next few days were spent meeting Embassy staff and generally getting our bearings. We had hardly been able to do much of this when a bizarre event occurred which was to drive home Peter Carrington's warning that the South Africans wanted to torpedo the Lusaka Conference if they could. Late one night Pik Botha rang me to say he had some ominous news. He had heard on good authority that the Rhodesian Government were so incensed by wild accusations made against them by certain African Commonwealth leaders at the CHOGM that they were contemplating some sort of punitive raid on Lusaka. He was passing this on to me as a friendly gesture, but there was nothing more he could tell me and I should realise that the matter was completely out of his hands. I decided that I must send a telegram straightaway to my old friend, Tony Duff, in the British delegation in Lusaka, and I summoned the duty cipher clerk to meet me in the office. But how to get there? My driver, Jim Hlongwane, was nowhere around and I was not sure enough of the route to drive myself. So I asked Albert, our butler, to act as my guide, while I got into the Rolls and found out, after pressing many a wrong switch, how to drive it. That achieved, I sent off the telegram explaining what Pik had told

Our Cape Town digs

me and saying that while I did not know how to evaluate his message I felt bound to pass it on. In fact nothing happened, no raid, nothing, and I heard later from Tony that a rather different version of events had come from General Peter Walls, the Head of the Rhodesian Armed Forces. He insisted that it was the South Africans who had been pressing the Rhodesians to take action. If that was indeed the correct version – and I cannot be sure of this – Pik was presumably using his call to me as a means of covering South Africa's involvement in advance of a Rhodesian attack. In any event I was inclined thereafter to take things the Foreign Minister told me with a large pinch of salt.

This happened before I had presented my credentials and officially taken up my ambassadorial appointment, or had even made a preliminary unofficial call on Pik Botha in the usual way. The ceremony of handing my letters to the State President, Marais Viljoen, took place on Friday 3 August, a week after our arrival, which was fairly speedy by local standards. There was one distinctly hair-raising moment when on lifting my hired top hat for the National Anthem in front of the Guard of Honour drawn up outside I found that attached to the back of it was a substantial fringe of my all too sparse coiffure. This caused some amusement when I checked in at the cloakroom later, but was not all that funny at the time.

Whoever had temporarily taken out the lining of the hat to make it more easily fit my big head had neglected to cover the sticky residue underneath. Luckily the press photos were all taken inside the Presidential house.

There followed the time-wasting chore of exchanging calls with other Heads of Mission, as protocol demanded. Because of South Africa's pariah international status the list was mercifully short, but I found it a bore all the same. Anne did not get off so lightly. I remember her coming into lunch one day with a slightly dazed look on her face having just returned from a call on Elise Botha, the Prime Minister's wife. She was a large imposing woman (Anne later gave her the nickname of "Pink Blancmange") and having got through the preliminary courtesies she proceeded to criticise in no uncertain terms HMG's lack of understanding about what her husband's government was trying to do. The wife of the recently arrived Israeli Ambassador was also present and, by way of contrast, was told how much Israel's friendly attitude was appreciated. Anne said she had been left speechless and was cross with me for not having warned her what might happen. Unfortunately I had no idea myself.

We were still settling in when the Embassy was suddenly called upon to organise a Service of Remembrance for Lord Mountbatten, who had been assassinated in Ireland a short while before, at St. Alban's Cathedral in Pretoria. To my surprise, there was a good turn-out of Ministers and senior members of the South African armed forces. I was soon to learn that on a personal level there was residual fellow feeling between the British and South African military, despite our arms embargo and the RN's departure from the Simonstown naval base. A Trafalgar Day Dinner continued to be held every year in the Rand Club in Johannesburg, to which I was invited (and went).

The South African secret intelligence service, the NIS (previously better known as BOSS) was not so friendly. Indeed it treated the Embassy as a hostile target and tried to suborn at least one member of the local staff, who came to see me in tears and asked for my advice. Through a contact we told them to lay off. We worked on the assumption that our telephones were being tapped and took precautions about listening devices in our offices. We also installed a safe speech chamber in the Chancery, where we could talk freely amongst ourselves. The NIS were also active in targeting members of the ANC living in London, and, if for no other reason, our own intelligence people took more than a passing interest in what went on at South Africa House.

As foreshadowed, Rhodesia and South African intentions towards it dominated my first six months or more. But there were of course many other calls on my time: many places to visit, including Soweto and other black townships, many people to meet of all colours and persuasions, and many things to learn, including Afrikaans. I have a scrapbook of press cuttings showing the wide range of these contacts. It was new and exciting work, for us both I should add, because Anne was involved in much of what went on. One thing we did, not long after our arrival, was to acquire a new Cairn terrier puppy, whom we named Bonnie, on the strength of which I was graciously invited to become an "Honorary Vice-President of the South African Short-Legged Terrier Club". So we were already making inroads into South African society.

There was much political static in the South African atmosphere and the local press took a close interest in British policies and attitudes. It was not difficult to get a message across, but I had to be careful because things I said were sometimes picked up by the British press and given a different twist, for example by the Anti-Apartheid Movement, whose basic view was that we should be lambasting the South African Government all the time. For their part, South African Ministers could react badly to perceived ambassadorial criticism. My first major public speech, to the Johannesburg Chamber of Commerce on 23 October 1979, got me into hot water straightaway. Its main theme was that while Britain valued its economic and commercial relations with South Africa we had to weigh these against similar interests elsewhere in the world, which in total were of course much greater. As was well known, HMG opposed attempts to introduce economic sanctions against South Africa, but, I went on, "I should be misleading you if I were to give you a cast-iron guarantee that we shall not, in any circumstances, feel obliged to go along with sanctions of some sort. Whether we succeed in avoiding sanctions will depend to a very large extent on whether South Africa is willing, particularly in the Namibian context, to help us help it. We cannot do it all alone and it takes at least two to make an agreement". The speech in general was well received by the audience and was widely reported in the press and television, with special emphasis, of course, on the passage quoted above. But the Foreign Minister, Pik Botha, rang me up in a fury and berated me for "threatening" South Africa with sanctions and undermining our Prime Minister's desire to maintain good bilateral relations. He was, he said, instructing the South African Ambassador in London to draw the attention of the FCO to my remarks and ask them whether they reflected official government policy. As a normal rule, I was not expected to clear my speeches with Central and Southern Africa Department, but on this occasion I had told them what I was intending to say and they had not objected. My reason for including the passage was that it was already clear to me after only a short time in the country that the South African Government tended to ignore the pressures on us in the Commonwealth and the UN to go along with sanctions and took our opposition to them for granted. I did not regret saying what I did, but I must confess I was taken aback at the time by Pik's heated response.

Although this mini crisis soon blew over, in general relations between our two governments remained tense. The Prime Minister, P.W. Botha, had a notoriously short fuse and was quick to take offence at things both real and imaginary. On more than one occasion I remember Pik Botha ringing me up early in the morning asking for my help because PW had heard on the radio about something HMG was reported to have said or done that had sent him into a fury. He, Pik, could not get hold of my opposite number in London, Dawie de Villiers, at that hour (two hours behind South African time) to obtain an explanation from the FCO and he practically implored me to do so without delay. Another time, when Tony Duff, who was visiting Cape Town from Salisbury, and I went to see PW, Tony made a fairly innocuous remark that so annoyed him I thought for a moment he was going to throw us out.

Pik himself constantly bent my ear about the folly of what we were trying to do in Rhodesia. All you British are concerned about, he would say, is handing over your responsibilities and getting out as soon as possible, while we in South Africa will have to live with the consequences; you are surrendering at the conference table what the terrorists cannot win by force of arms. On the contrary, I would reply, despite all the help you are giving them the Rhodesian Security Forces are gradually losing the armed struggle against the guerrilla forces of the ZANU/ZAPU Patriotic Front led by Robert Mugabe and Joshua Nkomo and in due course the PF will enter Salisbury by force of arms. He also complained that when the Conservative Party was in opposition he had been assured by some of its leading members that a Conservative Government would lose no time in recognising an independent Rhodesia led by Bishop Abel Muzorewa. I told him that he seemed to me to be clutching at straws, because the international community at large would never accept this.

As time went by following the Lancaster House Conference and preparations began in earnest to hold an election in Rhodesia, what struck me particularly about such conversations was that, for all their strong military and civilian presence on the ground in Rhodesia, the South Africans were apt to indulge in wishful thinking and harbour unrealistic expectations about both the military situation and the electoral clout of their political lackey, Bishop Muzorewa. If all else failed, they thought, he could form a coalition with Joshua Nkomo, who had fallen out with Mugabe. In his memoirs Carrington records that some right wing members of the Conservative Party were under the same delusion, so there may have been some cross fertilisation with the South Africans there. Increasingly, as the date for the election approached, Pik and others complained about the intimidation of voters by the Patriotic Front and asserted that HMG would have either to call the election off or to declare the result null and void. The interim Governor, Lord Soames, took the view that while there had been intimidation it was not on such a scale as to justify calling off the election. Then newspaper reports appeared in the South African press to the effect that a military intervention would take place if civil war broke out in Rhodesia after the election. These were taken sufficiently seriously for me to be instructed by the FO to go and see Brand Fourie, the Secretary for Foreign Affairs (PUS), in the absence of Pik Botha, immediately, on 21 February 1980, and tell him of HMG's serious concern. In London the FO Spokesman said that the British Government "deprecated any statement which held out the prospect of such intervention" and the *Cape Town Argus* splashed the news over its front page.

The election was held over two days, 27/28 February. Knowing how anxious the South African Government were about it and how badly they were likely to react to an unfavourable result, I asked, and was granted, several hours grace to give them advance notice before the announcement of the result, so that they could compose themselves and make a fully considered, rather than a strident off-the-cuff, response. In the event the result was worse than they might have feared: Zanu (Mugabe) 57 seats, Zapu (N'Komo) 20, UANC (Muzorewa) 3. I braced myself and telephoned Pik. He breathed heavily at the other end of the line as I began to read out the numbers. I had not got far when he burst in "And the little bishop?" As soon as I had finished, his immediate reaction was that the election had been a travesty of justice because of the rampant intimidation of voters and he assumed we would declare it null and void. When I disabused him of this, he snorted and put the phone down. A few moments later he rang back to say that the Prime Minister, P.W. Botha, was by his side and wanted to speak to me. Where Pik had been all sound and fury, P.W. was icily cold. He said that while we would have to live with the knowledge that we had given way to an unacceptable level of intimidation and shamefully abandoned our responsibility for bringing

Rhodesia to independence in an orderly way, South Africa would be left to live with the consequences of our action. When the official governmental statement appeared shortly afterwards, it was in strong, but reasonably measured, language. More to the point it was not followed by any threats of military intervention across the border. For a few days, however, there was a distinct possibility that General Walls would stage a military coup within Rhodesia. Laurence van der Post, amongst other things a close confidant of Margaret Thatcher, was staying with us at the time in Cape Town and involved himself as a self-appointed intermediary between Walls and the Prime Minister, somewhat to the annoyance of Christopher Soames and his staff. To his credit Walls decided against taking action. In retrospect, P.W. Botha's forebodings about what would happen in Zimbabwe may appear to have been vindicated. Even so, Mugabe's appalling behaviour represents more of an embarrassment than a threat to the government of post-apartheid South Africa.

While all this was going on, the problem of Namibian independence had still to be resolved and was being actively pursued in various diplomatic arenas. Ever since the end of the Second World War it had had a long and difficult history, with South Africa resisting attempts in the UN to give up its mandate over the former German Colony of South-West Africa. In 1978 the Security Council produced an outline plan for free elections and had given the task of bringing it to fruition to a "Contact Group" of five Western countries, the USA, the UK, Canada, France, and Germany, working in conjunction with the UN Commissioner for Namibia, Martti Ahtisaari, a former Finnish diplomat and since 1977 a senior UN mediator (he later became President of Finland). Sir James Murray, an old colleague from Paris Embassy days who had just retired, was also involved as "Special Envoy" of the five governments. So there was no shortage of important visitors and in one way or another negotiation gave the five resident Ambassadors plenty to do. Fortunately for me, the Embassy Minister, Martin Reid, was a real expert on the subject and could give me the benefit of his extensive knowledge. We made some headway, but it was slow progress and several times, just at a moment when we thought the Contact Group was on the point of a breakthrough, our efforts were frustrated by deliberately timed cross-border raids into Angola by the South African security forces. It is possible that Pik Botha himself was not informed in advance when these raids were to take place, because such decisions were the closely guarded preserve of the national security apparatus reporting directly to the Prime Minister. In any case, they had the intended effect of derailing our efforts. It also has to be said that the way in which events had unfolded north of the Limpopo in Zimbabwe did not incline the South Africans to cede ground in Namibia. Gradually, however, the human and economic costs of waging this increasingly unpopular campaign wore the South African Government down and in 1988 Namibia finally received its independence, six years after I had left South Africa.

Back to the domestic South African scene. I have often been asked whether we enjoyed our time in South Africa. My answer is always the same. "Enjoyed" is not the right word; it was a too unhappy place and a too unjust society for that. The contrast between the life-styles of the affluent whites and the impoverished blacks was too stark. It was a repressive and intolerant political regime, bolstered by blinkered, bigoted elements of the Dutch Reformed Church. As British Ambassador I was constantly involved in argument and heated debate in the highly charged political atmosphere, both in public and round private dinner tables. Of course, as the title of Alan Paton's book, *Ah, But Your Land Is Beautiful* (David Philip, Cape Town, 1981), suggested, there was so much for a casual observer to see and admire about South Africa's scenery and its people, it cried out to be enjoyed; and you could do so if you averted your eyes as a tourist or even a junior member of the Embassy. It was not so easy if you were sitting in the back of the Embassy Rolls Royce, driven by your black driver and waiting at traffic lights, when a police prison truck packed with blacks incarcerated in a cage drew up in the next lane; typically they would be people who had been rounded up for transgressing the pass laws that ruled their lives. What must have gone through the mind of Jim Hlongwane? I know what went through mine – a mixture of guilt, shame and disgust. I vividly remember another occasion when one of the Embassy gardeners staggered through the gates pouring blood from a nasty stab wound in his neck inflicted in a gang attack on the way to work from his township. It was clear that he had to go immediately to hospital, but I could not take him to the nearest one because it was reserved for white people, and instead had to drive him to another one much further away. On arriving there we found a long line of waiting blacks, but I am ashamed to say I pulled my rank to get him to the front of the queue. I should also say that, for a charge of one rand, he was well treated.

Of course, the consequences of apartheid went much wider and deeper than episodes such as these. As the word itself indicates, the policy was designed to keep people of the different races apart. The blacks, the whites, the mixed-race coloureds and the Indians had to live in quite separate areas, be it urban townships or rural homelands. Peoples' movements were strictly controlled: black people could go into white areas to work during the day but, with one or two exceptions, notably domestic servants, they had to return to their townships at night. This meant long and time-consuming journeys because the townships were always situated some way out of town. White people, for their part, had to obtain special permission to enter the townships. Few of them went, with the result that they had little idea of how the blacks lived. There was greater contact on the farms where the black workforce was generally well looked after in a paternalistic sort of way, and also in the gold mines, where the black miners were adequately housed and fed for the arduous and often dangerous work they had to do. But even these were essentially master and servant relationships.

Life was anything but easy for our own servants. As explained already, the gardeners commuted each day from their townships, while the domestic staff lived on the spot in servants' quarters. But there was no room for their families and they lived apart, with the consequent disruption of family life and a proliferation of extramarital relationships. This was compounded by the fact that all Diplomatic Missions, following in the footsteps of the government itself, moved down to Cape Town for the five months or so of the Parliamentary session. This caused big upheavals for everyone involved, including members of the Embassy with young families, and our domestic staff, who were removed even further from their own families and some of whom found solace in new liaisons or the bottle, or both.

Unlike white South Africans, as a member of the diplomatic corps I was able to come and go in the townships as I pleased, and I did, as did Anne and members of the Embassy staff. The contrast between the crowded, cramped, forlorn conditions in which the underprivileged people of Soweto or Crossroads eked out a living and the spacious affluence of the white suburbs of Johannesburg and Cape Town never ceased to shock me. Not long after our arrival in South Africa we took some visiting friends to a memorable service in a Soweto church. Memorable for several reasons; the swaying ranks of chanting, smiling people, the women in colourful dress, the length of the service (more than three hours) and, last but not least, the uplifting character of the local priest, the Rev. David N'kwe. We soon got to know him and his wife, Maggie, well and much admired the pastoral work they did, often getting round, or simply defying, apartheid rules and regulations. With his help and the efforts of a member of the Johannesburg Consulate-General whose full-time job was to cultivate relations with the residents of Soweto and Alexandra, we established and equipped a library and reading room in Soweto and organised one or two film shows. In general we made a point of visiting schools and social centres in townships all over the country and showing our support for them by donating practical things like desks, typewriters, duplicating machines, cookers, heaters, sewing machines and portable radios. The FCO provided me with a special fund for this purpose. The local Council Chairmen were by and large government stooges without a popular mandate, but since they were nominally responsible for important things like housing and electrification I kept in touch with them too.

Virtually all black political leaders of any real importance were either out of the country or in prison, where one could not visit them. Chief Gatsha Buthelezi, the KwaZulu leader, was still on the scene. Some people unfairly accused him of being a puppet too, but in fact he stood up to the government on a number of important issues. I saw him several times and judged him to be a shrewd politician, if somewhat prickly and vain. He eventually became one of the Vice-Presidents in the post-apartheid regime, but this was a figurehead position and, perhaps because he was essentially a provincial leader, albeit a powerful one, he never played the part in the governance of the rainbow country that many people hoped he might. Winnie Mandela, Nelson's firebrand wife, after being detained without trial in solitary confinement for seventeen months had been banned under house arrest for seven years in a miserable, out-of-the-way township called Brandfort in the Orange Free State. Bishop, later Archbishop, Desmond Tutu was a formidable opponent of the regime and knew how to get under their skins. He also got at me once or twice for some perceived sin of omission or commission by HMG. Another brave, if lesser known, black activist I saw occasionally was Dr Nthato Motlana, a Soweto physician and civic leader. He was Chairman of the so-called Soweto Committee of Ten and was one of 136 prominent blacks who had been detained without trial after the 1976 Soweto riots.

Relations with white people were variable. I have mentioned already how I got on with the two Bothas, P.W. and Pik. My contacts with other Ministers were sporadic, but with a few exceptions I found them to be approachable and friendly in a superficial sort of way. A few invited us into their homes. We were impressed how simply and unostentatiously, almost cosily, they lived. One I got to know was a middle-ranking member of the Cabinet called F.W. de Klerk, later to play, with Nelson Mandela, such a pivotal role in the transition to post-apartheid South Africa. He had once been selected to go to Britain on a COI (Central Office of

Information) special visitors' programme, an invitation our talent-spotters reserved for up-and-coming political leaders. At this time his main claim to fame was that he held the important and influential position of Chairman of the Transvaal branch of the governing National Party. He struck me as a careful middle of the road man who liked to tread cautiously and watch where he was putting his feet. A moderate conservative, but certainly not a great reformer or risk-taker. How wrong I was – or how much he changed in a short time. Both he and Nelson Mandela showed a high degree of moral, and physical, courage in facing down their own extremist hotheads who could only think in terms of a struggle to the death. They also demonstrated the ability to rise above their own pasts and put aside the burden of history, and to imagine how a new South Africa could arise out of the ashes of the old through a process of reconciliation between the races. They were worthy recipients of the Nobel Peace Prize.

It was only natural that I mixed with English-speaking whites more than Afrikaners. Anne and I had made some progress with our language lessons and with careful preparation I once delivered a speech in Afrikaans at Stellenbosch University. I did this as a matter of courtesy, because Afrikaners tended to be touchy about perceived attempts to downgrade their language. In daily life the Afrikaners we came across spoke English fluently. South African English-speakers by and large made little effort to reciprocate. They had made their home in South Africa, but were apt to hedge their bets about the length of time they stayed there, depending on how the political scene unfolded. So they renewed their British passports as a form of reinsurance. They were fond of criticising both their home country and their country of adoption. Many of them were doing good business; few of them took a direct part in the running of the country.

Margaret Thatcher once told me, when she had already been Prime Minister for five years, that apartheid was all the fault of "the Boers". I replied that on the contrary many hard-line racists could be found in English-speaking areas like Natal and the Eastern Cape, and there were some notable liberals among the Afrikaners. At least they thought of themselves as Africans, as their name implied, and were committed to stay in the country. She took that well enough, but I doubt whether she was convinced. In fact most of the whites we got to know well were well-meaning, decent people who, while not racist as such and disapproving of the worst excesses of apartheid, nevertheless enjoyed the good life-style that went with cheap black labour. The surprising thing was that despite all the humiliations to which the blacks were subjected under apartheid, outwardly they remained long-suffering, even docile.

Helen Suzman was a shining light in the darkness of South African politics and deserves a whole chapter to herself. To anyone who has not read it, I recommend her autobiography *In No Uncertain Terms* (Sinclair-Stevenson, 1993). She was a really inspiring person and great fun too. To sit at her lunch table in the parliamentary dining room and hear her loud stage whispers mocking stony-faced government ministers at adjoining tables was something not to be forgotten. I was delighted when she accepted my invitation to be guest of honour at the final dinner of my year as Master of the Skinners' Company in June 1994. There were of course other bonny fighters in the Progressive Party, such as Colin Eglin and Ray Swart, but for many years she stood alone in Parliament. Other prominent people, like the Vice-Chancellor of the University of Cape Town, Sir Richard Luyt, and Mollie Blackburn of the women's' Black Sash movement were not afraid to express their opposition loud and clear.

Amongst Afrikaners who had the moral courage to step outside their "tribal" backgrounds and, in their different ways, challenge the regime, three people stand out in my mind. One, Tertius Myburgh, the editor of the *Johannesburg Sunday Times*, became a good friend. He was a clever man who knew how to get under ministerial skins, while avoiding making out-and-out enemies. The second was Jan Steyn, a former judge who was the first chairman of the Urban Foundation established in 1976 by Harry Oppenheimer, Chairman of Anglo-American, and Anton Rupert, Chairman of Rembrandt and Richemont, to provide substantial non-governmental support for black development. After I retired from the Diplomatic Service, Steyn roped me in to head the Foundation's fund-raising office in London. The third, Beyers Naude, paid dearly for his outspoken opposition to the government. He had once been a senior member of the Broederbond and of the Synod of the Dutch Reformed Church in the Transvaal. He resigned from the former when he became Director of the Christian Institute and simultaneously his church proceeded to defrock him as a Minister. In 1977 the government used the Suppression of Communism Act to ban both the Institute itself and Beyers Naude, who was detained under strict house arrest outside Johannesburg. A year or more after our arrival on the scene I heard how he had been treated and rang him up at home. Realising the line would be tapped I did not come straight to the point, but after a few minutes non-committal chat I eventually asked him in a fairly casual way whether or not he would welcome a courtesy visit from me. He immediately said yes and we fixed a date. At the appointed time I drove up in the Rolls Royce, Union Jack flying, and walked up the path to find him waiting at the front door – all the while being photographed by the policeman at the gate. Once in the sitting room he offered me a cup of tea. Of course we both realised that the room was bugged by the security police, but the conversation flowed easily despite that. I was struck by the fact that he expressed no bitterness whatsoever at his treatment. He was obviously a lonely man, but he was sustained by his abiding faith and the strength of his convictions. He also read a great deal. I asked him whether I could send him any books, but he said he had enough. After half an hour or so, I got up to leave and he thanked me warmly for coming. It cost me nothing to go and see him, but he was clearly pleased that I did. At the very least it would have reminded him that British people had not forgotten him. A remarkable man and an uplifting experience for me.

Despite South Africa's pariah status in the world, British companies continued to do good business in the country and there was a constant flow of visits by company chairmen and other senior executives. One or two tried to enlist my help in circumventing the arms embargo to which HMG had committed themselves, albeit reluctantly, and I had to tread carefully. In contrast to the businessmen, government Ministers gave South Africa a wide berth and the only one to visit in my time was Richard Luce, then a junior Minister (Parliamentary Under-Secretary) in the FCO, who came with his wife for three days in September 1980. The visit was in itself uneventful, but it had an unfortunate sequel which could have had serious consequences for both of us. A month or so later I was back in London on a short visit, in the course of which I had my briefcase stolen while doing some last-minute shopping. Amongst other things in the case was a copy of the confidential report Luce had sent the Secretary of State about his visit, including some frank comments on some of the people he had met. I was naturally mortified and reported the loss immediately to the police and the security people in the FCO. I also owned up shamefacedly to the Minister. He was very nice about it, but added rather chillingly that if the contents of his report became public he would have to resign. I returned to South Africa and waited anxiously to see what emerged. Mercifully nothing. It seems likely that the thief was an opportunist who took the case on an impulse and was only interested in the wallet and credit cards inside, as well as the case itself, and dumped the rest in a rubbish bin. Some time later I received a letter from Sir Michael Palliser, the Permanent Under-Secretary, containing an official reprimand for my carelessness and warning me not to do it again. The fact that not long after that I received another letter, this time from the Honours Section of the FCO, intimating that my name was being submitted to the Queen for the award of the KCMG in the 1981 Birthday Honours List might make an outsider's eyebrows go up. Left hand, right hand perhaps, but it seemed a good idea to me.

In 1980, Harold Macmillan, then 86 years old, had had a serious attack of pleurisy and as part of his recuperation he was offered a round trip to Cape Town on a container ship belonging to the South African shipping line, Safmarine. Sir Anthony (later Lord) Barber, one time Chancellor of the Exchequer and Parliamentary Private Secretary to Macmillan, took charge of the arrangements. He told me that as this would be the first time Macmillan had been back to South Africa since his famous "Winds of Change" speech in 1960, it was expected that the South African Government would want to pay him special attentions. He said Mac was feeling quite frail after his illness and it would be appreciated if I could explain this to the South African authorities and head them off. Which I duly did. On arrival towards the end of February he was put up at the Mount Nelson hotel and he only left it once or twice during his short stay. Early on he insisted on coming to the Embassy to sign the visitors' book, although I had made it clear to him that there was no need to do so. He also accepted an invitation to join a small, informal lunch we had arranged at our house in Bishopscourt for Lord Nelson of Stafford, Chairman of G.E.C. When I went to fetch him at the Mount Nelson I found him sitting in the front hall and chatting to people rather like a bishop surrounded by confirmation candidates. He raised his hooded eyes and having looked me over said in an all too loud voice "I must say, Ambassador, you work for a pretty rum government". (For the uninitiated I should explain that he disliked Margaret Thatcher and her brand of Toryism.) Anyway, back at the house he was as good as gold. When the conversation at the table did not interest him he closed his eyes and said nothing, but every now and then when he heard mention of something he knew about like "publishing" or "Hong Kong" the trigger word brought him back to life and he would hold forth. He drank quite a lot both before and during the meal and seemed to be blessed with hollow legs. At some point I committed a gaffe when I told a story about a visit by the Soviet leaders, Bulganin and Khrushchev, to the Indian Staff College, when on being asked what they would like to drink before lunch they opted for whisky. Their rather stiff-necked hosts had learnt from their British predecessors that gentlemen did not drink whisky before lunch and were clearly quite shocked. Anyway, at the end of our own lunch, it being about 4 o'clock by then, Mac sidled up to me and said with a wicked look in his eye "Ambassador, it's after lunch, do you think I could have a whisky?"

Some British visitors I was under strict instructions from the FCO to have nothing to do with. When the British Lions rugby team toured South Africa in May/June 1980, HMG refused to give the visit their approval. This was a consequence of the Gleneagles Agreement, which, as I have already explained, I had had a hand in drafting two years earlier. So neither I nor members of my staff were allowed to attend the matches or offer the players any entertainment. However, I could not resist letting it be known that I was looking forward to watching the Lions beat the Springboks on SABC television and this duly made its way into the local newspapers.

I mentioned earlier the twice yearly migration between Pretoria and Cape Town and how upsetting it was for many people, not least our servants. Anne and I were the least affected in that the chore of the move itself was undertaken by the staff and we did not have any children with us. In fact we enjoyed the change and did not mind having to make fresh starts in two different places. Twice we did the journey in the famous Blue Train, which was an experience in itself. Other times we went by car. The summer in the Cape was especially agreeable and we had this lovely thatched house, Cape Dutch in style, in the exclusive suburb of Bishopscourt. The house in Pretoria was a modern, purpose-built brick affair of a functional but not very attractive kind. Cape Town itself is also a much nicer place than Pretoria and it is of our stays there that we retain our happiest memories.

Funny ones too. There is a photo of Anne and me standing in my Cape Town office all dressed up, me in diplomatic uniform, waiting to go to the state opening of parliament in January 1982. Thereby hangs a tale, or tail. On the same occasion in earlier years I had worn a morning coat and was outshone by a number of other Ambassadors, including my French colleague, who turned up in their full diplomatic finery. (I had not had my own uniform upgraded with all the scrambled egg due to one of Ambassadorial rank.) My old friend, John Killick, retired from the Diplomatic Service and living with his South African wife in the Cape, had been upset to discover this from press photographs and insisted that I wore his next time. Which I did. There was one snag. John's uniform looks all right in the photo, with me standing, but it was in fact such a tight fit that I could hardly sit down. Indeed I found it easier to walk beside the Rolls Royce for the short drive from the office to the Parliament Building, while Anne sat

In borrowed finery

alone on the back seat. On arrival it took me some time to find my French colleague and I eventually came across him soberly attired in a morning coat. Since the previous year there had been a change of government and a new climate of austerity in Paris, the ramifications of which had reached the Embassy in South Africa. After the struggle I had had to get into the uniform, I am not really sure who had the last laugh.

In July 1981 we had our mid-tour home leave. Fairly early on Michael Palliser took me out to lunch at his club. He told me that despite the expectation that Julian Bullard would succeed him as PUS, the Prime

KCMG, October 1981

Minister had opted for Antony Acland. He also gave me to understand that, although I had been in the running for the Paris Embassy, the PM wanted to have John Fretwell there because of his direct experience of EEC affairs. I told him that I had just about achieved all I could in South Africa and I would like to move sooner rather than later. We returned to South Africa in late October, after my leave had been extended to allow us to attend an investiture at Buckingham Palace. At the beginning of January 1982, I was informed that I would be returning to the FCO in March to succeed Johnny Graham as Deputy Under-Secretary for Africa and the Middle East; and that my successor in South Africa would be Ewen Fergusson,

This account of our stay in South Africa has inevitably concentrated on the political scene. We were there at a time when the walls of apartheid were beginning to crack, but they did not come tumbling down until eight years later. As before in Iran, we were pre-revolutionaries. I envy those of my successors whose tours of duty coincided with the emergence of the New Jerusalem, as well as those who have been lucky enough to serve since then in modern-day South Africa. It has often been claimed that international sanctions of various kinds were mainly responsible for bringing the apartheid regime to its knees and I can understand why those who campaigned for them for so long should think that. It is certainly true that sanctions did hurt, particularly the drying up of overseas investment in the country and the pariah status of South Africa in the sporting world. There was, however, more to it than that. Slowly but surely, it dawned on leading members of the government, De Klerk in particular and others too, that apartheid was not working and could not be made to work. The so-called

Umfalosi Trail

independent homelands or "bantustans", which were the core of the system, were just not viable, while in the townships, such as Soweto, the unrest was getting out of hand. The war against SWAPO, the Namibian liberation movement, was grinding on, without any prospect of bringing it to an end quickly. The cost of continuing it became an intolerable financial drain on the government's resources and the mounting loss of life among the young white conscripts involved in the fighting had reached an untenable level in terms of political unpopularity. On top of all this Nelson Mandela's health was beginning to cause anxiety and the government, realising they could not afford to let him die in prison for fear of making him a martyr, were forced to the conclusion they could not delay releasing him. They also calculated that by letting him out they were creating the best prospect of finding a peaceful way out of the political impasse into which they had backed themselves. This was the critical turning point without which there would have been a different and more violent transition from the old to the new South Africa.

At this point and on a different plane, I will briefly mention a few reminiscences of various personal experiences we had during our two and a half years in the country. For a start, our visits to various wildlife parks, including a trail, or guided walk, through Umfalosi, where I experienced the almost mystical excitement of keeping lone watch round the dying embers of the campfire and listening out for the grunts of lions and other wild animals under the brilliant African night sky.

Then, the rather different sensation of lying on a stretcher in the operating theatre of a hospital in Pretoria run by Irish nuns, where I was about to have a minor operation, and hearing the anaesthetist say as he stuck the needle into my arm "Now, Sister, here's your chance, that's the British Ambassador"!

Next another hospital story, one that may have changed the life of our younger daughter, Alice. During her gap year between leaving school and going up to Cambridge, she joined us in South Africa. Knowing she would be bored with the social round of diplomatic life we found her a temporary job as Assistant Occupational Therapist at a mission hospital run by German nuns in Zululand. She threw herself into it with her usual energy and amongst other things learnt how to converse in Zulu with the patients. Despite the fact that many were terminally ill, she thoroughly enjoyed the experience, so much so indeed that she decided then and there that she wanted to become a doctor, which she eventually did.

The other children, Emma, Peter and James, came out at various times. Peter, who has always been interested in wine, worked first for the Stellenbosch Farmers' Wine Cooperative and subsequently for African Distillers in Zimbabwe. He met Clarissa Youngleson, the daughter of a Durban-based family, in Cape Town and soon fell in love. James, more artistically inclined than his brother, followed a course in graphic art at the Michaelis School of Fine Art attached to Cape Town University.

Peter's and Clarissa's engagement was officially announced at the beginning of January 1982. Because of our impending departure the wedding date was brought forward to 6 March. It took place in the impressive setting of the chapel of Michaelhouse School near Nottingham Road in Natal, where Clarissa's father, Mike Youngleson, and her brother, Simon, had been as boys. James was best man. There were some 200 guests, including my sister Betty and her husband, Phil, on a visit from England. Gatsha Buthelezi was another one. The reception was held in a marquee in the grounds of Rawdon's Hotel, a well-known watering-place not far away. A local newspaper rated it "Natal's wedding-of-the-year". Be that as it may, we thought it was a very happy occasion.

A week before this we had given a farewell party on board RMS *St. Helena*, a ship that plied regular sailings between Cape Town and the eponymous Atlantic island. My brother, Patrick, and his wife, Ailsa, also on a

Farewell party

visit from England, came to this, as well as Bet and Phil. We also had to cram into a very short period the usual round of farewell parties and calls on ministers and diplomatic colleagues. Most of these were strictly courtesy affairs, but Pik Botha and Piet Koornhof, the Minister of Cooperation and Development, wrote me nice letters as well. The Prime Minister, on the other hand, could not resist a parting shot when I called on him. With a wintry half-smile P.W. said words to the effect that he had not always appreciated the things I had had to say, but at least I had not said them behind his back. A double edged compliment, I suppose, which showed that I had got under his tough old skin at times. He was very much a political hardliner ("verkrampt") who, despite his much-quoted remark that it was necessary to "adapt or die", was never able to reconcile himself to any meaningful change. His namesake Pik was more flexible and forward-looking ("verligt").

Sadly Anne and I had to make our separate ways back to England. I was told I had to take up my new job on Monday 15 March. We flew up to Johannesburg on the 12th for a party given by Alan Titchener, the Consul-General, to say good-bye to our friends and acquaintances there. We also took leave of the staff in Pretoria. Next day I took the BA flight back to London and Anne returned to Cape Town to supervise the final packing up. Ten days later she boarded an Ellerman Line container ship for a more leisurely voyage back home and a well-deserved rest in the comfort of the owner's cabin. More leisurely perhaps, but not without its excitement, because during the voyage the Falklands crisis came to a head and the Captain received a message warning him that the ship might be requisitioned for active service and diverted to another port. In the event it was not, and she docked at Southampton as planned in the first week of April. Things were humming in the FCO by then and there was a feverish air of excitement, even among those, like myself, who were not directly involved in the mounting crisis over the Falklands. So I could not easily absent myself to meet her and arranged for Emma to do so instead, together with Juan and Alice, in our newly acquired Austin Metro. A new chapter was opening …

Deputy Under-Secretary

… and it opened in a rush. Unlike my recent predecessors in the job, I was not an Arabist and my previous experience of the Middle East had been in Iran, which was a case apart. I was now thrown in at the deep end of Middle East politics and, two weeks after getting my feet under the desk, I found myself accompanying the Secretary of State, Lord Carrington, on a visit to Israel. It turned out to be a very short visit – and a momentous one. In his memoirs, *Reflect on Things Past* (Collins, 1988), Carrington says that he has been criticised, "very naturally", for making the journey at all and "with hindsight I wish I hadn't." In saying that he means, of course, that with the Falklands crisis at boiling point he should have stayed in London. Moreover, Anglo-Israeli relations were quite strained at the time and the visit was likely to prove a difficult one. As it happened, Carrington was able to see all the Israeli leaders, including Prime Minister Begin, and he felt afterwards that his talks had gone some way to repairing relations.

It is worth giving a fuller account of the meeting with Begin, at which I was present. It took place in his office in the Knesset building. Begin was suffering from gout at the time and throughout the meeting he kept one leg out in front of him on a stool. For a time he did all the talking and lectured Carrington about his insistence that sooner or later Israel would have to negotiate a settlement with the Arabs. Why should he expect Israel to try to come to terms with the PLO terrorists whose very Charter was dedicated to its destruction? "It is like asking us to commit suicide". When Carrington could get a word in, he said that, during the years of bringing colonial rule to an end, British governments had discovered that they could not choose whom to negotiate with, they had to deal with whoever had the power to deliver an agreement. This often meant people they had once regarded as terrorists, such as Kenyatta in Kenya or Makarios in Cyprus. He was about to add Mugabe's name when Begin broke in and said, with a slight smile, "Not me, I hope"(in the days of the British Mandate in Palestine Begin had been a member of the Stern Gang who, amongst other acts of violence, blew up the King David Hotel in Jerusalem). Finally, as the meeting was breaking up he invited Carrington and the rest of us to go up to the big window and look up at the hills of Judaea and Samaria, from where Jordanian artillery had once bombarded Jerusalem, including the Knesset building. Israel could never let that happen again, he said.

Notwithstanding Carrington's own assessment, the visit was not a success. The Israelis had long believed that he was anti-Israel and from the outset they gave him a distinctly chilly public reception; and in the private talks they showed no inclination to moderate their uncompromising views. They also refused his request to visit the West Bank. To demonstrate to the Palestinians that we were not ignoring them, he instructed me to go instead and to call on some of the local mayors. Even then the Israeli police were in close attendance and tried to put obstacles in my way. At one stop I had to resort to the ludicrous device of attaching a message to a stone and throwing it over the mayor's garden wall. I managed to call on one or two of the others, and we made sure this was given as much publicity as possible. During an official dinner on the second day a message came from London asking Carrington to cut short his visit and return to London.

From that moment the speed of events accelerated. The next day, Thursday 1 April, Carrington was back at his desk in the FCO. The following day the Argentines invaded the Falklands. On the morning of Monday 5 April, Carrington resigned, and with him went his number two, Humphrey Atkins, and Richard Luce. Francis Pym replaced Carrington and the latter held a drinks party in his office the same evening to say good-bye to his colleagues and senior officials and to welcome his successor. As I recall, he himself put on a brave face, but his wife, Iona, seemed distressed and on the verge of tears. The rest of us felt very sad indeed. He was a superb man to work for and great fun. Above all, he did his job supremely well and, rightly or wrongly, we did not think that he should take the rap for what had happened. However, he himself was convinced that he was the sacrifice that had to be made in order to assuage the anger felt in the country because the Argentines had stolen a march on us, and to unite public opinion behind the government in the days ahead.

It was over the Falklands that I found myself embroiled with the Israelis once again. We knew from intelligence sources that they were supplying military hardware to the Argentines and I was instructed to summon the Ambassador, Shlomo Argov, and demand that they put a stop to it. He said that he knew nothing about this and asked for further details, which because of the sensitive source of our information I was not able to give him. He said he would report to his government. A day or two later he came back with a prevaricating reply and I pressed him further, without any apparent success. We subsequently learnt from the same intelligence source that the deliveries had been quietly suspended.

Another crisis in our relations blew up on 6 June, when an estimated 60,000 Israeli troops invaded the Lebanon. Their stated goal was to secure the territory north of the border with Israel in order to stop PLO raids. Their unavowed aim was to destroy the PLO and establish in power a compliant Lebanese government. In the process the Syrian forces present in the country were defeated and the PLO retreated to West Beirut. I went through the motions of expressing our strong disapproval to Argov, but we were faced with a *fait accompli* and I doubt whether what I had to say cut much ice with him.

The last time I saw Argov was later in the month when we were both guests at the annual diplomatic dinner given at the Dorchester Hotel by the De La Rue Company. As he was leaving and about to get into his car, he was shot at point blank range by the side of the road. He was severely injured and left permanently paralysed. Poor man, he did not deserve that. Just over a year later Anne and I attended a big dinner given in his honour by British Jewry in the presence of the Prime Minister, Margaret Thatcher.

Over the next two years I travelled through a large part of sub-Saharan Africa and visited most of the countries of the Middle East. I will not attempt to list them all, but memories of one or two are worth recording. Being sent to the Lebanon in order to assess whether in the disturbed security situation it would be safe for Princess Anne to visit the country as President of the Save The Children Fund – she was determined to go in any case, and did. In Mogadishu, holding hands on the table with the Foreign Minister in total darkness during a power cut. In Togo being summoned to meet the dictatorial President Ayedema at 6.30am. In Bahrain meeting the Ruler, Sheikh Issa, and being showered with generous presents, both for me and for Anne, which FO rules did not allow me to keep. In Oman flying up by helicopter to spend the day with the Minister of Defence, Sayyid Fahad and his Welsh-born wife at their plush holiday home near the Straits of Hormuz – more embarrassing presents. Accompanying Francis Pym on visits to Jordan, where we had a meeting with King Hussein, and to Saudi Arabia, where King Fahd received us in the air-conditioned desert camp to which he retired from time to time away from Riyadh. And so on.

It is worth saying a little more on the much-vexed question of presents. It is a tradition of Middle Eastern hospitality for hosts to give generous presents to their guests. It is a strictly enforced anti-corruption rule in this country that government servants may not receive presents in their official capacity. In my time attempts to resolve the problem by dissuading local rulers from giving presents in the first place had always run into the sands. Who were we to dictate to them anyway? So we fell back on a typical British compromise: we accepted the presents and sent elaborate letters of thanks, and subsequently were obliged either to pay the Treasury the market price, minus a very small discount, or to hand them in to be disposed of by Customs & Excise along with other confiscated goods. Occasionally one was allowed to keep, say, a Rolex watch for the rest of one's current appointment, so as to be able to flash it in the face of the said ruler if and when he visited London, only to hand it in thereafter. The upshot of all this was that the donor thought you were venal because you had accepted his present and at the same time HMG made sure you were not. It also grated with the FCO Minister of State, Richard Luce, and me that at the conclusion of one state visit to London both he and I had to adhere to this rule, while members of the Royal family and household were allowed to keep their even more expensive presents. The absurdity of the situation has recently been thrown into sharp relief by the publication of a list of the presents given to ministers by foreign dignitaries, showing which they agreed to "buy", and for how much, and which they handed over for official disposal. This follows earlier disclosures about the way in which Prince Charles' butler was instructed to sell off unwanted presents to private dealers. All very embarrassing in foreign relations terms, but I suppose that eventually it might have the beneficial effect of drying up the flow of presents.

The Libyan Government was causing us many problems. In particular their agents were all too often attacking, and murdering, on the streets of London fugitive opponents of the regime. When the efforts of the police to stop them proved unsuccessful, I was detailed to go to Tripoli, accompanied by Oliver Miles, the Head of Near East & North Africa Department, to try to persuade their security people to call them off. Behind the scenes it was also discreetly arranged for us to meet Muammar Gadaffi in his private tent at the Tripoli International Horse Show. It was a fascinating experience, but as later events were to show, nothing came of it and the attacks continued. Gadaffi was polite enough, but that was all; he showed no inclination to give serious attention to the issue on top of our minds. A government minister might well have made more impression on him, but in London Gadaffi was regarded as a pariah and off limits for ministerial visits.

Matters came to a head in St. James's Square on 17 April 1984. In the course of a peaceful demonstration outside the so-called Libyan People's Bureau, i.e. embassy, a policewoman on duty, Yvonne Fletcher, was killed by gunfire from inside the building. It was soon surrounded by armed police and a virtual siege ensued over the next few days, including the Easter weekend. COBRA, the Cabinet Office Briefing Room which had been set up to deal with emergencies, was activated under the chairmanship of the Home Secretary, Leon Brittan, and I represented the FCO. We met twice a day to decide how best to handle the tense situation. Public feelings were running high and there was a universal demand that whoever was responsible for the shooting should be arrested. The Libyans refused to hand anyone over and in order to increase the pressure on them we arranged for a specialist unit of the SAS to be openly deployed near Heathrow with the ostensible purpose of storming the building. Meanwhile some backstairs talking was going on and our Embassy in Tripoli naturally became involved. They pointed out, reasonably enough, that they and the some 10,000 Britons living or working in Libya were vulnerable to retaliation by the Libyans for any action we took. The SAS were champing at the bit, with the smell of cordite in their nostrils. However, the stand-off was eventually broken without their intervention, when agreement was reached that all those inside the building should be escorted to the airport and expelled from the country. HMG severed diplomatic relations with Libya and the People's Bureau was shut down. In Libya retaliation followed quickly. Our Embassy was attacked and set on fire (though not burnt to the ground) and members of the British community were expelled or put under pressure in other ways. All in all an unsatisfactory ending to an unhappy episode.

The grass was not allowed to grow under my feet. The following month I was sent on an unusual mission to Angola to bring back sixteen British diamond miners who had been captured and held hostage by rebel UNITA forces. Jonas Savimbi, the UNITA leader, had wanted HMG to send a government minister to his HQ at Jamba, in the southeast of the country, to collect them, thereby securing political kudos and recognition for his movement. When the government baulked at this he accepted me as the next best thing.

Savimbi's sponsors, the South African Government, agreed to fly me, and a member of our Pretoria Embassy, Ric Todd, to Jamba. We made the first part of the journey from Johannesburg in a small chartered aircraft and the last stage in a SADF helicopter. The pilot of the latter had obviously been ordered not to let us follow the exact route he was taking,

Rescue mission, May 1984 (Savimbi on my left). Cape Times

because he kept changing direction and flying in a series of confusing tacks. Eventually we touched down in a jungle clearing, where we found UNITA soldiers waiting for us. After a rough truck ride of about an hour we were deposited outside a big stadium, where Savimbi and a group of about thirty journalists and television cameramen were waiting for us. He then took us through throngs of people into the stadium, where some 4,000 men, women and children sat or stood around a large parade ground. Savimbi was a consummate showman. The ceremony that followed our entry involved a band, a drill display, a women's' choir, much colourful flag-waving by children and speeches by him and me.

Savimbi then took us off in his Toyota Land Cruiser to meet the captive Britons. They were in better physical shape than I had expected. They said the long forced march and truck ride from the diamond mine at Cafunfo in the North to Jamba had been hard going, but they had not otherwise been ill-treated. They were certainly pleased with the mail, whisky and cigarettes I brought them. I said that I would be seeing them again later. We then went off for a late lunch and a long private talk with Savimbi and UNITA's representative in Europe, Tito Chingunji, accompanied by four other members of the Central Committee.

The meeting lasted three hours. Afterwards Savimbi and I spoke to the waiting journalists and told them that our talk had covered a wide range of regional questions. This pandered to his sense of self-importance, and there was no doubt that he was well-informed on a number of current international issues. However, most of our discussion was about our bilateral relations and UNITA's wish for more high-level contacts and "recognition" of the movement. These were not new issues and I did not have any difficulty in dealing with them. In the end nothing of any significance emerged from the meeting. Nor, I suspect, had Savimbi expected that it would. For him the fact of the meeting was what really mattered in his projection of himself to the outside world and it was his price for releasing the "captives" – he insisted that they were not "hostages".

After a short rest Ric Todd and I were taken at about midnight to a smaller floodlit stadium. There was more singing and dancing and then a brief ceremony took place in which Savimbi, in a further display of showmanship, symbolically handed over two of the hostages to me. At the ensuing press conference I said, amongst other things, that I had been asked before leaving London whether it was not humiliating for HMG to have to send me to Jamba; I could say now that since my arrival I had not had to beg for anything and if the reception I had received amounted to humiliation I could take a lot more of it. This seemingly off-the-cuff remark was widely reported in the British press, as I meant it to be.

The journey back to Johannesburg was uncomfortable, to say the least. The South African Government were willing to fly Todd and me out the same way we came, i.e. by helicopter and private aircraft, but would not extend their offer to include the released hostages. There was, of course, no way we could accept this. So we all bumped our way in the backs of two military trucks driven in low gear for nine hours through the night to the Caprivi Strip in Namibia, where a chartered C130 aircraft with bucket seats was waiting to fly us back to Johannesburg. We spent the next 24 hours in Johannesburg indulging in some R and R and, in my case, drafting a preliminary report to the FCO for the Minister of State, Malcolm Rifkind, before he made a statement to the House of Commons the next day. We then flew back as a group to London overnight and on landing early in the morning were met by a contingent of journalists and interviewed on BBC Breakfast Television. The whole episode had obviously been a good media story. For myself, I can only say that was it was an extraordinary, one-off experience in a not uneventful diplomatic career. I was pleased to read subsequently in Hansard that, when Rifkind made his report to the House of Commons, a number of MPs spoke approvingly of the way I had conducted the operation.

Two weeks later, on 2 June, I was at Heathrow to meet P.W. and Pik Botha, who had been invited by Margaret Thatcher for talks. There was much public opposition to their visit and a mass protest march was due to take place in central London. The meeting was, therefore, to be held at Chequers and I was detailed to escort them there by helicopter from Heathrow. Including lunch, the meeting lasted some five hours and I remember that the Prime Minister spoke quite strongly about the bad impression left by television pictures she had seen of the forced resettlement of black communities taking place in South Africa. Some months later the Foreign Secretary, Geoffrey Howe, and I admitted to one another in conversation something we both thought highly amusing but had not dared tell the PM at Chequers, namely that his son, Alec, along with James and Alice, were among the marchers.

The next thing I had to cope with had a bit of opera buffe about it, but it could also have had fatal consequences. On 5 July, Umaru Dikko, a former Nigerian government minister who had taken refuge in London, was kidnapped. He was subsequently found heavily drugged in a crate that had been delivered by van to Stansted Airport en route to Lagos from the Nigerian High Commission. In a probably life-saving Freudian slip, the driver had taken the crate to the passenger terminal instead of the freight depot and suspicions were soon aroused. After hurried consultations with the FCO the crate was opened. With the comatose Dikko another man was found, fully awake and armed with drugs and syringes. The Nigerian Government denied any knowledge of the affair and for a time relations between the two governments were put on hold, both High Commissioners being unable to return to their posts. Three men, two of them Israelis, were subsequently tried and sent to prison for the crime.

By now I was 56 years old and my final posting before retirement at 60 was looming. I had known for some time that it was likely to be either Canada or Australia and during the Commonwealth Heads of Government Meeting in New Delhi in November 1983 I learnt that it was to be Australia in the autumn of the following year. Anne and I were both pleased about this. The following month we completed the sale of our house in Kensington and moved to a converted flint barn we had bought in Bishopstone, East Sussex. This was to be our retirement home, for we had already decided that we did not want to go on living in London any longer than necessary. However, it was clear to us that for the remaining nine months or so of my current job we needed to retain a base there. So we rented a small furnished flat near Holland Park, which served us well for that busy period.

During the two or more years I had the Deputy Under-Secretary job, I had the opportunity to observe both the Queen and the Prime Minister at close hand on several occasions. I also met for the first time Tiny Rowland, who was to make quite an impact on my life later. At the risk of being accused of name-dropping, I will say something about each of them.

When the Queen receives Foreign Ambassadors for the presentation of their credentials, the Permanent Under-Secretary of the FCO or, in his absence a Deputy Under-Secretary (or whatever the title is these days), is in full-uniformed attendance. I did this a number of times. I kept my uniform (by this time I had discarded John Killick's tight-fitting number) in my office cupboard and I recall that on one occasion I could not find my black socks in the usual rush to get ready. So I wore the grey ones I already had on. When I arrived at Buckingham Palace, I was informed that, because of work going on, the usual room was not available and I was escorted along another corridor. My guide warned me to tread carefully as the wooden floor had recently been polished and was rather slippery. I did as he told me, although for some unaccountable reason my boots felt tighter than usual at that moment and my feet were beginning to go numb. Anyway, I got there without mishap and as I stood by the Queen's side it suddenly dawned on me what was the matter: I had stuffed the missing socks down the toes of the boots and my feet were feeling the pinch. I would have loved to share the joke with the Queen as I am sure she would have enjoyed it, but I forbore to do so. A pity, because as I took my leave, she repeated the advice to tread carefully along the corridor.

The person in attendance on such occasions has to be well briefed on what is going on in the world since it is the custom to have a short conversation with the Queen after the Ambassador has left, during which she often asks some pertinent questions. On one such occasion, for example, just after the American invasion of Grenada in October 1983, the Queen asked me for the latest news and expressed her concern for the safety of the Governor, Sir Paul Scoon. Unlike her Prime Minister or Foreign Secretary, she had been to Grenada and knew exactly the exposed position of his official residence. Another time was when Samora Machel, the President of Mozambique, was on an official visit to London in 1984. Margaret Thatcher was not at all pleased at the prospect of meeting this communist leader, but when he came to No.10 for talks and lunch she was won over by his charm and handsome looks. So much so that, when in the hour's private talk they had before lunch he talked so much she could hardly get a word in edgeways, she seemed not to mind at all. Next day I was in attendance on the Queen again and she said Samora Machel was coming to lunch and asked how his visit was going. I told her about the talk at No.10 the previous day and a broad smile crossed her face. A reflection, no doubt, of who did most of the talking during the PM's weekly audiences with her. She certainly has a lively sense of humour and is a good mimic. Shortly after I retired in 1988 Anne and I went with a number of other colleagues and their wives to Buckingham Palace to take our formal leave of her. In the course of conversation she asked me what I could tell her about Bill Hayden, the Australian Foreign Minister, who had just been nominated as the new Governor-General. I told her, amongst other things, that he was someone who disliked formality and preferred not to be called "Minister", to which she replied "You don't think I should call him "Mite"?

In the nature of things I saw more of Margaret Thatcher than of the Queen. As I suggested earlier, she disliked the FCO as an institution, but admired some of its officials. I was not one of her special favourites, but we got on all right and after a time I felt confident enough to contradict her when I thought she was wrong. She was not by nature a good listener, but provided you knew what you were talking about and did not irritate her with what she called "FCO waffle", she would hear you out. Even if she pooh-poohed an idea at first, she would sometimes adopt it as her own later.

One could not but admire her political courage. I witnessed a good example of this at a hastily called meeting one Saturday morning at Chequers. Terrorists had let off a number of bombs in Amman the day before and the urgent question was whether or not to advise the Queen to cancel a visit she was due to make there in 36 hours' time. We were a mixed group gathered at short notice. Among those present were the Minister of Defence, Michael Heseltine, the FCO Minister of State, Richard Luce, The Cabinet Secretary, Robert Armstrong, the Queen's Private Secretary, Philip Moore, the Chairman of the JIC, Tony Duff, and myself. The PM made it clear she would take the final decision, but first she wanted to hear what each one of us had to say. The Ministers laid emphasis on the fact that the government would be severely criticised if anything happened to the Queen, to which the PM retorted that she was all too aware of that, indeed she herself would have to resign within the hour. Philip Moore said that the argument would have to be a very strong one if the Queen was to be dissuaded from going. The rest of us in one degree or another thought that on balance she should go. It was of course easier for officials to say this because we would not have to carry the can if anything went wrong. Summing up, the PM said that it would be giving in to the terrorists if the visit were called off. She then left the room to take a telephone call from King Hussein. When she came back she reported that the King had told her he would stake his life on protecting the Queen. That clinched it. The visit went ahead without incident.

It is almost banal to add the following personal reminiscence, but I do so because it demonstrates how observant and considerate Margaret Thatcher could be to people around her. A year or two after the events described above, during a visit to London from Canberra, I was unexpectedly summoned to see her in No.10. I was told by her Private Secretary, Charles Powell, that she wanted to canvas my view of an idea that Laurence van der Post had mentioned to her of encouraging the establishment of a white homeland in South Africa as an Afrikaner independent state. I thought it was a non-starter and said so as politely as possible. But it was the very first thing she had said as I entered the room that impressed me most: she remarked that I had lost weight. As indeed I had done after going on a diet, but to my chagrin not one of our children had noticed it. From the moment I went as Ambassador to South Africa I had admired Margaret Thatcher, because thanks to her Britain quickly ceased to be regarded as the sick man of Europe and became a much easier country to represent abroad. Now I positively warmed to her. But only for a time, I regret. In her later years she listened to advice less and less and in particular became more and more opposed to any suggestion that Britain should play a constructive role in the European Community. As far as she was concerned, the Community's ambitions were incompatible with the maintenance of Britain's sovereignty and its encroachments had to be resisted at every turn. If Britain was no longer the sick man of Europe, it now became the odd man out – and she gloried in it. She lost my support then. If only she had retired from No. 10 a year or two before she was forced out ...

Lastly, Tiny Rowland. Ever since May 1973 when the Prime Minister, Edward Heath, had characterised Lonrho as "the unpleasant and unacceptable face of capitalism" Rowland's relations with HMG veered between bad and non-existent. While Lonrho continued to expand its large commercial stake in Africa and Rowland himself played an influential role in the politics of a number of African countries through his assiduous cultivation of their leaders, he had no contacts with our diplomatic missions, let alone the FCO, but made a point of keeping in touch with the Americans. It seemed obvious to me that it would be to the advantage of both the FCO and Lonrho if we were each aware of what the other was trying to do and, better still, could avoid working at cross purposes. I suggested, therefore, to my political masters that I should initiate contact with Rowland on a personal basis and this was agreed. Our first meeting took place in my office and was pretty frosty, with Tiny accusing us of doing various things to try to undermine him. He was also understandably suspicious of my intentions. But further meetings followed, mostly over lunch in the Berkeley Hotel or Claridges (I was never invited to Lonrho) and the atmosphere began to improve to the point where Tiny let his hair down more and more. I was also able to arrange an invitation for him to the lunch Margaret Thatcher gave President Samora Machel at No. 10. This represented a breaking of the ice for him and he readily accepted. For his part, he claimed to have smoothed the way with Jonas Savimbi for me when I went to collect the hostages and I have no reason to doubt this. By the time I went off to Australia our relations had not had time to develop very far, but they were reasonably relaxed and friendly. The bust-up came ten years later.

Australia

We arrived in Canberra on Saturday 13 October 1984, as the sombre news of the IRA's bomb attack at the Conservative Party Conference at Brighton was filling the airwaves. The following day, when I went to see Bob Hawke, the Australian Prime Minister, to present my letter of introduction from Margaret Thatcher, he began by asking me to convey his sympathy to her and his relief that she had not been injured. That I should be seeing him so quickly and on a Sunday, at that, was unusual. Even odder that at the time Hawke was standing in front of a cricket pavilion in his flannels and padded up as he waited to go into bat at the fall of the next wicket. It was indeed a bizarre occasion and I explained the circumstances in a formal letter to the Secretary of State a few days later in the following terms.

In accordance with the instructions contained in the despatch dated 14 September, I delivered my Letter of Introduction to the Prime Minister of Australia on 14 October. This was my second day in Australia and a Sunday. Mr Hawke was dressed in white flannels and an open-necked shirt; I more formally in grey flannels and a blue blazer. I drank beer from a can; he does not do that any more.

The occasion was a cricket match between Mr Hawke's selection from his staff and a team drawn from the parliamentary press gallery. It was also the last occasion when I was likely to be able to see him until after the General Election in seven weeks' time, because he was almost immediately setting out on the campaign trail. The assignation was cleverly thought up by the Deputy High Commissioner, Charles Cullimore, and readily agreed to by Mr Hawke himself.

When we arrived at the small ground where the match was being played, Mr Hawke was already padded up waiting on his own in front of the pavilion to bat next. We went straight up to him and introduced ourselves. Naturally he had half an eye on what was going on in the middle, but otherwise the conversation flowed freely, if not profoundly, and he was as relaxed as any 54 year old Prime Minister would be, with a cricketing reputation to live up to and the TV cameramen all waiting to see him get out first ball. Some of these same vultures

My first meeting with Bob Hawke, 1984

turned their attention to the two of us as we talked and I thought it would somehow not be in keeping with the dignity of the Prime Minister's letter if I made a show of handing it to him then. There was also the practical consideration that Mr Hawke could not easily have read it or handed it to anyone before going out to the wicket. With Mr Hawke's agreement, I therefore passed it shortly afterwards to his Private Secretary, who, I regret to report, treated it with even less respect by stuffing it into the back pocket of his somewhat off-white flannels. I feared it might be lost in the wash, but fortunately it survived.

I stayed to watch Mr Hawke bat. This he did to great effect – he was 12th man for Oxford when Colin Cowdrey was Captain – until after scoring a brisk 27 runs he was hit on the head in attempting an ambitious hook and had to retire hurt. I can only hope that he will not attribute any of the blame for this to my having shaken his hand a few minutes before. Anyway I enjoyed our first meeting and have subsequently heard that he did too.

This may seem a somewhat unorthodox way to have delivered my Letter of Introduction from Britain's Prime Minister to the Prime Minister of Australia. But I believe it provides an apt illustration of the nature of the relationship between our two countries. We should try to keep it that way.

The warm glow lasted just 48 hours, at which point one local journalist reported that I had made "a controversial start". It happened like this. On the Monday following our arrival I agreed to meet journalists at the

Westminster House

residence, Westminster House. Most of the exchanges were of a routine nature, but my answer to a question relating to the conduct of the British nuclear tests at Maralinga and the Monte Bello Islands in the 1950s received prominent media coverage. For some months an Australian Royal Commission, chaired by Judge James McLelland, had been looking into the effectiveness of our clean-up of radioactive materials at the sites in the 1960s. At least that had seemed to us to be its principal purpose, but in practice its terms of reference were sufficiently wide to allow it to range over such questions as the mistreatment of the aboriginal population in the vicinity of the Maralinga site and the sufferings of servicemen and civilians carelessly exposed to radiation. Lurid allegations along these lines were being presented unchallenged to the Commission and widely reported in the press. When one of the journalists asked me when the British Government was going to give its own evidence, I said that a decision on that rather depended on the way the Commission went about its business in the future: obviously we were not happy to see reports of one-sided hearings and what looked like snap prejudgments of conclusions appearing in the press. Britain's name was being unfairly dragged in the mud. When reported, these remarks got under McLelland's skin. "Diamond Jim", as he was known, was a veteran Irish-Australian Labor politician and had a flamboyant personality. In a statement released to the *Sydney Morning Herald* entitled "Message to Britain: Show Up or Shut Up" he took me to task and said that, if I wanted the Royal Commission to be fully apprised of the British

Government's view of the way the nuclear tests were conducted, I should advise them to do what they had been repeatedly invited, but not yet deigned, to do, namely be represented before the Commission.

What Diamond Jim had said did in fact make sense and, though I was not about to tell him that, I thought it best to stop the war of words. So I invited him to lunch at the Union Club in Sydney and we patched things up on a personal level without either of us giving any obvious ground. However, in his book *Stirring the Possum* (Penguin Books Australia, 1988) he referred to me as someone "who turned out to be a charming man ... and he had got the message". This was shown, he suggested, by the fact that "shortly afterwards senior and junior counsel were despatched from Britain and represented the British government before the Commission for the rest of its life". McLelland and I had no further run-ins, but in the coming months I had to write a number of letters to newspaper editors in order to set the record straight on continuing distorted reports and allegations in the press.

The proceedings of the Royal Commission rumbled on for another year or more and it finally produced its report in December 1985. In the intervening period it had visited London and I had visited Maralinga to see things for myself, in the company of the Australian Solicitor-General, Gavan Griffith, who became a personal friend. There seemed to be little doubt that, by more modern standards, the original clean-up of the contamination hazards in 1967 had not been good enough, and it came as no surprise when the Commission recommended that a new clean-up should be undertaken at both main sites, to the satisfaction of the Australian Government and at the expense of the British Government. Protracted negotiations followed between the two governments on the precise scope and cost of implementing this recommendation and these continued for some time after I left Australia in February 1988.

The other major political problem I had to deal with, the so-called "Spycatcher Case", came to a head in March 1987. The bare facts are sufficiently well known not to need repeating here. They have been fully set out, albeit with a certain bias, in Chapman Pincher's *A Web of Deception* (Sidgwick and Jackson, 1987). Although I was HMG's principal representative in Australia at the time, I was not consulted by ministers in London about the decision to take Peter Wright, who was now living in Tasmania, to court in Australia or the subsequent conduct of our case. I am not sure how much difference it would have made to the eventual outcome, if I had been, but some mistakes might have been avoided. In particular I could have emphasised that it would be wrong to assume that the same procedures would be followed in an Australian court as in an English one. Thus it would not have come as a surprise in London when the judge in the New South Wales Court, Justice Powell, intervened time and time again during the trial to express his irritation with arguments being advanced by the Plaintiff's lawyer, Theo Simos QC; or when he allowed Peter Wright's lawyer, Malcolm Turnbull, to take all manner of liberties that would not have been permitted in an English court.

After the first round was lost and it was decided to appeal to the NSW Court of Appeal I received private advice from Gavan Griffith to the effect that we would be well advised to bring in a new lead advocate in place of Simos, to give fresh impetus to our case. He even mentioned one or two names. I took the opportunity of a brief visit to London to pass this on to Sir Patrick Mayhew, the newly appointed Attorney-General and an old school acquaintance. When he demurred on the grounds that to change horses in midstream might suggest a lack of confidence in the strength of our case and in addition would be demeaning for Simos, I suggested he should telephone Griffith direct. He subsequently did so, but was unwilling to change his mind. In the event it was almost certainly not a critical point, because by the time the Court of Appeal decided by a 2-1 majority against HMG, publication of the book was already under way in North America and elsewhere and the horse had bolted. It was left to me to pick up the pieces and put on a brave face with the local press and television. I still cherish one slightly sarcastic report in *The Australian* entitled "Upper hand lost, upper lip intact". A mauvais quart d'heure, for sure, but I did not lose much sleep over it.

With the advantage of hindsight it is easy to see that it had been a serious error of judgment in the first place to try to stop publication of the book because it contained one or two embarrassing passages about the activities of the Security Service. Ministers should have realised that once the issue of publication became a cause célèbre, any injunction against it in the UK would not stop publication overseas and, worse, would positively encourage it. At the same time HMG's action drew attention to those very passages in the book which in the normal course of events might have caused less of a fuss. If any action was to be taken, it would have been better to concentrate efforts on preventing Wright from making any money out of publication of the book by taking legal steps to "distrain", or seize, any profits that he or the publishers might make. Such an action could have been undertaken on the grounds that in writing the book he had breached the duty of confidentiality he had assumed on signing the Official Secrets Act, a fact he himself did not deny, and it could well have succeeded.

Other problems I encountered during our time in Australia were of a relatively routine kind and for the most part I could get on and enjoy the many agreeable things the job, and the country, had to offer. The press went in for quite a lot of "pom-bashing", but for the most part it was good-natured and one could either let it pass or answer in the same vein. To the extent that it was meant more seriously, it was partly because many Australians felt an instinctive urge to assert their own identity after many years of not being quite sure of their place in the world. The so-called "cultural cringe" still rankled. The easiest way of getting rid of it was to have a go at the mother country and assert their own superiority. It was something they needed to get out of their systems and we, for our part, soon learnt to live with it. However, unfair and sustained press attacks on Britain could not be left unanswered and on such occasions I had no hesitation in writing letters to the editors or, occasionally, appearing on television. I have kept copies of some of them covering a wide variety of topics. Perhaps it is the Irish in me, but I quite enjoy a bit of controversy and since I retired I have written a number of letters to *The Times* on various topics.

We all know that Australia is a big country, but you have to go there to understand what that means. It was quickly brought home to us when shortly after our arrival Dame Elizabeth Murdoch invited us to a lunch party to celebrate the award of The A.C. (Companion of the Order of Australia) to her son, Rupert. I reckoned it would be a good opportunity to meet a lot of important people and was keen to go. The snag was that it was taking place in Melbourne and the only feasible way to get there was by air. I had never before flown anywhere just for lunch and wondered how I could justify the payment of our air fares from the High Commission's travel funds. In the end I decided it was too good an opportunity to miss, and we went. Subsequently, I felt less compunction about flying to Sydney or Melbourne for a lunch and a couple of meetings: the return journey from Canberra took less than two hours by air, as opposed to eight hours by rail or road.

The Australian Capital Territory, of which the city of Canberra forms the principal feature, is the seat of the federal government and parliament and other national institutions such as the War Memorial and the National Art Gallery. It has a shifting population of politicians who come and go as the sittings of parliament dictate and a resident population of civil servants, senior military people and diplomats. There is no industry or commerce of note. Most Australians tend to see it as a place that contributes little, if anything, to the wealth of the nation and, worse than that, squanders what they themselves contribute in taxes. The fact that it was purpose-built and for a long time had a rather soulless air about it has only added to its unpopularity. People who live there – and this now includes quite a large number of people who choose to spend their retirement there – find it very agreeable. We certainly did. Plenty of space, no overcrowding, a gratifying absence of traffic jams or polluted air, well-planned amenities, some lovely pastoral country close by, and last but not least a number of friendly, interesting people. The only trouble was that to do my job properly I could not stay rooted to the spot and was obliged to make frequent forays from Canberra in order to attend, say, a business function in one of the major cities. In 1986/7, when the England cricket team were touring Australia, I managed to find plausible excuses to visit four of the five cities where the test matches were being played. Naturally, with my support they won the series and retained the Ashes, so who can say it was not money well spent? They lost them two years later in England, after I had retired, and it was to be another seventeen years before they managed to regain them. Again I watched them, but this time only on television.

Australia being a sports-mad country and not being averse to it ourselves, we were often invited to other encounters apart from cricket. Among those we attended were the Melbourne Cup, the Australian Open Tennis Championship, America's Cup yacht racing off Fremantle, an international gliding competition (where I had my first and only flight) and a Grand Prix motor race in Adelaide (where mercifully I was not given a ride). Twice we watched the start of the Sydney/Hobart sailing race on Boxing Day. I seem to think we missed out on Australian Rules ("footie"), soccer and rugby. Spectating apart, I myself played a lot of tennis and golf at a social level.

We also took every other opportunity of travelling round the country In order to show our faces and fly the flag. In doing so we saw more of it than most Australians do in a lifetime. The vast majority of them live round the seaboard and do not venture into the interior any more than they have to. It is foreigners like us who tend to go on about the attractions of the "outback". We travelled the length and breadth of it, by road, train, and light aircraft, taking in remote parts of New South Wales, Queensland, Western Australia and the Northern Territory.

We saw coal, diamond, opal and iron ore mines, Flying Doctor clinics, cattle-ranching, cotton-growing, some very good wineries and much else besides. And of course crocodiles. Names like Alice Springs, Ayers Rock,

Bourke (the outback is sometimes referred to as being "back of Bourke"), Bunbury, Broken Hill, Dampier, Esperance, Kakadu, Katherine, Kalgoorlie, Kununurra, Nullarbor, Tibooburra and Tom Price bring back happy memories. We also met some very interesting people having a distinct character and life-style of their own.

On one occasion I went off to Papua New Guinea, which before its independence had been governed by Australia as a UN Trust Territory. The name of Leahy (pronounced "Lie", as it is in Australia) was well known there, and three brothers, Michael, Daniel, and James, had figured in a series of expeditions in the 1930s into the hitherto unexplored central highlands. They made some remarkable cinefilms of the primitive tribesmen they came across and these have been brought together in a video cassette entitled *First Contact* and a book of the same name (Viking Penguin Inc, 1987). Some years ago the youngest brother, Daniel, was knighted and as another beknighted Leahy I wrote to congratulate him, but sadly I did not get a reply. I would have liked to ask him, amongst other things, whether he was aware of a Daniel a generation or two back in his lineage. Too much of a coincidence, perhaps.

Australia was a popular place for our ministers, the heads of the armed forces, company chairmen and other senior British figures to visit and we had a steady stream of official guests staying at Westminster House. Baroness Young, Minister of State at the FO, was the first to come, just a week after our arrival. Not all of them stayed with us. As monarch of Australia, the Queen stayed with the Governor-General, as did other members of the royal family and, on one occasion, the Archbishop of Canterbury. For reasons of his own, Alan Clark, at that time a Defence Minister, scorned our hospitality in favour of a rather second-class hotel, but he did deign to have a meal with us. Those who did stay with us were treated to a first-class service by our admirable Chinese domestic staff.

Relations with Australian Ministers were relaxed and informal. Bob Hawke was outgoing and approachable, but since he was also a calculating, opportunist politician who kept his decision-making antennae closely attuned to the shifting strengths of public opinion, his reactions could be erratic and difficult to predict with confidence. It still rankles with me, by the way, that he failed to honour a bet of a box of cigars I had with him over the result of the Ashes test series! I found the Foreign Minister, Bill Hayden, more straightforward and predictable, but he was also a bit more buttoned-up than Hawke. I saw Paul Keating, the Minister of Finance, from time to time and, despite his fearsome reputation as a dirty fighter in the Australian political arena, he also knew when to turn on the charm in dealing with diplomats. I enjoyed friendly relations with the Attorney-General, Gareth Evans, and with the Minister of Defence, Kim Beazley, both of whom I had cause to meet quite often.

The Governor-General, Sir Ninian Stephen, and his wife, Val, were very friendly towards Anne and me and we enjoyed their hospitality on a number of occasions. He was born in Scotland and, after emigrating to Australia and serving in the Australian army during the Second World War, had a distinguished legal career, ending up as a High Court Judge. Subsequently, in 1992, after he had finished his Governor-General stint, he was appointed by the British Government to chair one phase of the complex political negotiations taking place in Belfast on the Northern Ireland peace process.

During official visits to the separate Australian States we were entertained, and in several cases given a bed, by the Governor at Government House. A particular favourite of ours was Sir James Plimsoll, the Governor of Tasmania. He had been a top Australian diplomat and, though a confirmed bachelor, he went to great pains to look after the comfort of his house guests and to invite interesting people for them to meet. Sir Walter Campbell in Queensland was also a generous host and we particularly enjoyed staying with him and his wife during a test match at the "Gabba" ground in Brisbane, when amongst other things he invited representatives of both teams to a memorable dinner. Another Governor I remember for less auspicious reasons. In September 1985, the Labor Premier of Victoria, John Cain, sent me a message asking me to go and see him urgently and, if possible, to make my way incognito. I was intrigued by the surrounding mystery, but had no idea what he wanted. When I arrived hot foot, he said he had a delicate request to put to me. The Governor, Rear-Admiral Sir Brian Murray, together with his wife, Jan (who incidentally had once been a nun), had been found to have abused his position by accepting financial favours in the form of free holidays and airline tickets and he, Cain, had decided that he should be dismissed. Since the Governor was formally appointed by the Queen he would like me to arrange for a message to this effect to be conveyed to her by the Foreign and Commonwealth Office. He explained that because this was a matter of State prerogative rather than a direct concern of the Australian Government as such, he preferred to act in this way rather than through Canberra and he would like me to keep it to myself. That did not stop me on my return to Canberra from telephoning Geoff Yeend, the Secretary of the Cabinet, and telling him of the tricky position I was in. He thanked me for telling him and agreed that I had no option but to do as John Cain had asked. Which I duly did and, somewhat reluctantly, the FCO went into action with the Palace. Murray departed on 3 October.

At the beginning of June 1986, we went on home leave and in the process had a most enjoyable round-the-world trip. On the outward leg we stayed in Bangkok, Kashmir, and Istanbul, where we went on a 10-day cruise along the Aegean Coast of Turkey. This was followed by two or so months at home in Bishopstone doing the rounds of family and friends and visiting Collobrières. As is customary, I also spent some time touching base with my bosses in the FCO and my correspondents in Whitehall and in the business community. On the return trip we once again broke our journey, with stops in Ottawa, Los Angeles, Tahiti and Christchurch, where we stayed with my first cousin, Michael, and his wife, Pamela. By the time we got back to Canberra in August we felt we had recharged our batteries and were ready to enter the fray again for what promised to be an intensive period of eighteen months before my retirement.

The Australians were making preparations for a large-scale, countrywide celebration of the bicentenary in January 1988 of the arrival in Port Jackson (now Sydney) of the so-called First Fleet under Captain Phillip. Although the motley complement of convicts he brought with him were not the first inhabitants, most of the population, except of course the aborigines themselves, regarded 26 January 1788 as the foundation date of Australia as it is today. Many countries were planning to mark the occasion with gifts of one kind or another and Britain would be expected to make a major contribution, as indeed Prime Minister Bob Hawke had made clear in a letter he wrote to Margaret Thatcher on 25 September 1985. Various ideas for what form it should take were mooted in London and in the High Commission, including an English rose garden in Canberra, the establishment of a British room in a museum, a specially commissioned painting, and a new bilateral scholarship scheme. None of these seemed to fill the bill and serious consideration began to be given to the idea of building a sail training ship (STS) and sailing it to Australia. Who first had the idea I am not sure – there are a number of claimants and it does not really matter now. For my part I remember discussing the practicalities of it in Canberra with Arthur Weller, a wealthy Scotsman with an Australian wife and an abiding interest in tall ships. He was convinced it could be done and his enthusiasm quickly infected me. In no time at all he picked up the ball and ran with it. He devised a scheme for designing, building and financing the ship. Somewhat to my surprise, HMG agreed to contribute £850,000, roughly half of the estimated cost, and the rest was to come from private sponsors. Arthur Weller was appointed Chairman of the Britain-Australia Bicentennial

Foreign Secretary's visit, 1987

Schooner Trust and put in charge of bringing the project to fruition. On 13 January 1986 Margaret Thatcher sent a letter communicating the decision to Bob Hawke and received an enthusiastic response two weeks later. It was agreed that the ship would be sailed out to Australia by a crew consisting of 24 young people from both countries, and both sexes, under the supervision of a small cadre of professional sailors.

The hard work then began and it was to prove anything but plain sailing. The original budget soon overran and the Brooke Marine shipyard in Lowestoft, who were building the ship, went bankrupt before the ship could be launched. Arthur Weller's energy and drive and his willingness to dig deep into his own pocket saved the day. I do not propose to go into further details here about the unfolding of events concerning the construction of the ship, since I was not closely involved in this aspect of the project. Those who would like to know more about that and indeed the complete story of *Young Endeavour*, as the brigantine came to be called, could turn to *The Life & Times of Young Endeavour* by David Iggulden (C. Pierson, Australia, 1995).

There was plenty to do at the Australian end. The High Commission had to be in almost daily contact with the Australian Bicentennial Authority and the R.A.N. over many detailed matters, including the selection of the young Australian crew members and the arrangements for the arrival of *Young Endeavour* in Australia and the handover ceremony in Sydney on the eve of Australia Day, 26 January 1988. I also had to raise public awareness of Britain's gift and to persuade British companies represented in Australia to become sponsors.

In April 1987, the Foreign Secretary, Geoffrey Howe, visited Australia as part of a round-the-world trip. When the visit was first mooted with me his idea had apparently been to stay for no more than 36 hours and he made it clear that there would be no time for sightseeing or any such frivolity. He was no doubt influenced by the fact that Margaret Thatcher had been annoyed to see a press photograph of another of her ministers on a beach in Spain, glass in hand, while he was on an official visit to the country. In the event he and his wife, Elspeth, stayed two nights with us and managed to fit in a launch trip round Sydney Harbour. He also gave a speech to the Canberra Press Club and attended, with me, the annual dawn service at the National War Memorial on Anzac Day. In a nice message he later sent me on my retirement he congratulated me, amongst other things, on my "achievement in getting a visiting Foreign Secretary out of bed earlier than any other head of mission ever has". The visit culminated with a private dinner at Westminster House for them and the Prime Minister, Bob Hawke, and his wife, Hazel, just the six of us. It was a relaxed occasion and, although no serious business was done, it provided a useful opportunity for the principals to get to know one another away from the glare of publicity.

June 1987 was an eventful month. We flew back to England in time to attend, on the 2nd of the month, the launch of *Young Endeavour* in Lowestoft by the Duchess of Kent. The 11th was the day of the General Election and despite some last minute campaign wobbles Margaret Thatcher led the Conservative Government back to power. On the 13th James and Alison Davies were married at St. George's, Hanover Square. Following the reception at the Oriental Club, Anne and I gave a dinner at the Ritz. We had hardly caught our breath when Emma, who had divorced Juan some years before, announced that she and her American boyfriend, Gary Campbell, wanted to get married at the beginning of October. At the time Gary was Bureau Chief for CNN in Paris and Emma was working for the French pay-as-you-go television channel, Canal Plus. She and Anne put their heads together straightaway to get the planning underway before we returned to Canberra.

Papal visit

With Emma in Paris and Anne across the other side of the world it was not going to be easy to get the preparations right. But they managed it somehow and Anne arrived back in England a week in advance to provide the finishing touches. I came a few days later and Gary's family flew in from New England. As Emma was a divorcée, it was a two-stage affair, Registry Office ceremony followed by blessing of the marriage in Bishopstone Church. The wedding breakfast for some 70 people was held in Manor Stables and involved, amongst other things, the removal to storage of the sitting room furniture to make space for the trestle dining tables supplied by the caterer. Despite this and many other complications the whole thing went off well. It was also our good fortune that it did not take place a couple of weeks later, when the great hurricane hit the southern parts of England (followed hard on its heels by the stock exchange crash). By then Anne and I were back in Canberra and, worried as we were at first about the safety of our families and the extent of any damage to Manor Stables (minor, as it turned out), we were soon immersed again in the hurly-burly of diplomatic activity and, in particular, the preparations for the coming arrival of *Young Endeavour* in Australia.

In the meantime, *Young Endeavour* had set sail from Cowes on 3 August and, following the same course as the First Fleet, arrived in Fremantle on 1

Young Endeavour

November, after an eventful but successful voyage. There were many people there to welcome her, including Arthur Weller and myself carrying bottles of chilled champagne. After a brief stay she set off for Sydney, with no less than fifteen ports of call en route. She also took line honours and first place in her class in the Tall Ships Race from Hobart to Sydney, where she finally arrived on 19 January 1988.

In the midst of all these jollifications we received the sad news that my brother, Peter, had died on 24 November. He had been suffering for some time from cancer of the colon, but after radiology treatment had been in remission. When we saw him at Emma's wedding he had appeared to be in quite good form. Not long after that I received a letter from him saying he was back in hospital. I still have the letter and whenever I read it I am moved to tears. He must have known the end was not far off, but in the letter he shows no self-pity and seems determined to be cheerful. Some members of the family did not find Pete an easy character to deal with, as he was quick to take, and give, offence, but he and I had always got on well. I wish I had gone to his funeral and feel guilty that I did not; with all that was going on in Canberra it would have been difficult, but not impossible. As a confirmed bachelor who did not take much exercise or cook for himself Pete had a distinctly unhealthy life-style in his latter years and he was only 62 when he died. He had a good brain, was widely

Young Endeavour's *handover, Sydney, 1988*

read, wrote well and loved opera and classical music, but frustratingly he never found quite the right outlet for his abilities and so failed to do himself justice.

On 25 January 1988, I handed over *Young Endeavour* to the Prime Minister, Bob Hawke, in a formal ceremony at Man O'War Steps by the Sydney Opera House. It was an impressive occasion, attended by the Prince and Princess of Wales, the Governor-General, the Premiers of all the Australian States and a large crowd of well-wishers, and it was carried live on national television. The next day, Bicentennial Day, *Young Endeavour* had the honour of leading the parade of Tall Ships out of Sydney Harbour. Anne and I were among those on board. It was an emotional occasion for us all, not least the young crew members who would be leaving the ship the following day and saying goodbye to their shipmates with whom they had formed close ties of friendship over the previous six months. The harbour was a truly amazing sight, packed solid with vessels of all shapes and sizes, and a fire tender had to go in front of us to clear a path with its hoses. One commentator remarked, "Bob Hawke really could walk on water today". It made a wonderful climax to our stay in

Australia and to my diplomatic career. As Geoffrey Howe put it, "not a bad note to go out on".

There were just a few days to go before my 60 birthday and with it the onset of retirement. In between times we had fitted in the usual round of farewell visits to each of the States, and a large number of dinner parties and receptions, and by the end we were feeling pretty tired. To help us wind down we left Canberra a couple of days early and went for a gentle sail on the Hawkesbury River (north of Sydney) in a hired motor cruiser, stopping off at a well-known restaurant in Berowra Waters for my birthday dinner.

Before leaving I sent the traditional farewell despatch of a departing Head of Mission to the Secretary of State. It covered not only my thoughts on leaving Australia but also on leaving the Service. One of the main points I made was that for various reasons our two countries had been drifting apart and that in due course Australia would inevitably give up the monarchy and become a republic. With the hindsight of today I would say that under Australia's present Liberal (Conservative) Government both trends have been somewhat slowed down, but not reversed.

In relation to my time in the Diplomatic Service, I said that I would be leaving with happy memories, but few regrets. I took the opportunity to get one or two gripes off my chest. I would not, for example, miss the tendency of officials to disguise individual responsibility for things that happened by taking shared decisions in committee or sheltering behind their political masters; I had, I said, always found it "much more stimulating to take decisions oneself and then to live with them". Nor would I miss the propensity of officials to tell ministers why something could not be done, instead of finding ways and means of getting it done. I concluded by saying that having avoided doing so-called "commercial work" in my diplomatic posts – something I always thought was overblown – I welcomed the prospect of being free to do the real thing in the private sector for a few years. Little did I know how those words would come back to haunt me later on.

Having recharged our batteries on the Hawkesbury River we set off on a long, circuitous journey home, featuring a guided tour of China, in the company of one other couple and lasting nine or ten days, and a visit of about the same length to see old friends in South Africa. In the process we went from the extreme cold of a Peking winter to the heat of summer in the Cape and to make things easier for ourselves we discarded some well-worn winter garments in various hotel rooms on the China leg of the journey. We noticed that they were quickly snapped up. In South Africa, amongst other things, I was smitten with tick-bite fever after an overnight, stay in a safari park. Thanks to the prompt attentions of a doctor in Johannesburg, I recovered just in time to give the address at the funeral of our old friend, Harold Hawkins. During the years of UDI (Unilateral Declaration of Independence) in Rhodesia he had been the regime's representative in South Africa and, more than that, a very useful backstairs channel for contacts between Ian Smith and HMG. Anne and I had become good friends with him and his wife, Eve, and I was glad to be able to pay my tribute to him.

Retirement

Some members of the Diplomatic Service are quite good at planning for their retirement and setting themselves up for well-paid jobs in the private sector. I was not one of them. Partly because I was more than usually busy in my last year of service and partly, I suspect, because I was too casual about it, I had made no plans at all. One interesting proposition had been put to me shortly before we left Canberra, in the form of a personal message from the Chief Clerk, Mark Russell. The Security Service (MI5) would shortly be appointing a new Director-General on Tony Duff's retirement, he said, and my name had been suggested as one possible candidate. Was I interested? I said I would be, and shortly after we returned to England I was asked to go and see the Cabinet Secretary, Robert Armstrong, to discuss it further. He made it clear that the Security Service was keen to have one of its own people take over after a succession of outsiders and would obviously be pressing hard for this, but nothing had yet been decided. He suggested that I should have a word with Tony Duff to find out more about what the job entailed, which I did. Tony confirmed that the front runner was an insider, and in the event the choice went that way.

Not long after arriving home, we embarked on a programme of major improvements to Manor Stables: notably the installation of a heated swimming pool in the small kitchen orchard (a priority for Anne's exercising), laying out a new garden, sprucing up the little courtyard and making a new doorway to give direct access to it from the kitchen, converting the old pigsty into a tool shed and workshop, replacing the garden door in the sitting room and, a little later, the installation of a burglar alarm system. This last was in response to a burglary that took place one night while we were away in London. Fortunately for us, the burglar was incompetent and, thanks to some smart work by the police, we recovered virtually all the stuff that was taken.

In June 1988 I joined the Court of the Skinners' Company, one of the "Great Twelve" livery companies, as Renter Warden. I had been a Liveryman since 1954, but because of spending much time abroad I had

Manor Stables, front

Manor Stables, back

not played an active part in the life of the company before. In 1993, having climbed up the five-year promotional ladder, I was elected Master. It was a busy year for both Anne and me and, because it meant that we spent a lot of time in London, we made good use of the Master's flat in Skinners' Hall. Reflecting later, as "Past Masters" do, on what they may or may not have achieved in their year of office, I was particularly proud of having made a couple of breaches in the male-only exclusiveness of the upper echelons of the company. Other companies had appointed women to their courts and even made them Masters, but the Skinners had not done so. One of my initiatives was to persuade the Court to invite

Mary Soames to become the first Honorary Freewoman of the Company in modern times, and to sugar the pill I arranged for a simultaneous invitation to that renowned bachelor, Cardinal Basil Hume, to be an Honorary Freeman. The climax of the Master's year in office comes at the Feast of Corpus Christi, normally in June, and, as I mentioned earlier, I persuaded our old friend, Helen Suzman, to be the Guest of Honour at the dinner and make the main speech. Mary Soames and Lynda Chalker, the Minister for Overseas Development, also sat at the top table. Only a few years before women guests still dined in a separate room and were graciously allowed to witness the goings on in the banqueting hall from the gallery above. I am pleased to say that women are now elected to the Court, something I also promoted when I later chaired the relevant committee dealing with the selection of likely candidates. I like to think that one day the Court will put a woman in the chair, but how long, O Lord, how long?

The Skinners Company is responsible, amongst other things, for the governance of Tonbridge School and, after stepping down from the chair, I did a five-year stint as Chairman of the Tonbridge School Committee, to all intents and purposes Chairman of the Governors. In view of the family connection – three brothers and one son at the school – I was pleased to be able to do this. It was a big responsibility and the job had its fair share of problems, but I was able to see for myself that overall the school was in excellent shape and could be numbered among the leading schools in the country. I broke new ground here as well in bringing outside members on to the governing body for the first time, despite the misgivings of some of my colleagues on the Court. Anne did her stuff too: in 1994/5 she organised a large group of volunteers from people connected with the school to make 150 kneelers for the new school chapel (the old one was burnt down in 1988). I am pleased to say the family connection with the school continues, with two grandsons also going there.

In the next year or two I took on a number of other part-time positions: Chairman of the British Section of the Franco-British Council, a quango financed by the FO; Governor of the English-Speaking Union; Chairman of the London branch of the South African Urban Foundation charity; Chairman of the Council/Pro-Chancellor of City University in London; Chairman of the Britain-Australia Society and the associated Cook Society. In their different ways they were all worthwhile things to do and two were modestly remunerated. Some involved travel overseas and two were kind enough to honour me for my services, Officier of the Légion d'Honneur at the hands of the French Ambassador, Jean Guéginou, and an Honorary Doctorate in Civil Law from City University. One further appointment had important consequences and is worth mentioning separately: in November 1989 I was invited to take Lord Windlesham's place as one of the five Independent Non-Executive Directors of the *Observer*. Lonrho owned the paper at the time and it is possible Tiny Rowland had something to do with my appointment, but since the whole purpose of HMG's insistence on having Independent Directors was to ensure that there was no improper interference by Tiny with the presentation of news, his would not have been a deciding voice. It did mean that our paths crossed again and it was the beginning of a painful saga involving us both.

During the nearly four years I was a member of the *Observer* Board, I do not recall Tiny ever coming to a meeting, his place in the chair being taken by one of his trusty lieutenants, Terry Robinson, Paul Spicer or Robert Dunlop. He was careful to be seen to keep his distance in public and was content to exert his influence on the output of the *Observer* through backstairs contact with the Editor, Donald Trelford. Away from the *Observer*, he began to pay some attention to me. At his invitation, we had a number of one-to-one lunches, at Claridge's or the Berkeley Hotel, during which he spoke quite frankly about his political involvement in various African countries, including Libya, as well as about certain problems he continued to have with Margaret Thatcher and her government. It was as if he was testing out ideas on me. Flattering, perhaps, but I was not at all sure why he was doing it. Thinking back on it, I wonder whether every now and then he felt the need to hear the reactions of someone outside the close-knit circle of deferential cronies with whom he had surrounded himself in the company. In the early part of 1993 he invited me, for the first time, to several board lunches at Lonrho's Cheapside head office. He did not say as much, but it seemed to me fairly obvious that he wanted me to meet Dieter Bock, whom he had just brought into the company as Joint Chief Executive, and the other directors, with a view to my joining the board at some stage. Things got to the point where I thought it necessary to write to Tiny to say that as one of the Independent Directors of the *Observer* I had to avoid any possible conflict of interest being seen to arise from what might be construed as too close an association with the newspaper's proprietors: so if he had something in mind for me in Lonrho the sooner the matter could be clarified the better. Tiny replied that he was just off to South Africa and we could talk about it when he got back. We did, but not immediately, and at the beginning of July my question was overtaken when Lonrho sold the *Observer* to the *Guardian* and I ceased to be a Director.

Lonrho

Over the years Tiny had made it clear that he had no time for Non-Executive Directors and ever since he saw off the "Straight Eight" led by Sir Basil Smallpiece, who had sought his resignation for "unacceptable behaviour" in 1973, he was resolved to do without them. At best they were, he said, "Christmas tree decorations". But Dieter Bock had different ideas. He wanted the management of Lonrho to be more transparent than in the past and more willing to conform to the corporate governance rules of the stock exchange. In future Lonrho should be seen as a normal, modern company, instead of retaining the anachronistic features of a personal fiefdom. For these reasons he was keen to bring in Non-Executive Directors from outside and in so doing to end the monopoly of Tiny's clique of "yes men" on the board. The two men argued about it, but eventually Tiny let Dieter have his way and they agreed to bring in three non-executives, two being chosen by Dieter and one by Tiny.

The two chosen by Dieter were both accountants and experienced businessmen: Peter Harper, Chairman of the Industrial Division of Hanson plc, and Stephen Walls, Chief Executive of the Albert Fisher Group plc and, before that, a Director of the Plessey Electronics Group. I was Tiny's choice and had neither of their attributes. Rather he saw me as a counterweight to the others and as someone who would take his side. It was over lunch at Claridges, with Paul Spicer and Robert Dunlop present, that he offered me the job. Not wishing to seem too eager I thanked him and said that I would like to sleep on it. I also made the point that as a Non-Executive Director I could not just do his bidding: I would have to make up my own mind about things and I might feel obliged on occasions to do or say something he did not like. I had the impression that he heard what I said, but did not listen, so I repeated the point later in the conversation. From the way he reacted to his eventual dismissal from the board of the company, it is clear he really thought he had bought my unswerving allegiance and I had betrayed him. That was his way with people and I was not the first to discover it. "Don't forget I put you on the board" was a favourite expression of his, along with the equally revealing "everyone has his price".

I understood, of course, that Lonrho would not be plain sailing and I might be out of my depth, but I was excited by the prospect and willing to learn. I also thought optimistically that I could get along with Tiny. Nor was the director's fee of £30,000 a year something to be sniffed at. What I did not realise was the full extent of the bad blood that had already made itself felt between the two Joint Chief Executives. Had I taken this in, as I perhaps should have done, I might not have gone ahead. As it was, I accepted the invitation. I was now entering a minefield and when it became public one or two old friends drew in their breath and advised me to take extreme care.

The three non-executives were appointed on 19 October 1993. We soon agreed among ourselves that we were not going to be played off one against another on the board and as far as possible would act in unison. We even signed a note to the Company Secretary delegating our vote to one of the others in the event of an absence. I am happy to say that we stuck to our pact.

Before outlining the turbulent course of events that followed over the next eighteen months, we need to understand the motivations of the two principal antagonists. Why did Tiny bring Dieter into the company and what was Dieter hoping to get out of it?

By February 1993 the company was in a bad financial way, the share price had tumbled and Tiny's personal fortune with it. Tiny was no Robert Maxwell, but after the latter's disgrace the so-called "tycoon factor" made itself felt and there was no question of an investment bank underwriting a Lonrho share issue at this time. Other options for raising money through selling assets were rejected. A remaining possibility was to bring in a private investor who could temporarily relieve the pressure. Dieter Bock, a 53-year-old German property developer, was introduced to Tiny, who went to work on him. Bock had the double attraction for Tiny of having money to invest and of understanding virtually nothing about the business, so Tiny figured he would be able to continue running it for the time being. Despite beginning to feel his age and realising he could not go on for ever, he could not bear the thought of handing over "his" company to anyone else, let alone a man who was not as steeped in the business as he was. So his natural instinct in his negotiations with Dieter would be to avoid naming a day for passing on the torch. At most he would have alluded to the possibility of his taking over from him in a year or two, without committing himself in so many words. In such situations people often come away with differing impressions of what had been agreed and it is quite possible that Dieter was misled into thinking Tiny's words meant more than they did. What is clear is that no sooner had Tiny done the financial deal than he began to harbour serious doubts about Dieter's fitness to be his successor. A less charitable explanation of his conduct is that he never intended him to be.

What was Dieter looking for? He was not temperamentally inclined to share his innermost thoughts, even with people close to him. So there is a certain amount of speculation in what follows. According to Tom Bower in *Tiny Rowland a Rebel Tycoon* (Heinemann, 1993), he let it be known that he saw Lonrho as a vehicle for expansion into Eastern Europe. He must also have concluded that Lonrho was underperforming as an unwieldy conglomerate of some 800 disparate companies and needed streamlining. With Tiny out of the way, he would be in a position to introduce the changes that he felt were necessary to modernise the company and bring him a good return on his investment. The prospect, therefore, of succeeding Tiny sooner rather than later must have weighed heavily in his thinking. Under the terms of the financial deal the two men had struck Dieter had bought almost half of Tiny's 14% stake in the company straightaway, with the right (and obligation) to buy the rest after three years or when Tiny ceased to be a Director. In addition, his underwriting of a simultaneous rights issue brought his total holding in the company to nearly 19%. So he should have felt both confident of the eventual outcome and impatient for it to materialise.

The conflicting aspirations of the two men were compounded by the decision they took to appoint themselves Joint Chief Executives, without any attempt to delineate separate spheres of responsibility. This was a recipe for constant discord, and so it proved. In January 1994 they did agree to set down in writing some ground rules for cooperation, but it soon came to be honoured in the breach. The suspicions each of them harboured about what the other was up to was such that increasingly they kept themselves apart and did not speak any more than they had to. Attempts by me and others to bridge the gap were of no avail. A private initiative taken by Dieter to negotiate a merger of Lonrho's platinum interests in South Africa with those of General Mining (Gencor) aroused deep suspicion and resentment in Tiny's mind. He was even more upset by the speed with which Dieter insisted on enforcing the retirement of Tiny's old guard on the board, Paul Spicer, Robert Dunlop and the Chairman, René Leclézio. Their departures were staggered: Spicer at the end of July, Dunlop at the end of September, and Leclézio at the end of October. At some time in this process, I am not sure exactly when, Dieter put the proposition to me that, failing the appointment of a new

Chairman by the time Leclézio left, I should take over the chair on a temporary basis until a permanent successor was appointed. Thinking that it would be a matter of months, I agreed and so did the Board, but the first announcement on 7 July merely stated that I was appointed Vice-Chairman and in that capacity would chair a Nomination Committee to recommend the appointment of a new Chairman. All too soon it became blindingly obvious that the chances of finding an outsider to take on what in the current circumstances amounted to a can of worms were virtually non-existent and I would be stuck with the job for the foreseeable future. On 6 October it was announced that I had agreed "to take the chair from 1 November, pending the appointment in due course of a new Chairman". In the event it took two and a half years for that due course to materialise.

With these changes the balance of power on the board had tilted decisively against Tiny and in order to put an end to the destabilising effects on the company of the constant feuding, which had become public knowledge, we took immediate steps to bring about his retirement too. Given the fact that he was the virtual father of the company and also had a large following of loyal shareholders ("Tiny's Army"), we were clearly embarking on a highly controversial course and for that reason were keen to offer him honourable terms, including remaining on the board until the next AGM, generous salary and other financial benefits, including use of the company's aircraft for a further year, and his appointment to the new position of Company President. Peter Harper and I were deputed to put these terms to Tiny and over a fraught lunch at the Ambassadors Club on 1 November we handed him a letter setting them out. He reacted indignantly and rejected them out of hand.

However, Tiny soon thought better of it and over the next two days intensive negotiations took place in Cheapside between him and members of his old guard and team of lawyers ensconced on one floor and me and my company colleagues and lawyers in our offices on the floor below. Because of the bad blood between the two camps, the direct exchanges took place between the lawyers. After the main terms had been agreed, there was still much haggling on various financial matters, but eventually an agreement was hammered out and announced on the afternoon of 3 November. It was not to last.

Over the Christmas holiday Anne and I paid a visit of inspection to Lonrho's hotel and sugar subsidiaries in Mauritius, an undisguised Chairman's perk. In February 1995, I went on a familiarisation visit to the platinum and coal mining companies in South Africa. By the time I returned, there were clear signs that Tiny was going back on the agreement. He was doing everything he could to discredit Dieter and had engaged, at his own expense and without consulting his fellow board members, a firm of forensic accountants to conduct extensive enquiries into Dieter's background and finances. The climax came when I returned to my office after lunch one day to find a copy of the accountants' report had been left on my desk. It was also in the offices of other directors. That was the final straw. It was quite unacceptable that he should behave in this way from the privileged position he held on the board and while he was still on the company payroll. Although he would be leaving the board anyway at the AGM in three weeks' time, in consulting board members I found general agreement that we should dismiss him at once. We did so at a board meeting, at which Tiny was present, on 2 March.

Reading again the minutes of the meeting provides a full account of the discussion, but cannot convey the drama of the occasion. Because Peter Harper's arrival was delayed I took some other agenda items first. When the moment arrived there was some preliminary skirmishing, until eventually I produced from my pocket the text of an official notice removing him as a Director forthwith. As required by company law, it was signed by three quarters of the Directors, in this case nine. When I handed it to Tiny he went white with shock. Obviously he never thought we would have the guts to do it. But he soon recovered and said in an icy tone that he would see each of the signatories in court. He also asked if the intended Presidency was to continue, to which I replied that it was no longer on offer. Nor would he continue to receive any salary or expenses. After a few more exchanges he gathered up his papers and left the room. As he did so he pointed at each signatory and repeated that he had appointed him to the board and would sue him personally. We adjourned the meeting briefly in order to put out a press statement and then went back to complete our business.

In the circumstances the AGM scheduled for three weeks later was always going to be a highly charged occasion. In the run-up journalists were licking their lips in anticipation of a punch-up between Tiny and his supporters and Dieter and me. I was warned in various articles to expect a rough ride from "Tiny's Army" and I prepared myself carefully. On the day, 24 March, some 1,700 shareholders crowded into the Barbican, facing the stage in two or three banks of seats, and waiting excitedly for the bull-fight to begin. It was an intimidating sight and I had not experienced anything like it in my diplomatic career. However, I felt better as soon as the meeting got under way. As Chairman, I had the advantage of making the opening statement and I took the opportunity to explain the background to the board's recent decision to sack Tiny (Appendix II). Since Tiny had issued a writ against the company for wrongful dismissal our lawyers advised me not to say too much for fear of prejudicing any proceedings, but I told the shareholders that I thought they had a right to know as much as possible. What I was able to say seemed to hit the right note, because they listened intently and, when I sat down, one or two complimented me from the floor on the tone and clarity of my remarks. In the discussion that followed, however, most of the questions came from the Rowland camp and were predictably hostile. I was keen to let them have their say and on a number of occasions succeeded in defusing their indignation with a light-hearted response that got the audience laughing. In the end the board won the day, but after four and a half hours of answering questions and managing what could easily have become an unruly assembly I felt absolutely drained. I would have loved a stiff drink, but unfortunately I had gone on the wagon for Lent. Afterwards I was pleased to receive a number of congratulatory letters about my performance, and the press reports were for the most part positive.

Whatever relief I may have felt at the time over winning the immediate battle, looking back on it later I think of it more as a tragedy and, perhaps, a Pyrrhic victory. For all his faults, Tiny Rowland had had a glittering career at the head of Lonrho and as a mover and shaker on the African political scene. In his time he had pulled off some spectacular commercial deals. The trouble was that the management style that had served him so well in his buccaneering days was by now distinctly out of fashion. He showed no interest in the rules of corporate governance the Stock Exchange were now applying and resented being asked by the Non-Executive Directors on the company's Audit Committee detailed questions about such things as his claims for reimbursement of the costs incurred in the upkeep of his house at Hedsor Wharf and in entertaining guests there. If only he had fully grasped the olive branch we offered him and become President of the Company, he would have retired with honour. Instead he obliged us to commit what amounted to an act of regicide and very unpleasant it was. He later wrote me an angry letter accusing me amongst other things of being a "Quisling". Not perhaps the most appropriate name for a one-time member of the Hitler Youth to choose. "Brutus" I might have understood – and Tiny would not have minded being equated with Caesar, I feel sure.

My next two years in the chair were something of an anti-climax, but I was kept busy in my office three times a week on average, not to mention frequent telephone and fax calls at weekends. I presided over two more AGMs and three EGMs (Extraordinary General Meetings), less controversial, certainly, than the earlier rowdy occasion but still demanding my close attention. I also did three further overseas visits for the company. The first, in May 1995, was to Kenya, where I called on President Arap Moi, Zambia, where I did the same with President Chiluba, and Zimbabwe, where I met amongst others the influential Minister of Justice, Emmerson Mnangagwa. The next one, in January 1996, was a bit of a doddle: together with Anne I did a "chairman's tour of inspection" of two Lonrho-associated hotels in Acapulco and Barbados. Lastly, in May 1996, I attended a meeting of the Southern African Economic Summit in Cape Town organised by the Davos World Economic Forum. All things considered I reckon I earned my annual remuneration of £120,000.

Now that Tiny had gone and the old order with him, it was easier to get things agreed, including a decision to move the office from Cheapside into a more suitable building in Grosvenor Place. Tiny kept up his attacks on the board in various missives to shareholders and in menacing letters from his solicitors, but it was all done at arm's length. Moreover we knew that his threats to see us in court were little more than bravado, because he would never have submitted himself to cross-examination in the witness box. Lawyers in London would have queued up for the chance to put him through it. Nevertheless, Tiny's antics, combined it has to be said with Dieter's inability, or unwillingness, to confide in other people, had the effect of making the Chairman's job look unattractive to potential aspirants and it soon became clear that I would not be leaving yet.

For some time a major problem for the company had been its high level of indebtedness. Tiny had set his face against selling assets he had acquired, but it was now easier to do so and two of the EGMs mentioned above paved the way for the sale of the Metropole chain of hotels. Some smaller companies were also sold and in order to improve profitability the idea of demerging the mining interests and the various other African operations began to take shape.

In March 1996, Dieter dropped a bombshell. He decided to sell the extra 5.9% shareholding in Lonrho he had acquired from Tiny, under their put and call option agreement, to the Anglo-American Corporation. At the same time he entered into an agreement giving Anglo the right of first refusal over his remaining 18.5% during the next eighteen months. Following that, he had discussions with Anglo about converting this right into a put and call option. At the time this was coming to a head, Anne and I were staying with Emma and Gary in Andover, Massachusetts, and after several telephone exchanges with Dieter we decided to convene a special meeting of the board on the morning of 11 April to discuss it. I caught an overnight flight from Boston and, after a shower and shave at Heathrow, arrived in time to start the meeting at 10am. We had a full discussion of the implications of the proposed change for the company, in particular Anglo's representation on the board, but agreed that it was up to Dieter to decide whether to proceed in this way. That was that, so we thought, and I flew back to Boston the same day.

It was by no means the end of the story. Towards the end of October Dieter told me that he was thinking of exercising his option to sell his remaining shares to Anglo. In a long hand-written letter I sent him on 24 October I explained in unambiguous terms why he should not do it, but he had already made up his mind and an announcement was made a few days later, on the 29th. It stated, amongst other things, that Dieter would hand over to Nick Morrell as Chief Executive and become a Non-Executive Director. He bailed out at a generous premium over the current share price, and in so doing predictably earned the opprobrium of ordinary shareholders. One can only suppose that he had been planning his move for some time, but true to form he did not let on to anybody. A clever man, but not someone I could warm to or even get to know.

A few months earlier I had stepped up the pressure, in communication with Dieter and my fellow non-executives, for finding and appointing a new Chairman. I now set about it in earnest in collaboration with Nick Morrell. We soon agreed that Sir John Craven, Chairman of Deutsche Morgan Grenfell, who as our merchant banker already knew the company well, would be the best man for the job, if we could persuade him to take it on. So we went to see him together and put the proposition to him. Understandably he asked for clarification on a variety of questions, but eventually, and much to my relief, he agreed. He took over from me at the AGM on 26 March. Dieter retired from the board and I stayed on as a Non-Executive Director for a further year, when having reached the age of 70, I was obliged by company rules to retire.

Would I have joined Lonrho in the first place had I been able to foresee what was in store for me? May be not, but looking back on it after the event I can say that I would not have wanted to miss the experience. It certainly represented an invigorating challenge that kept me on my toes at a time of life when I might have been tempted to take things easy. It was not exactly the kind of commercial activity I had been anticipating in my farewell missive on leaving the Diplomatic Service, but it did give me an insight into the ways of a quite different world from the one in which I had spent most of my life.

Senior Citizen

On leaving the Diplomatic Service at the age of 60, I had said to myself that the next ten years would be the time to try my hand at other things, and after that I would do my own things in my own time. It could never work out in quite that clear-cut way, but certainly by the time I reached the age of 70 I found I was slowing down and taking longer to do things. I also felt less inclined to go on travelling up to London three days a week. This was my touchstone. I am not a Londoner and have always thought of it as my workplace; and commuting by train had become an increasingly onerous chore. So had putting on a coat and tie. It came as a great relief no longer to have to do these things regularly.

One thing we did miss was our canal boat, *Rosella*. We had bought our first narrowboat in 1990 and had taken to canal touring like ducks to water. Many of the best navigable canals are in the Midlands and we explored many of them, seeing in the process lovely parts of the country we hardly knew existed. Twice we journeyed from our base at Braunston, near Daventry, to London and back on the Grand Union Canal and on one of those occasions we had the great thrill, for a narrowboater, of sailing along the Thames through the centre of London. In a reversal of the normal roles, Anne was generally the driver – and a good one too – and I was the deckhand who attended to the locks. She chatted up her macho male counterparts while waiting in the locks, while I did the same with their womenfolk, who were normally assigned the heavy work of opening the gates. We eventually had a brand new 60-foot boat built which was comfort itself and we might have continued with it (no nautical genders on the canals!) for some time. Sadly, however, the years caught up with us and we became less agile at jumping on and off and performing other necessary contortions. So reluctantly we sold *Rosella* and, although we then bought a share in a small Dutch-type barge based at Auxerre on the River Yonne in France, we gave that up too after a couple of years. Our inland boating days were over.

I must also mention our dogs, because they too gave us a lot of pleasure. First of all our much-travelled Cairn terrier, Bonnie. As I have already

Rosella II *(and Zach)*

mentioned, we acquired her as a puppy shortly after we arrived in South Africa in 1979. She was a lovely little dog and had had to put up with no less than fourteen months of quarantine in all by the time we returned from Australia. She died at the ripe old age of fifteen in 1994 and after a year's gap we acquired a Manchester Terrier, whom we named Zach. Not a well-known breed, but a handsome dog looking like a small Doberman (the breeds are related). I took him to one or two training classes, but I can't say he learnt very much, and he remained unreliable about running off when the urge took him. With her short legs, Bonnie had found getting about on the narrowboat not to her liking. Zach had longer legs and took to it better, although he enjoyed it most when I took him ashore to walk to the next lock. I was very fond of him and was upset at having to find a new home for him when we moved from our house in Bishopstone to a flat in Eastbourne. We hear news of him from his present owners every year at Christmas and he is now 12 years old.

On 31 July 1999, Alice was married. I should of course have mentioned this before the dogs, but I hope she will understand that the dogs came first, chronologically speaking. Like her, the bridegroom, Oliver ("Ollie") Ross, is a doctor. He is also a very nice chap. It was just about the hottest day of the year and, after the ceremony in Lewes Registry Office, there was a reception in a marquee on our lawn at Manor Stables. It was sweltering and as the afternoon wore on and we drank more champagne many of us began to look a little bedraggled, if that is the right word. All in all, it was a very happy occasion. Ollie and Alice now live in Winchester with five children (four daughters and a son, in that order). Ollie is a

Anne's 70th party

consultant anaesthetist at Southampton General Hospital and Alice is a part-time paediatric consultant there. Ollie ran in this year's London marathon and in so doing raised some £1,800 for a children's' hospice in Winchester; he also did it in the very creditable time of 4 hours 11 minutes.

Our move from Manor Stables in 2000 was a great wrench. We loved the house, it had something really special about it and we always felt glad to return to it after being away. We were its first two-legged inhabitants and had put a lot of ourselves into it. We also felt much attached to Bishopstone. We had thought vaguely about making a move before and had even had the house valued, but had not pursued the idea. But, as in the case of our narrowboat, with the passage of time physical things like mowing a rather uneven and difficult lawn and looking after the swimming pool began to become a bit of a drag. We also came to the conclusion that the longer we left it the more difficult it would be for us to contemplate a move. So we bit the bullet and put Manor Stables on the market. In no time at all our good friends, Patrick and Jane Thomas, who lived in Bishopstone House, made us a good offer and we had to set about finding a flat quickly. Having found nothing to our liking in Seaford, we eventually settled on our present penthouse flat on the top of a purpose-built block in the old town part of Eastbourne. I will not go into the details of the move itself, because everyone knows what is involved, except to say that in the process of "downsizing" it was not easy to find a home for all our belongings. Having to dump a large number of books was particularly upsetting. That apart, we soon got used to flat life. Naturally Anne missed the garden very much and busied herself putting pots of plants on our balcony. As for me, I took some time to get used to not having Zach around.

If one purpose of moving to a flat had been to simplify our lives, it did not take us long to complicate it again. It had been in our minds to acquire a flat in France as well with the residual proceeds of the sale of Manor Stables, and in February 2001 we found what we wanted in Mandelieu-La-Napoule, near Cannes. A two-bedroom flat on a private estate, with a nice terrace overlooking an inland golf course nearby, and the Esterel range of hills in the distance, together with the chance to buy the furniture and fittings at a very reasonable price. So now we have two homes and we can move easily between the two, either by air from Gatwick to Nice or by car and the Channel Tunnel. We also keep a car in Mandelieu. We regard our Eastbourne flat as our base and the one in France as our home from home. How long we will keep it up I am not sure. We may sell it sooner rather than later and use the proceeds to do some more travelling, if the mood takes us and we remain fit enough to enjoy it. Then again we may not. Long-distance journeys, for example to Australia, have lost their appeal, but there are plenty of attractive places in this country and elsewhere in Europe we have not seen and would like to visit.

Latter-Day Free-Thinker

The world of today has changed out of all recognition from the one I grew up in. For a start, seventy years ago the map of the world in my atlas was still covered in red and it was said that the sun never set on the British Empire. The Empire is gone and Britain no longer rules the waves. We are a second-rank, overcrowded, increasingly multicultural country, on the fringe of continental Europe, but still retaining some influence on what goes on in the wider world. As Douglas Hurd, then Foreign Secretary, once said, we manage to punch above our weight. Britain's industrial and economic decline, in comparison with the United States and Germany, had begun long before I was born, but I do not remember hearing about that during my school days. What I was led to believe was that the label "Made in Britain" was a byword for manufacturing excellence throughout the world. Our manufacturing industry has continued to decline in recent years and it is sometimes said that we are on the way to becoming a "post-industrial society". I am not altogether sure what that means, but I can only assume the increasing pace of globalisation and the advent of new industrial powers such as China and India will hasten the process.

A good summary of the numerous changes that have occurred in our life-styles and attitudes during these years is contained in the following note entitled "We are Survivors – For those born before 1940", which somebody, I do not remember who, sent me.

We were born before television, penicillin, polio shots, frozen foods, Xerox, plastic, contact lenses, videos, freebies and the Pill. We were before radar, credit cards, split atoms, laser beams, and ballpoint pens; before dish-washers, tumble-dryers, electric blankets, air conditioners, drip-dry clothes, and before man walked on the moon.

We got married first and then lived together (how quaint can you be?). We thought fast food was what you ate in Lent. A "Big Mac" was an oversized raincoat and "crumpet" you had for tea. We existed before house-husbands, computer dating, dual careers and at a time when a "meaningful relationship" meant getting along with cousins, and "sheltered accommodation" was where you waited for a bus.

We were before day care centres, group homes and disposable nappies. We never heard of FM radio, tape decks, electric typewriters, artificial hearts, word processors, yoghurt and young men wearing earrings. For us "time-sharing" meant togetherness, a "chip" was a piece of wood or fried potato, "hardware" meant nuts and bolts, and "software" wasn't a word.

Before 1940 "made in Japan" meant junk, the term "making out" referred to how you did in your exams, "stud" was something that fastened a collar to the shirt and "going all the way" meant staying on a double-decker to the bus, or tram, depot. Pizzas, McDonald and instant coffee were unheard of. In our day cigarette smoking was fashionable, "grass" was mown, "coke" was kept in the coal shed, a "joint" was a piece of meat you had on Sundays and "pot" was something you cooked in. "Rock music" was a grandmother's lullaby, "Eldorado" was an ice cream, a "gay person" was the life and soul of the party and nothing more, while "aids" just meant beauty treatment or help for someone in trouble.

We who were born before 1940 must be a hardy bunch when you think of the way in which the world has changed and the adjustments we have had to make. No wonder we are so confused and there is a generation gap today .... BUT by the grace of God, we have survived. What a hardy lot we are!

Against this background, I have been re-examining the received wisdom I grew up with to see how it has withstood the test of time. This has led me, step by step, into thinking what for my parents would have been unthinkable thoughts. My short term memory seems to be deteriorating fast, and I find it very frustrating. My longer-term memory is erratic and, no doubt selective. I can still recall, quite vividly, certain things that occurred when I was young and I have a fairly good general picture in my mind of the world I grew up in.

All too many people of my age are apt to bemoan the passing of the "good old days" when, they say, things were simpler and more ordered, people went to church, and family life was strong, in contrast to the one-parent families of today, empty churches, drug-taking, binge-drinking, violence in our streets and permissive behaviour generally. Such cosy nostalgia sometimes strikes a chord with me, but when I think about it more deeply I conclude that most of our population live in a more compassionate society than their forebears of, say, 100 years ago and are better off in almost every way. Edwardian England was fine for the prosperous few, but it was a more class-ridden society than today and for many people life was anything but genteel or free of drunkenness and disorderly behaviour. The gap between rich and poor was wide and not easily bridged.

In looking to the past the unwary can fall into another trap, of the opposite kind: unlike professional historians, we risk taking things out of context. It is, for example, all too easy for people who have never had the misfortune to experience what total war means to be unfairly critical of the terrible carnage their forebears took part in during the Second World War. I could cite a number of examples to explain what I mean. Suffice it to mention the tendency to condemn as war crimes the saturation bombing by the RAF and USAAF of Dresden and Cologne and the consequent killing of many thousands of "innocent" German civilians. To which I vigorously respond that the elemental reaction of most British people at the time was that, after what the Germans had done earlier to London and Coventry, they had it coming to them. War is a truly horrible aberration, but it ill behoves those who have been spared any first-hand knowledge of its effects for more than sixty years to be judgemental about people whose behaviour was conditioned by the world in which they lived, and died. *O tempora, O mores!* On a more positive note, I might add that the Germans themselves learnt a lesson they have never forgotten. Up to that time they had fought their wars on the territories of other countries and now experienced for the first time just how destructive it could be in their own homeland. Which goes some way to explain the anti-militarist provisions embedded in the Federal Republic's constitution today.

I am not naturally an introspective type and yet as I approach the last stage of my life I do find myself wondering what I have learnt from my experiences and how my attitudes towards many things have changed over the years. Having been born into a middle-class family of conventional outlook and modest means and subsequently educated in old-style boarding schools I grew up with an ingrained desire to conform to the traditional attitudes of my peers and the mores of the time. The English were the salt of the earth and I believed in king and country, "right or wrong". (Like most people, I stood rigidly to attention whenever the National Anthem was played, as it frequently was.) We were also snobs: when my mother said someone was not "out of the top drawer" I knew what she meant. "Common" people were to be avoided in case I caught something nasty from them, including the way they spoke. Black people – or "coolies" as both my parents called them from their time in India – were a lower order altogether, but I hardly saw any myself. It was taken for granted that I was a practising member of the Church of England and it was not uncommon to hear people refer to "dirty Jews". Indeed I once overstepped the mark myself at my prep school, when the boy to whom I had addressed the remark challenged me to a fight and gave me a beating I never forgot. It also went without saying that in political terms we were natural Conservatives, though not actively so; my father read the *Daily Telegraph* and my mother the *Daily Mail*.

In brief, I had a sheltered upbringing and grew up with little idea how the other half lived and no great desire to find out. The first time I had any prolonged exposure to the masses was during my National Service, when I was in my early twenties, and quite an eye-opener it was too. The experience both broadened and accelerated my education. During my subsequent career in the Diplomatic Service I obviously had to conform to certain rules of behaviour and toe the official line on policy matters. But the chance to live in a number of different foreign countries also opened my eyes to their different ways of doing things and permitted me to compare them with what we do in this country. Gradually I began to think heretical thoughts on a number of fundamental matters. In the interests of brevity, I will outline them here in a series of sweeping generalisations.

First, it struck me that countries where there were more egalitarian, less class-ridden societies were by and large more successful than ours in encouraging their young men and women to rise to the top and in enabling them to get there. People were more upwardly mobile and their economies did better than ours. As a whole they were better educated. Our best schools and universities were among the best in the world, but the fact that we virtually had two separate school streams, one more successful than the other in advancing people to the top, put us at a disadvantage. It was, and is, much easier to state this problem than to see a way of changing it, without throwing the educational baby out with the bath water. Perhaps a gradual way of bringing the two systems closer together which involves levelling up rather than down can be found. It will be difficult and require the exercise of much political will, and there's the rub.

I have also come to see the monarchy as another part of our problem, since it is at the apex of the pyramid of privilege that remains the basis of the class system. I cannot help thinking we would be better off without it. This is shocking, and some might say, treasonable thinking and I have kept it more or less to myself for a long time. Even now only a very few people know. Too many members of my family and friends would have been horrified if I had paraded myself as a republican. For the record Anne does not share my view. I feel nothing but admiration for the Queen herself and despite their antics I am not against the royal family per se; it is the institution of the monarchy that I have in my sights. I remember reading about the Civil War as a boy and instinctively sympathising with the Roundheads. So perhaps it was ordained that I would become a republican. One trouble about going down this road is that when I look around at republican countries, many of those who become Heads of State seem to be virtual nonentities. However, that is not, I believe, inherent in the republican ideal; it depends to a large extent on which system is adopted for choosing the President, direct or indirect election.

Despite going to church regularly in recent times, my Christian faith, never profound, has become shallower. As I sit in the pew and join in the service, I realise that I do so out of habit and because the parish church is the main focus of the community to which I belong. There has also been the drawing power of the recently retired vicar, an ebullient, all-embracing character whose personal magnetism is almost tangible. It is not the same without him. I envy others in the congregation who have preserved their faith intact. For myself, I find that I can no longer suppress increasing doubts about the virgin birth, the resurrection and an "after life" in paradise, all central tenets of the Christian faith. I must have known this for some time, but refused to admit it to myself before. As I move towards the closing stages of my life, I do not want to pretend any more. Now when I am told that those who die are going to their eternal rest, I take that to mean, in less poetic terms, that we enter a permanent state of unconsciousness. I may, of course, "live on" in the consciousness of those who come after me and what I am writing now may even encourage that process. But that is all. I willingly accept that Jesus Christ was a saintly man who preached the message of peace on earth and goodwill towards men and was eventually crucified. Moreover, I have no doubt that in the world of today practising Christians represent a force for good, even though at times the blinkered attitude of church institutions towards contemporary problems has hindered, rather than helped, the search for solutions. I could cite various examples I came across during my career to support that last remark, but to avoid any accusation of being selective I will refrain from doing so.

There has recently been much debate about the origins of the universe and of mankind, with the so-called creationists in one camp and Darwinian evolutionists in the other. Much of it has passed me by; but my own, perhaps simplistic, view is that it defies all reason to suppose that the creation of the universe, the order of the natural world and the astonishing complexity of the human brain all occurred haphazardly. Evolution cannot supply a complete answer. How, then, did it come about if not by some divine intervention? In plain language, do I not believe in god? Yes, I do, but with a small "g". What do I mean by that? That is a question too far and I cannot give a satisfactory answer.

As for politics, for some time I have not voted Conservative, mainly because of the party's anti-European stance, which goes against one of my core beliefs, but also because I am naturally drawn to the middle ground of politics at present occupied by New Labour. I say at present because, as I write, after nine years of the current government the political tide is turning. Tony Blair and his ministers are no longer trusted to come good on their promises and are said to be running out of steam. I came across the following pertinent words in the Preface to the *Book of Common Prayer* concerning the service of the church: "There was never anything by the wit of man so well devised, or so sure established, which in continuance of time hath not been corrupted". In a nutshell. I was, in any case, a firm opponent of the war in Iraq both as a matter of principle and because it put us at odds with our main EU partners. In my view Blair made a terrible mistake by not refusing to send British troops to fight alongside the Americans, as Harold Wilson had once done over Vietnam. All the more so, as we now know that George Bush had told him that he would understand if he had to do so because of his difficult position in the House of Commons. Might such a refusal even have given Bush a pause for further thought about going it alone?

Our so-called "special relationship" with the United States has bedevilled successive British governments since the war. In 1972, Dean Acheson, a former American Secretary of State, said that Britain had lost an empire and had not yet found a role. His words remain true today. For too long we have tried to hedge our bets and have the best of all worlds. On the one hand, that has meant avoiding committing ourselves to joining with our continental neighbours in transforming Europe into a political force to be reckoned with in the modern world. Perhaps we have been influenced in this, consciously or unconsciously, by a long history of having to resist a series of threats from combinations of European powers. Whatever the reason, we have clung instead to the chimera of acting as a bridge between the United States and Europe, ignoring the fact that, given the evident disequilibrium between our two countries and the self-imposed limitation of our present influence in the EU, such a bridge could not be equally poised between each side of the Atlantic or act as a channel of communication with Europe. There is no getting away from the basic truth that we cannot avoid making a choice, unless of course we are content to be little Englanders, as some would have us be. I myself have long felt we should take the plunge and decide that our future lies in our being a fully committed member of the EU, instead of continuing to regard it as a threat to our way of life and to all that we hold dear. As in the case of the monarchy, my views on this are very much minority ones today and I realise I am swimming against the current. I fear I will not live to see any significant change in public opinion on either issue.

I have always regarded myself as more of a doer than a thinker and I like to get on with things. I am naturally impatient in both senses of the word, that is to say I am often in too much of a hurry and sometimes take unkindly to criticism, particularly when people impart it from the sidelines, that is to say they do not have to accept the responsibility for taking any action themselves. Whichever party was in office during my time in the FO, I used to get fed up with the constant attacks of the political opposition. I realised they were only doing their job in the adversarial style that is part of our parliamentary tradition (as well as being an intrinsic feature of our system of administering justice in the law courts). But I disliked the negativity, the blinkered cynicism and hypocrisy of it all, and the knee-jerk determination to question the cost, and overlook the value, of anything the government did, whilst claiming, typically, that the money would be better spent on building more hospitals. Whether such a highly confrontational and misleading approach serves our country well in the modern world is open to question.

The same sort of thing may be said of our media. We have some of the best and some of the worst newspapers in the world. Good or bad, they all like to present themselves as the bastion of our society and the defenders of our liberty. They are in fact commercial businesses competing with one another for our patronage and for all their high-minded aspirations they are capable of stooping very low in order to outdo one another with dirty tricks and sensational scoops. The tabloids are the worst offenders and the hyperbole that is the stock in trade of their news presentation all too often encourages a mood of near hysteria among their readers that is not justified by the facts. At the same time none of our newspapers, or for that matter the electronic media, can resist the temptation to create news, as well as reporting it. Of course, the press plays an important role in a democratic society like ours and does more good than harm. At times, however, I am tempted to agree with the jaundiced view of Tom Stoppard's character, Ruth, when she says, "I am with you on the free press, it's the newspapers I can't stand". Many correspondents are highly professional and do a very good job, I know. It is at the editorial level where I am inclined to think conscious distortion, or "sexing up", of the facts and the seamless insertion of comment take place. I do not condone the "spinning" by politicians, especially the current Labour Government, of the information they see fit to impart to us, but it is a bit rich when members of the fourth estate criticise others for doing what they themselves do every day. I also get fed up with their tendency to trivialise the reporting of what is going on in the world by concentrating more on the personalities of people in the public eye than the merits of the issues in which they are involved. They can be swift to condemn and, in pursuit of their quarry, sometimes assume the role of a political lynch mob. Strong words may be, but not, I believe, unfair. They would no doubt reply that they are only giving their readers what they want. All right, I concede that they are the best judges of how to sell their wares, but I cannot help feeling they are also pandering to our worst instincts and should set their sights higher. Perhaps I am more old-fashioned than I like to admit, but I am glad to have got it off my chest.

Over and Out

At the time of writing both Anne and I continue to enjoy reasonably good health, although Anne, in particular, has lost some mobility in recent years and wears a metal calliper on her left leg. She still paints from time to time and her watercolour Christmas cards are much admired. For my part, I am still enjoying playing golf regularly, despite an artificial hip. We go to Glyndebourne as and when we can afford it and are lucky enough to get seats, though these are becoming exorbitantly expensive.

My two sisters and I are the remaining members of the family into which I was born. Betty is 93 and Pam 88. Both are widows: Betty's husband, Phil, died in 1985 and Pam's husband, Tudor, in 2005. My brother, Patrick, died in 1998 at the age of 83, his wife, Ailsa, having died in 1987. The deaths of my brothers, Roly and Peter, have been mentioned earlier. I am happy to say numerous nephews, nieces and cousins are still going strong. We are a big tribe.

Writing one's memoirs is an exercise in dredging up things from the past, as accurately as one can with the material to hand. In living my life, however, I have preferred not to dwell on the past and, as far as I can, to look to the future. This has sometimes meant striking a balance between hoping for the best and preparing for the worst. In practice, I am lucky enough to have had much more of one than the other. My bedrock has been a happy marriage and a family of which any man would be proud. Without Anne and our four children my life would not have been half as rewarding and it is a great comfort to think that we have twelve grandchildren to keep the family going. They are the sixth generation to figure in this chronicle and there should be many more to follow. I hope someone else will write about them.

Appendix I (see page 54)

22B, Balmoral Park,
Stevens Road,
Singapore 10

Friday evening: 10/5/57

[My Dearest Betty and Jack]

I would have given anything not to have had to send you that terrible telegram this morning. I know what an awful shock it must have been. I only hope I put things in the right way because it was not easy to convey the proper impression. However your telegram has just this moment arrived and we should have talked on the telephone by the time you get this. In the circumstances I think the best thing is for me to leave the "problems" aside for the moment and go right ahead and try and describe to you Annie's condition at the moment.

She has been in bed since Tuesday morning, when she succumbed to what seemed quite obviously flu. There is something of a flu epidemic here at the moment and she had all the usual symptoms: headache, temperature, aches and pains and a slight sick feeling; also she was rather depressed. I consulted a doctor, who told me to keep her in bed and to give her Disprin every two hours or so, which we did (as I will explain later, this was a point very much in Annie's favour when paralysis set in). She had a wretched night on Tuesday, tossing and turning without sleep, so I got the doctor to see her next morning. He confirmed flu (and you must remember that until paralysis starts the symptoms of flu and polio are to all intents and purposes identical) and gave her some pills to help her sleep during that day. By Wednesday evening the aches and pains had pretty well gone except for her legs, and apart from the fact that her temperature was still up and she felt sick every now and then, she seemed to be better and more cheerful. She had a reasonable night, but it was soon clear that she was very weak: I had to help her out of bed to the bathroom and in doing so we discovered that she could not support herself at all; her legs just gave way under her, particularly the left one. I got the doctor at once and he immediately diagnosed "suspected poliomyelitis" and we took her off to B.M.H in an ambulance. I might add here that Annie was told straightaway what it was (she told me she had guessed already) and she reacted wonderfully, in complete control of herself. I was terribly proud of her and I know you would have been.

Polio was confirmed that same afternoon in the hospital (Thursday). Both legs were paralysed, the left worse than the right but neither totally – that is, she retained and, according to the latest information, still retains some movement of the muscles (which is a good omen for her recovery if it gets no worse) – and her right arm is slightly affected to the extent that she finds it difficult to raise it from the shoulder. The doctor in charge also told me that there might be some stiffening of the lower part of her trunk, but it was difficult to confirm that at present as it would mean moving her about for the necessary examination, which at the present stage is something they want to avoid. There has been no extension of this paralysis so far, which is another good sign since in most cases the paralysis has normally done ist worst after about 24 hours. On the other hand her temperature is still up (about 102) and until it goes down the paralysis is still active, that is it can still extend and do damage. So every hour without extension at this stage is an hour gained and there is little one can do but hope and pray.

She is in isolation, in a room of her own, and has her own nurse, full-time. This is not so much because her case is considered grave – it is **not** – but because the Acting Commissioner-General, Angus MacKintosh, got the Army Chief of Staff here to take a personal interest in Annie's case and, as a result, she is getting V.I.P. treatment. The head army physician is looking after her with another more junior doctor, and at my request they called in Professor Gordon Ransome, who is Professor of Medicine at the University here and has good experience of treating polio, to give a second opinion. He has assured me that Annie is in the best of hands and that B.M.H. has all the necessary equipment (such as an iron-lung, which I pray will not be necessary) and know-how to deal with polio. He also said that when the time came for treatment to remedy the paralysis (this cannot start for about a week or at least until the fever has gone and the paralysis is no longer active) we might consider moving her to another hospital, the Middleton Hospital, where they have special experience of remedial therapy for polio. But that is looking ahead at the moment and I'm thinking much more of the immediate present at the moment, in fact living it hour by hour, constantly on the end of a telephone.

Annie is naturally not allowed any visitors at the moment, particularly as there is still a risk of infection in the early stages. It is heart breaking not to be able to see her, but for Emma's sake I have been advised to keep away. However, I was allowed to see her this morning for a short while and was delighted to find her so full of spirit. Of course it is difficult to know whether she was putting on an act – I certainly was for I felt anything but cheerful – but the doctors all say she is standing up to it remarkably well. And they very sensibly are not trying to hide things from her; as far as I can gather they explain to her what is happening quite naturally.

One important thing I forgot to mention earlier on. The doctors say that the polio should not affect the babe in any way. On the other hand the fact that Annie is pregnant may possibly aggravate the polio a little. One other thing: I mentioned earlier on that the fact that Annie had been resting in bed since the onset of the fever on Tuesday was a point in her favour. The thing is that at this stage even in hospital all that can be done for her is to try to bring her temperature down as soon as possible; that she has been doing that right from the start, instead of struggling up out of her bed to go shopping or something, is very much to the good, because activity only stimulates the polio.

Finally, all that the doctors will say at the moment – and I take it as a good sign that they say so much – is that if Annie gets no worse than she is now there should be few, if any, lasting after-effects, that is with physiotherapy and hard work by Annie she should lose the paralysis completely or practically so. As one of the doctors put it, "I have seen cases like her walking around after a couple of months". It would be foolish to count on this when the crisis is not yet over, but it does offer some encouragement.

As regards other things, numerous less immediate questions (which cannot be decided now until we know more definitely what we are up against) crop up; for example we should consider whether or not it would be wise to send Annie home to you (in an RAF ambulance aircraft), with E.J. and me following, and, if so, when. Or, on the other hand, if it would be wise to ask you to come out, as you so kindly suggested in your cable. Or if it is thought best to leave Annie here, where she would be best off? I am also wondering what to do about E.J. I think the best thing is for her to stay with me for the next fortnight, until the risk (apparently not great) of infection is over, as she is not meant to mix with other children. The office have also told me to stay away for the time being, so I can easily look after her, and am in fact delighted to do so because she is quite a handful and she gives me something to think about. I need hardly add that she is also very good company. Tan, our boy, and the new Amah, Ai Lean, are doing their parts magnificently, which is a great help. And numerous friends are rallying round with offers of all sorts of help, which I am temporarily refusing while Emma and I are infectioun risks. As I say, the risk is apparently quite small, but we cannot be too careful. So there is no need to worry on that score – we will manage perfectly well.

I have been advised to have Emma and me vaccinated with the polio serum after two or three months (it might be risky before that apparently). The original intention when we got back here was to have her done when she was two, which was the age recommended by the army doctors, so we have not had it done before. Annie would not have been done anyway while she was pregnant, so we need not have heart-searchings about that, thank God.

Well, dear Betty and Jack, there it is. Please don't get too distressed. God knows it's worrying, terribly so, but there are some hopeful signs. And I don't need to tell you that if there is anything that can be done for Annie, I will see to it that it is done. I am sorry if this letter is not always as lucid as it might be, but I am finding it hard to collect my thoughts and am a little short of sleep. It seems a century since yesterday morning.

All our love to you and the family – I will try to write again soon.

Johnnie

Appendix II (see page 173)

It is normal at this stage for the Chairman to comment on the year's results before inviting questions from the floor and I certainly do not wish to miss this opportunity of having a first-hand account of the company's achievements since we last met and an explanation of what we hope to achieve in future. You will be hearing from our Chief Executive, therefore, about our progress in a moment.

First, I think I must say something about the Board's decision on 2 March to put an immediate end to Mr Rowland's tenure of office. No doubt there will be many questions about this and I will do my best to see to it that a fair cross-section of shareholders get a hearing for their views. For this to be possible I will need your cooperation.

Ladies and Gentlemen, two years ago I sat as a guest at the AGM up there in the body of the auditorium and heard my predecessor introduce Dieter Bock with the words "This is the man we have all been waiting for". The inference I as an outsider drew from that remark and from other things that were said at the time was that this was the beginning of a process of transition in the direction of Lonrho's affairs and that over a period preparations would be made for Tiny Rowland to hand over the helm to Dieter Bock.

At the time I joined the Board as a Non-Executive Director seven months later, in October 1993, it was clear that the relationship between the two "Indivisible" Joint Chief Executives was anything but smooth. Amongst other things, some dissension had arisen over the appointment of Non-Executive Directors. My coming on to the Board was apparently a condition that Mr Rowland made for agreeing to have the two other appointees, Peter Harper and Stephen Walls. I might add in passing that there was a tendency in the press to typecast us as being in one or other of the Rowland or Bock "camps" so-called. As it was, the three of us worked closely together as independent directors in line with the Cadbury Code of corporate governance.

We have had to work very hard. We had no option. Over the following twelve months or so we and the Board as a whole became embroiled in a series of contretemps. What should have been a smooth transition period became more like an obstacle course. I do not intend to rake over the particular issues or to allocate blame for the arguments. Some of them were about matters that were relatively unimportant in themselves. But the cumulative effect of what in my letter of 8 March to shareholders I referred to as these "distracting wrangles" was twofold: inside the company, mainly but not exclusively at Board level, we found it difficult to concentrate on the business of doing business and planning for the future; outside, in the City and in the press, we were seen as a house divided.

Mr Rowland and Mr Bock made one notable attempt in January last year to patch up their differences and signed a memorandum to that end. I can only say that its effects wore off fairly quickly and despite other brief moments of reconciliation their differences continued. So much so that in November the Board came to the conclusion that the Joint Chief Executives formula was not workable and that for the good of the company the transition period could not be allowed to run on much longer. Hence the agreement with Mr Rowland that he should cease to be Chief Executive at the end of December last, retire from the Board at this AGM and become President.

As I mentioned in my letter to shareholders, for some time after that I was still hoping that we could move forward with Mr Rowland in a new and more constructive relationship, with him as our President. Certainly that was what the rest of the Board wanted. Unfortunately it was not to be.

Which brings me to the events of three weeks ago. Since Mr Rowland has issued a writ against the company for wrongful dismissal and in due course we shall be making our defence, I have been advised by the company's solicitors that I should refrain from saying anything that might prejudice those proceedings. Having said that, I do believe shareholders have a right to know, at least in general terms, what led the Board to take the action it did on 2 March, just three weeks before this Annual General Meeting.

I knew some time ago that Mr Rowland was planning to send a letter to shareholders. I fondly, and perhaps naively, imagined that it was by way of being his valedictory message, and I concluded that, odd as it might seem that a man who was still on the Board and indeed would be sitting on this platform here today should be sending a communication to shareholders that the Board had neither seen nor endorsed, nevertheless we should not try to stand in his way. In other words an exception should be made for an exceptional person.

Subsequently, it became clear that Mr Rowland was intent on making a sustained and detailed attack not only on Mr Bock but also on his and the Board's stewardship of Lonrho in recent times. It appeared that he was conducting extensive enquiries, involving one or more agents or agencies, into Mr Bock's background and finances, including the performance of other companies with which Mr Bock is or has been closely associated. His reasons for doing so are apparent in his letter to shareholders: in effect he thinks he made a mistake two years ago and he wants to redress it.

It would indeed have been understood if Mr Rowland had instituted such enquiries at the time he was considering bringing Mr Bock into the company. Or if his principal concern had been to submit the results of his investigations to the Board for their consideration.

As it was, there was apparently more to it than that and it was difficult to escape the conclusion that such concerns Mr Rowland might have had on behalf of the company were now overshadowed by his determination to call into question the reputation of the Chief Executive. Inevitably this would harm your company at the same time.

In the opinion of nearly all the members of the Board, including myself, it was unacceptable that he should behave in this way from a privileged position as a member of the Board or as someone on the company's payroll with an office in Cheapside House. Sad as it was, we felt this was the final straw and that our differences with Mr Rowland were now so acute that we had to ask him to leave at once.

Ladies and Gentlemen, a full account of how events unfolded will be canvassed, if necessary, in court. In the meantime I have tried to give you a general flavour of what brought matters to a head three weeks ago.

In a quite separate context I must tell you that we have recently said good-bye to other members of staff, some of whom have been with Lonrho for a long time. As part of a drive to economise on the cost of our headquarters operations, we felt that some slimming down of our establishment was called for. We therefore invited members of staff at Cheapside House to opt for voluntary redundancy on specially favourable terms. In all, 36 people have taken advantage of that. I wish them all well and thank them warmly for their service to the company.

I also wish to take this opportunity to thank all members of staff throughout the group for all they continue to do for us. I myself was particularly glad to have the chance to meet and thank some of them personally during visits that I recently made to Mauritius and South Africa. I am looking forward to visiting our companies in other countries as soon as I can.

I should like to end on a personal note. One of the things we have been distracted from doing in recent months is appointing a new Chairman. Apart from anything else, I very much doubt whether in existing circumstances it would have been possible to find the right person. But we would like to get on with this as soon as we can. I have made it clear that I am willing to hand over to someone else whenever my fellow Board members think it desirable. Moreover, since I am the sitting tenant, I have asked my fellow Non-Executive Director, Stephen Walls, to take my place as Chairman of the Nominations Committee, which is charged with finding and recommending a successor.

I will stop there and, as foreshadowed at the beginning of my remarks, ask Dieter Bock to tell you briefly how he sees the development of Lonrho at the present time.

Index

Acland, Antony 130
Alexander, Ebenezer 3
Allen, Denis 34
Anne, Princess 137
Argov, Shlomo 136–7
Armstrong, Robert 144, 164
Arthur, Geoffrey 68–9
Atkins, Humphrey 136
Ayedema, President 137

Barber, Sir Anthony 127
Beaumont, Sir Richard 73
Beazley, Kim 155
Begin, Prime Minister Menachem 135
Berrill, Sir Kenneth 108
Betjeman, John 102
Birch, Alex and Joan 69
Blair, Tony 185
Bock, Dieter 168–70, 172, 174–5
Booker, Eleanor 79
Botha, Elise 116
Botha, P. W. 118–19, 121, 124, 133, 142
Botha, Pik 112, 114–15, 117–21, 124, 133, 142
Bower, Tom 170
Brittan, Leon 139
Brooke Turner, Alan 34
Brown, George 81, 83
Bullard, Julian 40, 130
Burgoyne, John 79
Buthelezi, Chief Gatsha 124, 132

Cain, John 155–6

Caines, John 68
Callaghan, Jim 108
Campbell, Gary 158–9, 174
Campbell, Sir Walter 155
Carrington, Lord 112, 114, 119, 135–6
Chalker, Lynda 166
Charles, Prince of Wales 138, 161
Chiluba, President 174
Chou En-lai 87
Churchill, Winston 37
Clark, Alan 154
Conn, David 49
Cooper, Sir Frank 98
Cowdrey, Colin 11, 148
Craven, Sir John 175
Crawford, Anne (Brucie) and Hunter 46
Cullimore, Charles 147

Davies, Alison 158
de Gaulle, Charles 58, 60–2
de Klerk, F. W. 105, 123, 130
de Villiers, Dawie 118
Debré, Michel 62
Deedes, Bill 102
Diana, Princess of Wales 161
Dickie, John 83
Dikko, Umaru 142
Dixon, Sir Piers (Bob) 61
Douglas-Home, Sir Alec 70, 78, 80–90
Douglas-Home, Caroline 90
Douglas-Home, Elizabeth 82, 88, 90
Dreux Family 32, 33
Drumm, Maire 104

Duff, Tony 35–8, 41, 43, 114, 118, 144, 164
Dunlop, Robert 167–8, 170

Eden, Anthony 37, 38
Edinburgh, Duke of 70, 94
Eglin, Colin 126
Eisenhower, Dwight 60
Elizabeth II, Queen 113, 143–5, 183
Evans, Gareth 155
Ewart-Biggs, Christopher and Jane 92–3, 103

Fahad, Sayyid 137
Fahd, King 137
Farquharson, Robin and Joan 63
Fergusson, Ewen 130
Fitt, Gerry 98, 102
Fletcher, Yvonne 139
Flynn, Beatrice 36
Fourie, Brand 119
Fretwell, John 92, 130

Gadaffi, Muammar 138
Gallop, David 12–13
George VI, King 30
Gilchrist, Andrew 48
Gilmour, Ian 112
Goodman, Lord 84
Graham, Johnny 130
Green, Betty (Leahy) 6, 8, 132, 188
Green, Phil 9, 28, 30, 188
Greene, Graham 101–2
Greenhill, Sir Denis 80, 84–5, 87
Griffith, Gavan 150–1
Gromyko, Andrei 80–1
Guéginou, Jean 166

Hadow, Michael 61, 74
Hall, George 34
Hall, Ricky 39
Hammond, Professor Nick 15–16
Hancock, Pat 34, 57

Harper, Peter 168, 171–2
Hawke, Bob 147–8, 154, 156–8, 161–2
Hawkins, Harold and Eve 163
Hayden, Bill 144, 154
Haydon, Robin 78
Heath, Edward 94, 111, 145
Henniker-Major, John 32
Heseltine, Michael 144
Hills, Stuart and Dorothy 44–6, 51–2
Hlongwane, Jim 114, 121
Hollingsworth, Mirabelle 3
Holmer, Flight-Sergeant 25
Howe, Geoffrey and Elspeth 142, 158, 162
Hudson, Miles 82–3, 86
Hume, Cardinal Basil 166
Hurd, Douglas 180
Hussein, King 137, 145
Hussey, Susan 113

Ippolitov, Ivan 80
Issa, Sheikh 137

Jebb, Sir Gladwyn and Cynthia 38, 59–61
Jellicoe, George 44

Keating, Paul 154
Kennedy, John F 67
Kent, Duchess of 158
Kerby, Captain Henry, MP 28
Khomeini, Ayatollah 110
Khrushchev, Nikita 60, 127
Killick, John 129–30
Koornhof, Piet 133

Lawrence, Pam (Leahy) 6, 9, 188
Lawrence, Ro 4
Lawrence, Tudor 9, 188
Leahy, Ailsa 132, 188
Leahy, Alice (daughter) 49, 67, 68, 73, 76, 98, 132, 134, 142, 177–8
Leahy, Anne 30, 38–51, 53–62, 64, 67–9, 74, 89, 91–2, 97–8, 103,

105–6, 112–13, 116–17, 122, 124, 129–30, 133, 137, 142, 144, 155, 158–9, 161, 163, 165–6, 171, 174, 176, 179, 183, 188
Leahy, Daniel and Mary (great-grandparents) 1–3
Leahy, Emma (daughter) 49–50, 55–6, 58, 68, 73, 91, 93–4, 113, 132, 134, 158–60, 174
Leahy, Ethel (Sudlow) ("Ma") 4–7, 9, 10, 39, 44, 52, 74
Leahy, James (son) 60, 61, 68, 73, 94, 113, 132, 142, 158
Leahy, John and Alice (Nash) (grandparents) 1, 3
Leahy, Mary (great-aunt) 1, 3
Leahy, Michael and Pamela 156
Leahy, Patrick (brother) 6–7, 9, 132, 188
Leahy, Peter (brother) 6–7, 10, 39, 41, 160, 188
Leahy, Peter (son) 56, 58, 68, 71–3, 132
Leahy, Roly (brother) 6, 9–10, 45, 188
Leahy, William ("Pa") 1–2, 4–9
Leahy-Johnson, Joyce 1
Leclézio, René 170–71
Lewis, Ross 21
Lloyd, Selwyn 35–7, 43
Lowis, Joanna 114
Luce, Richard 126, 136, 138, 144
Luns, Joseph 90

Ma, Mr 87
MacDonald, Malcolm 48, 50–51
Machel, Samora 143, 146
Macmillan, Harold 60, 127–9
Maillard, Philippe 12–13
Maitland, Donald 82
Mandela, Nelson 105, 131
Mandela, Winnie 123
Mansell, Gerry 109
Mao Tse-tung 88
Margaret, Princess 61
Marshall, David 50

Mason, Roy 99
Maxwell, Robert 169
Mayhew, Sir Patrick 151
McBean, Jane 3
McCarthy, Senator Joe 19
McKay, Lt. Col. Pat 48
McLelland, Judge James 149–50
Mellon, Paul 17, 24
Miles, Oliver 138
Moi, President Arap 174
Moore, Philip 144
Morell, Nick 175
Motlana, Dr Nthato 124
Mountbatten, Lord Louis 117
Mugabe, Robert 118–20, 135
Murdoch, Dame Elizabeth 152
Murdoch, Rupert 152
Murphy, Father 101
Murray, James 59, 121
Murray, Rear-Admiral Sir Brian and Jan 155–6
Muzorewa, Bishop Abel 118–19
Myburgh, Tertius 126

N'kwe, Rev David and Maggie 122
Naude, Beyers 125
Nkomo, Joshua 84–5, 118–19
Noble, Pat 83, 85
Nutting, Anthony 43

O'Faolain, Sean 102
Oppenheimer, Harry 125
Ormsby Gore, David 36
Owen, David 107, 109

Paisley, Ian 103
Palliser, Sir Michael 34, 89, 126
Pearce, Lord 84
Perry, Anthea 83
Philip, Captain 156
Pitchford, Jack and Betty 39, 41–2, 49–50, 52, 56, 91
Pitchford, John and Betty (Bass) 67

Plimsoll, Sir James 155
Pompidou, President 94
Powell, Justice 151
Pym, Francis 136–7

Radji, Parviz 110
Rahman, Mujibur 86
Rawlinson, Sir Peter 84
Rees, Merlyn 97–101
Reid, Martin 120
Rendel, Sandy 78
Rifkind, Malcolm 141
Robinson, John 58
Robinson, Terry 167
Robles, Juan 91, 113, 134, 158
Rose, Sir Clive 67, 108
Ross, Oliver (Ollie) 177–8
Rowland, Tiny 143, 145–6, 167–74
Rupert, Anton 125
Russell, John 89
Russell, Mark 164

Sadat, President 111
Salan, General Raoul 61
Salisbury, Lord (Bobbety) 37
Savimbi, Jonas 139–41
Scott, Sir Robert (Rob) 51
Sears, Charlotte 17–18, 20, 23–4, 30, 38
Shah of Iran 70, 109–11
Shakespeare, John and Lalage 61–2
Simos, Theo QC 151
Smith, Ian 84, 163
Snow, Peter 83
Soames, Christopher 92, 119–20
Soames, Mary 166
Spicer, Paul 167–8, 170
Stephen, Sir Ninian 155
Steyn, Jan 126
Strang, Sir William 34
Sudlow, Anne (grandmother) 4
Sutherland, Iain 86
Suzman, Helen 125, 166

Swart, Ray 126
Sykes, Richard 43, 103

Tennyson, Lord Harry 64
Thatcher, Margaret 92, 110–11, 120, 124, 127, 137, 142–7, 156–8, 167
Thomas, Patrick and Jane 178
Todd, Ric 139, 141
Tomkins, Sir Edward (Eddie) 92
Trelford, Donald 167
Trimming, "Uncle G" and "Doolie" (Sudlow) 4, 41
Trimming, Teddy 53
Turnbull, Malcolm 151
Tutu, Desmond 123

Van der Post, Laurence 120, 145
Viljoen, State President Marais 115

Wake-Walker, Christopher and Anne 63
Walden, George 109
Walls, General Peter 115, 120–1
Walls, Stephen 168
Warner, Fred 34
Warren, Rhoddy and Rosemary 50
Weller, Arthur 156–7, 160
White, Bryan 66
White, Ted and Lucy 21–2
Wiggin, Charles and Maria 68, 71
Wilson, Harold 94–5, 185
Windsor, Duke and Duchess 64
Wisner, René and Geneviève 40
Wong, Ah 47–50
Wright, Peter 150–51
Wright, Sir Denis 70–72, 74, 111

Yeend, Geoff 155
Yew, Lee Kuan 50
Young, Baroness 154
Young, Gerry 58
Youngleson, Clarissa 132
Youngleson, Mike 132

Printed in the United Kingdom
by Lightning Source UK Ltd.
124219UK00001B/466-480/A